Campuses Respond to Violent Tragedy

Campuses Respond to Violent Tragedy

Dorothy Siegel

AMERICAN COUNCIL
ON EDUCATION
Series on Higher Education
ORYX PRESS
1994

The rare Arabian Oryx is believed to have inspired the myth of the unicorn. This desert antelope became virtually extinct in the early 1960s. At that time several groups of international conservationists arranged to have 9 animals sent to the Phoenix Zoo to be the nucleus of a captive breeding herd. Today the Oryx population is nearly 800, and over 400 have been returned to reserves in the Middle East.

© 1994 by American Council on Education and The Oryx Press
Published by The Oryx Press
4041 North Central at Indian School Road
Phoenix, Arizona 85012-3397

Published simultaneously in Canada

Printed and Bound in the United States of America

∞ The paper used in this publication meets the minimum requirements of American National Standard for Information Science—Permanence of Paper for Printed Library Materials, ANSI Z39.48, 1984

Library of Congress Cataloging-in-Publication Data
Siegel, Dorothy, 1928–
    Campuses respond to violent tragedy / by Dorothy Siegel.
      (American Council on Education/Oryx series on higher education)
    Includes bibliographical references and indexes.
    ISBN 0-89774-825-5
    1. Campus violence—United States—Case studies. 2. College students—Services for—United States—Case studies. 3. Universities and colleges—United States—Planning—Case studies.   I. Title. II. Series.
LB2345.S54   1994   94-21315
378.1'97'820973—dc20   CIP

To

Jessica and Alexa Siegel and Dylan and Allen Ford

TABLE OF CONTENTS

* * * * * * * *

ACKNOWLEDGMENTS

❖ ❖ ❖ ❖ ❖ ❖ ❖ ❖

This book has been the product of a lot of hard work and cooperation. Jan Mitchell Sherrill has been with the book from the beginning, shaping its design and content. Jan has been a significant part of the creation of the Campus Violence Prevention Center at Towson State University. Clarinda Harriss Raymond has read and reread, critically evaluated, and assured me it could be done. Cyndi Zimmerman has, in her usual and supportive way, patiently corrected and printed each draft. My longtime friend, Marcia Epstein, taught me first how to use the computer, and later she critically checked each page. I am indebted to Jay Bondar for the many things he did to help me complete this project.

Dr. Hoke Smith, president of Towson State University, has supported the study of campus violence from my first discussion of the topic in 1984. The Campus Violence Prevention Center, created at Towson State University in 1986, could only have happened because Dr. Smith was willing to acknowledge and openly discuss the existence of violence on campuses. He was considered daring by colleagues across the nation. This work could not have happened without the unique, open environment that Hoke Smith has fostered and the support he has given the center.

My work in student affairs began because Dr. James Fisher, then president of Towson State, decided to bet on me. I am grateful to him.

Dr. Charles Maloy, friend and colleague, and Robert Giordani, assistant and expediter, are among the many without whom this work could not have been done. Patricia Frawley and Jenifer Yolken helped continuously.

My family, Lisa and Larry Ford, John and Carole Siegel, and Kathy Siegel have been, as always, supportive and loving.

My thanks to Jim Murray who saw the possibilities of a book on campus violence in our first telephone conversation. Throughout the writing process, Jim gave me advice.

I am grateful to each of the following people who contributed to the making of this book: Francisco J. Hernandez, Karen Kinney, Ray Colvig, Vicky Harrison, W. Russell Ellis, John F. Cummins, Harry LeGrande, Laura Blake, Mja Shandera, Nad Permaul, Steve Lustig, Robert Cremer, Everett Stevens, James Scott, Art Sandeen, Edward Poppell, Linda Gray, Jack Heidler, Jim Grimm, Boyd Kellett, Jim Archer, Pamela Bernard, David Kratzer, Michael Brown, Paul Ferguson, Tim Susick, Carol Latronica, Linda Koch, Carol Cowder, Debbie Jackson, Tim Brooks, Larry Thornton, Tom Vasha, Mary Hempel, Nancy Geist, Cynthia Cummings, Janice Jordan, Gary Stokes, Linda Koch, Carol Crowder, Craig Willis, Leland Spangler, John Moyer, Max McGee, Steve Murphy, Dan McCarthy, Kathy Williams, Mary Lee Farlow, Art Taguding, Bill Schermerhorn, Ken Thompson, Don McCulloh, Calvin Handy, Eric Shoemaker, Cyrus Jollivette, Edward T. Foote II, Bill Butler, Robert Reddick, Luis Glazer, Paul Galagher, Dennis Wiedman, Andrea Goldblum, Olga Magnuson, Leonardo Roderigues, Lalo Gomez, Lyn Morgan, Dick Correnti, Susan Donovan, Joe Boylan, Kathy Clark, Michelle Espinosa, Steve Jones, Mark Kelly, and some whom I shall not name so that the anonymity of their institutions is not compromised.

Finally, my gratitude to Gary Pavella and Peter H. Hollister who read the manuscript and offered many fine suggestions.

INTRODUCTION

❋ ❋ ❋ ❋ ❋ ❋ ❋ ❋ ❋

I started working on this book because I have seen that colleges and universities throughout the nation are struggling alone as they respond to campus violence. Since the tragic events discussed here can happen anywhere, I believe that institutional leaders will profit from understanding how their colleagues responded and how they reflected on their experiences.

To get a broader picture of an institution's response, I have let those who were immediately affected tell their own stories. Some schools were better prepared for emergency situations than others. None, except the school that responded to a suicide, ever dreamed that its community would be called upon to react, to live through, and finally to heal from such disruption and sadness. (The one school was prepared for a suicide because suicide among college students has been discussed in the literature for many years. Most campuses have lost students to suicide, and several authors have described suicidal behavior among college students.[1])

In preparing case studies, I wrote to presidents of institutions where the press had reported violent tragedy, asking permission to interview those offices that had been immediately involved. At every school, a fellow vice president for student affairs arranged for me to visit.

The presidents of all the institutions included here gave me permission to study their universities' responses to tragedies on campus. They and their staffs arranged appointments and extended warm hospitality. Several people whom I interviewed told me that talking about their experiences was cathartic.

Not all institutions to which I wrote agreed to participate. In my letter, I said that I would telephone for their decision. Two institutions would not even answer my calls. (Some institutions feared that public statements would damage their position in cases currently under litigation.)

One university that declined to be studied did so because it was just beginning to heal, and the president feared reopening those wounds.

In all the universities studied, I found the leadership deeply devoted to the welfare of their students. They were concerned for the rights of students, and, where death had occurred, with the rights of the deceased and the care of their families. When faculty and staff were in danger, presidents were determined to offer help despite great difficulties. Each tragedy presented a sudden unexpected challenge, the kind of challenge for which no one is completely prepared. I finished my interviews with a new and higher regard for my colleagues across the country.

When I wrote to the campuses, I offered anonymity. Some accepted but several schools with well-publicized tragedies will be immediately recognizable to many readers.

The case studies that follow are not meant to serve as model responses. I'm only seeking to describe how institutions did respond. The participating schools did not see themselves as exemplary but rather survivors of difficult situations. In hindsight many were justly proud.

I am grateful to the many people who talked with me and to those who made the many arrangements for my visits.

ORGANIZATION

Part One consists of my interviews with campus administrators who have guided their institutions' responses to the violent behavior that affected their own campuses. Part One concludes with a paper by Dr. Gilles Gauthier, conseille au secretaire general et ombudsman, École Polytechnique de Montreal, presented at the Seventh Annual Conference of the Campus Violence Prevention Center, February 1993, Baltimore. He has generously allowed me to reproduce that report.

In Part Two, I present the responses of two schools to the natural disaster of Hurricane Andrew. At Florida International University (FIU) I interviewed the many who guided the campus response. The University of Miami (UM) experience is presented differently because President Edward T. Foote II graciously permitted me to include correspondence from UM senior administrators who had, at his request, chronicled events related to the hurricane. His own reflections are included.

Part Three presents a summary of the book as well as suggestions from others and useful checklists.

ABBREVIATIONS USED

For clarity, I have identified people by initials that designate their positions in the following manner. (Please note that some of these titles vary from university to university, though the position is largely the same.):

ACP	Assistant Chief of Police
AD	Athletic Director
ADS	Assistant Dean of Students
AHD	Assistant Housing Director
APR	Assistant to President
AT	Attorney
AVP	Associate V.P. for Student Affairs
AVPA	Associate V.P. for Administrative Affairs
BCH	Branch Campus Housing
BFA	Administrator for Business and Finance
CD	Director of Counseling
CM	Campus Ministry
DCP	Director of Career Placement
DCS	Dean of Continuing Studies
DO	Director of Orientation
DP	Director of Personnel
DPP	Director of Physical Plant
DS	Dean of Students
DUU	Director of University Union
EAP	Executive Assistant to the President
FUR	Faculty Union Representative
HD	Housing Director
HEO	Health Officer
HO	Housing Officer
HOM	Head of Maintenance
IO	Information Officer
JO	Judicial Officer
PA	President's Assistant
PAO	Public Affairs Officer
PC	Police Chief
PL	Placement Officer
PO	Police Officer
PP	Associate V.P. for Physical Plant
PR	President
PS	Chief of Public Safety
PV	Provost

RD   Residence Director
RL   Residence Life
RM   Risk Manager
SA   Student Activities Director
SGA   Student Government President
SI   Sports Information Officer
UC   University Counsel
VC   Vice Chancellor
VP   Senior Development Officer
VPA   Senior Academic Officer
VPB   Senior Business Officer
VPP   Associate V.P. for Personnel
VPS   Senior Student Affairs Officer

For some people whose positions were unique, I have assigned letters in the text.

AN EXPLANATION TO THE READER

Because colleges of any size are bureaucracies with departments such as security, finance, information, and student affairs, they are organized vertically. Campus police do the police work and train their own staffs in accordance with precepts for their profession as do people in campus housing, student affairs, and information offices. There is little cross-training. As a result, few people have a sense of how the other departments work and, therefore, how the whole institution operates. For that reason, I have presented each school's response by reporting what each campus office's response was to the crisis. I hope that when readers learn more about how their colleagues in other disciplines responded, they may be willing to integrate that knowledge into their staff development programs. That effort would result in a more interdisciplinary, comprehensive response to a campus crisis.

Some redundancy occurs as each person tells how that specific department responded. I have included digressions that I hope will give a better understanding both of the milieu and of the thinking that affected the decisions. I hope this book will help campus administrators think about what they would do if they were facing the same situations their comrades faced. When they consider what their actions would be, they will be able to better add items to their own preparation and response checklists.

REFERENCE

1. Schneidman, Edwin, Editor, *Death and the College Student: A Collection of Brief Essays on Death and Suicide by Harvard Youth*, New York: Human Sciences Press, 1972; Rickgarn, R.I.V. "Violence and Suicide: Deadly Connections." Paper presented at First National Conference on Campus Violence, Baltimore, January 7, 1987.

PART

1

❖ ❖ ❖ ❖ ❖ ❖ ❖ ❖ ❖

CHAPTER
one
* * * * * * * *

Multiple Tragedies
Off-Campus

BACKGROUND

UC, a prestigious state research university, has a total community of 38,000, including staff, faculty, and students. Some campus-owned residence halls are outside the perimeter of the campus.

The Emergency Response Committee

The university has been the site of many protests. Several years ago, the university appointed a committee to provide direction and to oversee the university's response to demonstrations. That committee consulted with and advised the police, who have the responsibility for direct response to demonstrations.

Later events caused the university to broaden the responsibilities of the protest committee. UC is located on a geological fault. The state administration has mandated that all political subdivisions, including universities, develop an earthquake disaster plan. Following the earthquake in 1989, a new vice chancellor for administration, who had been a city manager, appointed his assistant to organize an Emergency Response Committee. This committee would both prepare the university to respond to disasters, protests, and other emergencies, and oversee the management of such crises. It is comprised of 20 representatives from campus services, students, and faculty. Only those members (university officers) who will have to respond to a specific emergency are called to the command center. The command center is located in the police offices and is equipped with a television.

Each member of the emergency response team has been issued a wallet-sized card with the current phone number of every team member. The card also serves to inform the police that the holder of the card is a member of the emergency staff of the university and should be permitted to cross police barriers. These cards, which are updated every three months, include numbers of cellular phones.

The committee's first task was to develop emergency procedures for each building. The 1990 emergency plan emphasized that members of each campus community need to know their respective roles in the community's safety. The committee further developed and distributed an emergency plan for each student in the university as well as a plan for resident students and those in fraternity or sorority housing (Greek housing). To increase safety awareness, the committee sponsored an information fair for the entire campus.

According to the emergency preparedness officer, the committee had to develop an aggressive marketing plan promoting good prevention and appropriate emergency response because no one on campus cares about safety except when crises occur. The committee developed a campus-wide advertising program with brightly colored signs and information posted in lobbies and elevators, including maps of exits for each building. The information was also sent to all departments on campus. The committee plans to distribute a card to each student with emergency instructions. All the material emphasizes individual responsibility, and each department is responsible for educating its own staff.

According to committee's plan, each building has a coordinator, chosen from among the occupants, and an assigned assembly area outside, where all people evacuating the building are to meet. Assembly areas are marked on campus maps. Each coordinator has a two-way radio to receive messages from the Emergency Operation Command center.

In the event of an emergency, the emergency committee will communicate with the coordinator at the gathering site and will send emergency supplies, if necessary, to that location. A major disaster may leave people totally disabled and dependent on the local building response team. For that reason, the future work of the committee will be to create an on-site storage of food, clothing, and medical supplies. As the budget allows, supplies for one- and two-day periods will be stockpiled.

The committee is also adding a larger radio system with more radio channels and will investigate installing a remote public address system. Plans are for managers of housing and dining services to use their facilities to shelter and feed disaster victims.

In the future, the committee will work with The Red Cross to decide how to best coordinate their efforts. Providers of essential emergency services from the university and local municipality have been meeting to establish cooperative programs.

City and University Police Responsibilities at UC

An existing agreement between the university and the city designates city police as the appropriate emergency response unit for the Greek houses and campus police for the residence halls. Both the Greek houses and the residence halls are located off campus. The university owns the residence halls. The Greek houses are operated by private corporations distinct from the university.

On Thursday, Friday, and Saturday nights the university police supplement city patrols by patrolling the area where the Greek houses are located.

The university police are responsible for the campus, the residence halls, and for the students while they are on the campus. The area one mile outside of campus is subject to optional jurisdiction.

The university is dependent on the city fire department. The university fire marshall sets fire safety standards for the campus. The state fire marshall sets standards for Greek housing.

In the following pages three emergencies will be addressed, a fire, a bomb threat, and a hostage crisis.

THE FIRST EMERGENCY—THREE DIE IN FRATERNITY HOUSE FIRE OFF-CAMPUS

About 1:30 A.M. on Saturday morning, September 8, 1990, an arson fire in the Phi Kappa Sigma (PKΣ) fraternity house took the lives of three students, two of whom were found in the burned building 14 hours after the fire had begun. Two of the victims were members of the fraternity, and one was a visitor from a sorority. Fire fighters retrieved the body of the first victim soon after the fire broke out. Two other students were hurt escaping from the building, both of whom were treated and released from the hospital. Surviving fraternity members lost most of their personal effects, in addition to their housing. The discovery of arson as the cause of the fire was made some time after the fire occurred. The arsonist was later apprehended. Because of the close proximity of one sorority house, that building was also evacuated, although some of the occupants were able to return to the building that same day.

SA—Student Activities Director

The SA, at 3:00 A.M., was the first administrator to arrive at the scene of the fire. The university police chief had called the SA. One student was known to be dead.

All residents of the house had been evacuated, and they were waiting to see if everyone had been accounted for. In the sorority house nearby, the Red Cross already had a counselor to provide services. The student activities director (SA), while working with the Red Cross in their efforts to relocate displaced students, was also directing a search for unaccounted-for students and helping the acutely distressed fraternity members and their friends.

The SA called for help from the Greek advisor to account for the whereabouts of the occupants of the house to determine who might have been inside. Since many of the students were away at an athletic competition, the authorities needed to confirm their identities. Parents of the first-known victim arrived from Sacramento at 3:30 A.M. They had been called earlier by the police when the authorities failed to locate the young man. A sorority house made a private room available to the family; at the parent's request, the staff contacted the priest from the Newman Center. At 4:00 A.M. when the chancellor arrived, the SA introduced him to the parents. The chancellor devoted himself exclusively to the parents, accompanying them when they viewed the remains, and when they went to the coroner's office.

When the VP for administration arrived, the SA briefed him. He instructed the SA to continue directing the effort.

By 9:00 A.M., the SA had a report on the car of a missing student who was known to have entered the fraternity house before the fire. By noon, the van of the second missing student was discovered at that student's father's house. The SA spoke with the parent who said that his son was not with him.

The SA and staff had been searching for the two students. To try to locate the students, the SA had been calling parents. She had not been able to contact the parents of one of the missing students. At 3:00 P.M., a friend of the parents of that student called because the student's parents were out of the country.

The SA was sure that the two missing students were still in the building. One of the students was a fraternity member. The other was a sorority member. The SA relayed to the police her conclusion that the two students were still in the building. After several attempts, in the late afternoon the firemen brought out the remains of the two missing students. Official identification, from dental records, could not be made until almost one week later.

It was not clear who should have been responsible for informing parents in a situation such as this one. The SA invited the CARE office to meet with staff. (CARE is an employee assistance program, a part of health services, that offers counseling, assessment and referral services for faculty and staff.)

The student activities office called a meeting of all Greek advisers to let them know what was happening. An SA was on duty all day. The counseling center made information about their services available to all the Greek students. The dean of students (DS) and the SA met members, and their parents, of the Phi Kappa house, and they invited counselors to attend the meeting. The DS met with members of the fraternity and sorority to which the missing students had belonged to inform them about the discovered deaths.

The SA was sent home at 5:00 P.M.

The student activities office worked with the Red Cross to provide for the needs of the survivors like textbooks, clothing, and housing. A wheelchair-bound student, who had been evacuated from the sorority house, needed appropriate new housing.

The SA attended the funeral and the campus memorial service for the young man and women who died in the fire. A representative of the student activities department attended the funeral for each student.

A precedent was established with the memorial service. It was then expected that there would be a memorial service for victims of other tragedies.

The other Greeks announced in the *Daily Cal*, the student newspaper, a fundraising campaign for the Greek houses of the students that died. During Greek Week, they had a vigil as a memorial to the fire victims.

PC—Police Chief

Early on Saturday morning, September 8, the lieutenant on duty called the PC of the university to report the fire in the fraternity house. The university police were assisting the city police and the fire department. Fire engines were present. The building had been evacuated and the city fire chief was on the scene.

University police procedure specifies that the lieutenant calls the chief and the chief calls the vice chancellor for administration to whom the chief reports. The people who were called included the information director, the housing director, the vice chancellor for undergraduate studies, and the director of public safety. If there is a question of liability, the lieutenant will call the risk manager.

After midnight, there were four officers and a sergeant on duty. When university police learned of the fire, those officers who had come in for a dance were held over for continued duty. University police helped evacuate the buildings, managed the traffic, and worked with others at the scene in identifying victims.

The PC called the SA because she has responsibility for Greek affairs. The university had no on-call counselors, but the City Crisis Team started working immediately with students in need of crisis counseling.

When the chancellor arrived, he sat with the family of the then-known victim. When the body was evacuated, the chancellor stayed with the family to see the remains. The chancellor then went with the family to the priest, and later, to the coroner's office. The chancellor's actions had a dramatic positive effect on university personnel working that night.

Later, when two students were still unaccounted for, the university police helped the city police search for them throughout the town and in neighboring areas. As news of the fire was broadcast, police received calls from many families wanting more information. A lieutenant was assigned to stay in touch with the families of the fraternity house residents.

The fire department wanted the university police to contact the families of the dead and missing persons. This task went to the police officer who had been talking with the parents of two of the victims and had developed a relationship with them.

The university officers, who had worked long hours, were under a great deal of stress and pressure; they had been calling families all day to check the whereabouts of students who could not be accounted for. They served as intermediaries for parents and the university. When the deaths of the students were confirmed, these officers considered it their responsibility to inform the parents.

Although the dispatcher who had worked all day didn't want to leave, the chief sent him home. Three additional staff were asked to come in. All of the university police work done that night was done at the request of the city. If campus police had been in charge, they might have done some things differently, but it was their responsibility to follow the plan of the city police.

Reflecting on the tragedy and the role of the police, the PC described the campus police as enjoying a position of respect and equality on the campus. Officers serve on university committees including academic search committees. This relationship allows the force to identify more closely with the spirit and goals of the university.

HD—Housing Director

The housing director (HD) was called on the night of the fire and told that he might need to feed and house the evacuated students. As it turned out, Greeks in the other houses took in those students, and HD provided free meal cards for the displaced students.

Most of the residence-hall students were freshmen and did not know the victims, but nonetheless counseling was available immediately for all the resident students. A police officer and counselor were assigned to each hall for the semester.

IO—Information Officer

On the morning of the fire, the vice chancellor informed the information officer (IO) at 3:30 A.M. of the student who had died and the two missing students. University police were assisting city police.

At the scene, the IO prepared a statement for the media, including background information on the fraternity. The IO mentioned that the fraternity house was off-campus. By the time the IO released his statement, the body of one student had been discovered, and two students were known to be missing. Aware of deadlines for the news media, the IO faxed them information so that the press would know that the university was working and could take calls. The student press was treated the same as the other media and received copies of all officially released information.

The IO prepared statements for the chancellor and attached a booklet about the fraternity. He worked on a statement to be released to the media while he was also the sole university spokesperson to the media for two hours. When he made his first report, he told of the students, one dead and two missing. He kept updating and verifying the data in time for the news deadlines. He accommodated the television station, who set up their broadcasting equipment on campus.

Because of the many questions about the safety conditions of the fraternity house, the IO issued a report on the fire safety inspection completed just prior to the fire. He gave statements quoting the city fire marshall so that the public would see that the inspection had not been done by the university. He announced later that the state fire marshall would be inspecting the fire scene to determine the cause of the fire. The IO wanted the public to know that the fraternity house was not university property or the responsibility of the university.

The coroner reported that the victims had been drinking and concluded that their ability to escape was impaired. The president informed the parents about the coroner's report and that it had been given by the coroner to the press. The president wanted the families to know the university did not tell the press that the victims' ability to escape had been impaired because they had been drinking. The newspapers made the presence of alcohol in the victims prominent information.

At 9:30 A.M., the IO issued the following statement:

IO—Statement to the Press September 8

A U of C student died Saturday (September 8th) in an early morning fire that destroyed the Phi Kappa Sigma fraternity house at . . . near the . . . campus. Initial reports from university police and city firefighters indicate the fire broke out about 1:00 A.M., possibly in the living room area of the house. No cause has been determined.

The student who died was. . . .

U . . . Chancellor T. was at the scene of the tragedy early Saturday morning to be with the young man's family.

As of 9:00 A.M. Saturday, two other students, a resident of Phi Kappa Sigma and friend from a nearby sorority, were not accounted for, but campus officials do not want to speculate on whether they were at the Phi Kappa Sigma house at the time of the fire. The hope is they were elsewhere and are safe, and all indications at the fire scene as of 9:00 A.M. indicate they were not in the house.

The Phi Kappa Sigma house, built in 1958, currently housed 34 students, including many members of the C. water polo team and one member of the football team. Only 16 people were in the house. Both athletic teams are playing games out of town this weekend.

The remaining 15 residents of the house escaped with only one known injury—a broken ankle suffered by one man who jumped from either the roof or a ledge. He was treated and released from . . . Hospital.

Investigation of the cause of the fire is being handled by the City of . . . Fire Department. The university will cooperate in every way possible with the fire department.

As news became known, IO released more information.

An Advisory to the News Media 5:45 P.M. September 8, 1990:

Three people died Saturday (September 8th) in an early morning fire that destroyed the Phi Kappa Sigma fraternity house at . . . near the . . . campus.

Initial reports from university police and City of . . . firefighters indicate the . . . investigation is continuing.

Chancellor T., who was on the scene of the fire early Saturday, directed campus units to assist in every way possible to provide for housing, meals, and other needs, including personal counseling and academic arrangements, for the students who have been displaced by the fire.

Local Red Cross volunteers assisted the campus in responding to the tragedy. They worked with university staff to arrange temporary housing for displaced students, to feed the students, and to give them clothing vouchers for local stores. University staff also provided emergency counseling.

After the deaths of the second and third students were confirmed, the IO invited the community to gather at noon on Monday at the Campanile, the bell tower, to share the university's observance of a moment of silence in memory of the victims. He announced a memorial service for the following Wednesday.

IO—Special to The Student Newspaper September 10

A number of key services, some permanent on the campus and some arranged on an emergency basis, are available to those who lost housing and belongings in the Saturday morning fire—and to others who need help themselves or who want to provide help.

HOUSING AND FOOD SERVICE. The immediate needs of those displaced in the fire have been met through offers from fraternities and other living groups. Student Activities and Services (telephone number given) and The Red Cross are working together on this.

EMERGENCY LOANS. Loans are available from The Red Cross (telephone number given) and from the Financial Aid Office in . . .

CLOTHING for those who lost their belongings. The Red Cross (telephone number given) provides vouchers to purchase new clothing.

TEXTBOOKS. The Associated Students joining with The Red Cross (telephone number given), will assist students in replacing textbooks and other school materials lost in the fire.

The arsonist was later identified as a friend of one of the students in the fraternity house. No motive for the arson was reported. The chancellor issued the following statements on behalf of the university:

Chancellor's Statement—September 8, 10:00 A.M.

I know that I speak for the entire campus in expressing the deepest regrets and sympathy to the family and friends of. . . . In this time of sadness, I want to assure them that the people and the services of the campus stand ready to give help and comfort in every way possible.

I am also directing campus units to assist in all ways along with fraternities and other groups, to provide for housing, meals and other needs, including personal counseling and academic arrangements, for the students who have been displaced by the tragic fire.

In addition, I will direct the campus to assist city and other agencies in a thorough investigation of the fire as well as the safety conditions at other off-campus student living groups.

Chancellor's Statement (II) 5:45 P.M.

With still more sadness I am adding to the statement that I made earlier today. The news that two more victims died in the fire on . . . St. comes heavily upon the grief that has already spread through our community. Our deepest regrets and sympathy go out to the families and friends of all three victims. . . .

If there is a heartening note at the time of such loss, it must be in the knowledge that so many persons and so many agencies and services have come quickly to provide help and support for the families and for the students who have been displaced. I am confident this spirit and participation will continue in the days ahead.

The Chancellor's Message to the University Community
September 10

. . . at 11:00 A.M. today, the carillonneur at the Campanile will play the University Hymn, which begins with the words "O God, our help in ages past . . ." At that time I invite everyone to observe a moment of silence in respect for those who died. Also, through this week, campus flags will be lowered to signify a period of mourning. In addition, plans for a memorial service will be announced in a few days. . . .

The committee decided to have a memorial service on Wednesday and invited the students to help plan it.

PA—Assistant to the President for Public Affairs

At the time of the September 1990 fire, the assistant to the president for public affairs (PA) was in Wisconsin with the football team. The dean of students reached him at 1:00 P.M. the day after the fire to let him know about the tragedy. Some of the Greek residents of the building were on the football team. The DS feared the press would question athletes before the players knew what had happened to their fraternity brothers. The PA told the athletic director about the fire and deaths.

When the fire occurred, many of the services the university needed to respond to such an event were already in place. They included counseling services and procedures for notifying parents and the press. The committee wanted people informed about the availability of counseling services to assure maximum use of those services.

The campus needed to come together for healing. A time for the service was chosen that was respectful of the parents' wishes. Many students attended.

DS—Dean of Students

On the morning of the fire, the DS contacted the two traveling athletic teams to inform the fraternity members of the teams about the fire.

The DS and staff met at noon to determine how to proceed. While they made plans to meet as many of the needs of the students as possible, they also prepared recommendations about how to improve the student service response in the event that there was a future emergency. They were immediately aware that a better listing of emergency personnel was needed.

The DS met at 2:00 P.M. with members of the Greek system and told them what the university knew officially. At that time two students were still missing. By the time the DS met with the Phi Kappa fraternity members and some of their parents later that afternoon, he had learned the fate of the two missing students and told them about it. DS wanted the students to know the various services available to them. Counselors and Red Cross representatives were present for the second meeting.

The university had set up offices for replacement of checks, textbooks, clothing, and emergency supplies. The DS interceded with faculty on behalf of students for academic accommodations. The faculty cooperated in making appropriate allowances for missed work. The fire marshall inspected all of the fraternity and sorority houses the next day and sent its report to the university. The fire marshall directed a report of the fire to the fraternity and sent a copy to the dean of students. Arson was determined to be the cause of the fire. The fraternity gave no hints of possible suspects.

In a meeting the following day, the chancellor, counseling director, Red Cross, and health services director reviewed the following: the city fire department inspection of all Greek houses and cooperatives; updates on all actions to the moment and future plans including counseling services; replacement of school supplies for victims; housing accommodations for the displaced; and disbursement of meal cards and replacement of registration cards.

The DS and SA met with the fraternity and provided information about interim housing, meal cards, emergency loans, memorial services, fundraising, textbooks, and academic concerns. Staff of the DS and SA went to other Greek houses to inform residents about memorial services and available counseling. The same staff learned how many other students were displaced because of water damage in other buildings.

The next day the DS and SA staff arranged for the rest of the meal cards to be distributed, worked on long- and short-term housing possibilities, and rented vans so fraternity members without cars could get to the funeral of one of the victims. They coordinated receipts of donated funds for victims through the Development Office, responded to inquiries from press and parents about memorial services, student safety, insurance, and housing and loans, and arranged for survivors of the fraternity house to secure textbooks with Red Cross vouchers at the bookstore. Plans were developed for the campus memorial service.

Staff visited the sorority house that was accommodating some displaced students to talk about housing, meal cards, textbooks, academic considerations, available counseling, and memorial services.

Counselors conducted sessions with both the fraternity and the sorority. The counseling service sponsored a drop-in group session for all students who wished to come and talk.

The dean of students' office and the Office for Student Activities outlined a plan for how to stay in touch with the fraternity and sorority members and what responsibilities each person from each office would have.

The University Health Service issued the following flier in response to the tragedy.

University Health Service—Flier
Response to Fraternity Fire September 11, 1990

Grief/Loss/Fears

The sudden, traumatic death of someone you know or someone in your community may produce many kinds of feelings. These feelings are part of the normal grieving process, are usually temporary, and generally lessen with time. You or your friends may experience one or more of the following:

Shock, numbness	Sadness, crying
Fear for your own safety	Appetite changes
Denial that the loss occurred	Physical exhaustion
Physical discomfort	Despair
Sleeping pattern changes	Thinking about past losses and deaths
Guilt	Coping with grief
Inability to concentrate	Forgetfulness
Anxiety/worrying	

Experience your feelings—if not done now, healing may take longer.
Pay attention to diet, exercise, and substance abuse.
Talk to people about your feelings.

Be with friends and family you care about—don't let yourself become isolated.

Ask for support from friends, family and campus staff available to help.

Attend memorial services and/or set up your own rituals with other students.

If your symptoms persist, cause you excessive discomfort, or increase over time, you may want to seek professional assistance.

(A list of resources on campus followed.)

VC—Vice Chancellor for Undergraduate Affairs

The vice chancellor for undergraduate affairs (VC) reviewed how the Student Service offices responded to the fire. The VC learned that there had been no provision for counselors to be on-call at the site of emergencies like the fire. The VC decided that reorganization of some services would make for a better future response. The VC has a policy for informing parents of the students who die.

In the course of the year, the VC needed to inform a family of the death of a student. He has concluded that the university must aggressively address the problems of excessive drinking. Alcohol was not only central to the deaths in the fraternity house fire, but to a fatal accident six months later. The VC has proposed that alcohol parties be prohibited for Greek groups on Thursdays and is seeking to have that stipulation included in the annual agreement between the university and the individual chapters of the Interfraternity Council and the College Panhellenic Association. The agreement will include definitions of what constitutes a party. The VC is continuing discussions with the Greeks.

Fire Safety Committee

This committee reviewed the previous year's fire prevention program and began planning to upgrade fire safety standards for certain campus-owned student residence buildings. They arranged for the state fire marshall to inspect campus-owned student residences.

RM—Risk Manager

The risk manager (RM) had been notified at the time of the fire but had not been at the scene. When the fire was out, the fire marshall asked who would assume responsibility for the cost of boarding up the building. The VP for Administration agreed to assume the cost, although the fraternity house is a separate corporation, and as such, the university is not responsible for its bills. The RM was concerned about the responsibility the university was assuming by agreeing to pay for the boarding up of the building, since it is on private property. Eventually, the university collected the money it had paid out from the insurance company.

NP—Emergency Preparedness Officer

On the morning of the fraternity fire, the NP was not called until 6:00 A.M. By then, several members of the committee and the president were at the scene. The Red Cross was assisting displaced students in a headquarters set up in a nearby Greek house.

The Emergency Response Committee concluded, after a debriefing, that the emergency response to the fire had been poorly organized. Although many people were called to the site, no real command center existed, no one knew who should be in charge, and no one took overall responsibility for final decisions. There was some competition among the responders. Some services that were needed were not available until offices opened at their regularly scheduled times. The personnel present were police, the vice chancellor for administration, the vice chancellor for undergraduate affairs, the chancellor, the director of student activities, the dean of students, the information officer, and the public safety officer. The committee agreed that in the future the highest ranking vice chancellor present would assume charge.

Campus Evaluation of Response to the Fire

The following is the report of the vice chancellor for undergraduate affairs to the chancellor:

> The emergency contact system needs revisions including the development of a core contact list and contact lists for specific types of situations.
>
> Specific individuals should be designated as contact people for the parents of the deceased.
>
> University psychological and counseling staff need to be consulted early.
>
> Further discussion is needed about planning memorial services and when they are warranted.
>
> Praise should be extended to all staff and administrators, including senior staff, for their commitment.
>
> During the first two days, staff and administrators should have been rotated in and out on a regular basis.
>
> The emotional needs of staff/administrators should have been more directly addressed.

THE SECOND EMERGENCY—A BOMB THREAT FORCES THE CAMPUS TO CLOSE FOR THREE HOURS

In response to a bomb threat, UC closed all campus buildings at 4:00 P.M., Wednesday, September 19, 1990, and asked all students, faculty, and staff to evacuate the campus until 7:00 P.M. Thirty-eight thousand people left the campus. No bomb was found.

NP—Emergency Preparedness Officer

At 10:45 A.M., the university received a recorded message saying that four bombs placed on campus were scheduled to detonate at 5:26 P.M. The perpetrator had also sent a copy of the message to the nationally affiliated local television station.

At 11:00 A.M., NP and the vice chancellor for administration met in the police offices, which was the home of the Emergency Operations Command Center. They decided what persons should be called on in this emergency. They wanted to keep the number of people in the command center to a minimum. The police chief, medical, public relations, and information officers were present.

The FBI recommended that the university treat the threat seriously and evacuate the entire campus. The university could not use the alarm system because it might trigger the bomb. Building coordinators and the media informed the community of the need to evacuate the campus. The committee recommended that the campus close from 4:00 P.M. to 7:00 P.M. All buildings would be closed.

The following actions were taken by 4:00 P.M.:

- The committee set up a hotline in police quarters and asked the police chief VH to oversee answering calls.
- The chancellor was informed.
- Campus dogs inspected the dining areas.
- A statement was sent to the media.
- A flier announcing the closing was printed.
- The fire department was notified.
- City police were informed of the evacuation plan.
- Fifteen buildings were designated to be inspected first by university police.
- Residence halls were evacuated.
- Red Cross was notified.

- Building coordinators were informed by a designated calling group.
- Building coordinators were to distribute the fliers.
- Posters were made and delivered to building coordinators.

By 5:00 P.M., the fliers had been distributed, and many buildings had been inspected for the presence of a bomb. By 5:02 P.M., the campus had been cleared. Two surgeries had been in progress when the notice had been received, but all patients were evacuated from the hospital.

No bomb went off. The local television stations reported that information.

A statement was prepared for the media. Students were permitted to return to residence halls a few minutes before 7:00 P.M. The libraries were not able to open until the next morning. The emergency phones were shut down at the police station at 7:30 P.M., and the Emergency Operations Command was closed at 7:46 P.M.

One person called to report that one building had not been notified of the need to evacuate.

THE THIRD EMERGENCY—A HOSTAGE SITUATION OFF-CAMPUS— ONE STUDENT KILLED

On Wednesday evening, September 26, 1990, a gunman took 33 people hostage in a bar near UC campus and held them until police killed him at 7:00 A.M. the next morning. During the time the assailant held hostages, he killed one student and wounded nine others, including a city police officer. Most of the victims were UC students. The gunman was a former student.

PC—Police Chief

Between the time of the arson fire and the taking of the hostages, the acting chief had been named the police chief (PC). One of the first acts of the police chief was to require all persons on duty to wear bullet-proof vests.

On Wednesday night, September 26th, the director of a housing unit called police. A bloodied student reported escaping from Henry's Bar where a man armed with a gun was holding a number of people hostage. The university police responded immediately. A city police officer who had heard shots arrived at the scene at the same time as university police.

The city police chief was present; both city and university forces were working side by side. When the PC arrived, the city chief asked the PC if she would allow her officers to shoot the assailant. She agreed that if necessary she would. The PC was contemplating evacuating a residence hall but decided against it. Her concern was that if the gunman shot in the direction of the building, residents would be endangered. It was determined to be a better alternative to have the students remain in the building, however, than to chance the dangers of evacuation.

During the hostage taking, a city police officer was shot. He was outside the building. The PC knew the other officers would think the shot had killed him even though it had not; the police had immediately requested permission to return fire.

As officers were sent to surround the hotel in which Henry's is located, they went first to a safe zone, out of the line of fire, from which a sergeant assigned them to locations. One officer was placed at each door. The perimeter of the building was covered. The city and campus police had two different radio systems; the dispatcher had both systems and sent information to both forces. The city police captain visited the campus headquarters.

The two police forces were in constant contact. They were planning to negotiate with the assailant, but concurrently officers were preparing to enter and capture him. Chief D of the city police went to his command post, a mobile center. The PC was invited to join Chief D at his command post.

In addition to managing the university police action at the hostage scene, the PC was also part of the University Emergency Response Group Command Center; she stayed in both roles throughout the crisis. The PC continuously updated the campus committee. She also visited the city command post later in the crisis.

The two police forces had surrounded the hotel, waiting for the suspect to be in a position where it was possible to shoot him or to enter the building. The PC needed to delegate her role of managing each officer's assignment to lieutenants so she could devote herself to planning.

The PC arranged for a psychologist, skilled in working with the police, to be at campus police headquarters most of the night. As campus officers returned from the crisis scene, they met with the psychologist. (The state sponsors a three-day program for police officers to dispel the traumatic effect of police work. Everyone with three years' experience participates. The workshop focuses on the effects of major dangers and the cumulative effects of the unique work of the police. In the program, officers recognize that day-in and day-out tasks have special psychological effects, and they learn how to decrease the unfavorable consequences of such work. The consultant was associated with that program).

One of the officers secretly entered the lobby of the hotel and, while hiding, relayed information to an officer who kept the chief informed. Meanwhile, another officer outside the door was negotiating with the gunman. All officers who could were conveying information to the police chief.

The gunman had shot and killed a student. He reportedly told some of his hostages to get the victim out of his sight and out of the building. While the victim's body was being taken away by ambulance, the news of the victim's death was broadcast over television. A TV was playing in the bar, and when the assailant heard that his former hostage had died, he yelled that he was not a killer. Then he announced he was going to kill more hostages and he started shooting. The police were not able to determine whether he was shooting at individuals. Students were injured. As people were hurt, the assailant reportedly became increasingly violent and wanted those who were bloody to get out of his sight. He made some of the other hostages take away those who were hurt.

When the wounded hostages exited the scene, the officers rushed them out of the line of fire to the emergency medical teams. The ambulances had to be kept out of sight around the corner. As the released hostages were getting treatment, they told police what had been happening and who had been in the bar. Their information was continually relayed to the university police headquarters. Counseling services were immediately available to each of the victims. The PC learned from the escapees that hostages were being assaulted. She did not share that information with the policy team. When the decision was made to enter the building and kill the perpetrator, the PC did not inform the policy committee but told the vice chancellor, to whom she reports.

The hostage rescue team was, meanwhile, in the gym running over the entrance plan. Based on the information relayed to them, the police departments identified the perpetrator and secured pictures of him. They studied the pictures of the assailant so officers could make instant identification. Part of the police research during the crisis was to obtain those pictures. Police practiced making their entrance.

During the siege, the chancellor requested that he be allowed to get close enough to observe. The PC accompanied him through the cordoned-off area close to the hotel.

Those students who escaped asked why the police had waited so long to rescue them. The PC explained how much planning was required to enter the site.

Immediately after the gunman was killed, the president and the chancellor accompanied the PC to see the released hostages. The chancellor and the president visited with every hostage and spoke with each police officer. The chancellor and the president also spoke with the reporters who were standing by. Before anyone left that night, the PC assembled her staff and praised their outstanding performance. The university police chief held a debriefing, which is mandatory following such an event. The city police chief came to the university police station and thanked the officers. The chancellor met with the assembled university police in their offices and thanked them. The chief and the officers were exceptionally pleased by the chancellor's recognition of their work.

The PC first told the officers who had worked that night that they had to take a two-day leave; she later changed that to an option after consulting with the psychological consultant. Some officers wanted to work. One week later, the psychological consultant returned to work with the officers. CARE met with the nonpolice staff.

Since that time, three officers have become part of a peer counselor program for police from the whole county.

The emergency policy group convened again later. They discussed follow-up service with CARE and follow-up letters to students, staff, and families. They discussed the memorial service and who would be responsible for planning.

IO—Information Officer

On the night of the hostage crisis, the IO was called between 1:00 and 2:00 A.M. by the VC for administration. The IO and the public affairs officer (PAO), neither of whom knew the nature of the crisis, arrived together to find familiar streets guarded by officers with drawn guns and to learn of an armed man holding students hostage. The IO found the situation incredible.

The IO called additional staff. He gained more information about the student hostages. He was mindful that the situation did not arise from a university event, yet the majority of the people involved were students. When he learned the identity of the gunman, who had himself been a student in the past, he released that information. The IO issued a statement when the student hostage was killed. His intent was to inform, to express the university's grief and concern, and to identify the off-campus location of the crisis. The IO's public statements were carefully articulated to avoid any appearance or implication of university responsibility for the events.

After the episode ended, senior staff met to discuss whether and when there should be a press conference. Although the IO knew that there was too little time to prepare, the chancellor needed the opportunity to express publicly his concern and sorrow. The press conference was planned.

The IO's office issued statements of concern for the victims, and also included descriptions of Henry's off-campus location. At 10:30 A.M., the IO announced a press conference for 2:00 P.M. The IO knew that he did not have enough time to prepare the chancellor fully for what the IO anticipated the reporters would ask. At the conference, a reporter asked the chancellor why the university had the highest crime rates of any campus. The chancellor said that was the opposite of the truth and added that the reporter should check those statistics with the university offices. The chancellor had misstated the facts, but the reporter failed to verify them.

When the reporter included the misstatement by the chancellor, saying the campus had the lowest crime rate, and overemphasized that error without checking the facts, the IO sent a strongly worded letter to the newspaper complaining about unprofessional reporting. The newspaper printed a correction and removed the reporter from university coverage.

The IO's office puts out a biweekly newsletter with news of the campus. The independent student paper is published daily. Information about these events was fully reported in prominent places in each of the publications, but, the main means of communicating with the campus about this tragedy was through the public media.

The media questioned whether there could and should have been some earlier intervention and identification of the assailant as a troubled person who could cause trouble. IO found experts for the media to interview. He also drafted letters for the chancellor to send to the community.

In adverse situations, the IO tries to influence the references to the university. What happens at UC becomes national news.

PAO—Public Affairs Officer

On the night the hostages were taken, the PAO received a call at 1:10 A.M. The PAO called the IO, who had also received a message. They came to campus together. The PAO called the chancellor to tell him what had happened up to that point.

The PAO did not recommend that the chancellor come to campus then but said that he would call him later with an update. When the PAO arrived, he identified himself to police as an official on business for the university. The police were limiting access to the campus.

The PAO set up the command unit in its assigned area in the police offices as designated by the Emergency Response Committee. The PAO called the VC and a staff member who was responsible for admissions and registration data so those at the command center could get access to records.

The committee had a TV in the command center and could hear by means of the Berkeley police update just what was happening.

When the death of a student hostage had been confirmed, the PAO again briefed the chancellor. The PAO failed to reach the president of the university system who lived nearby; they could only get his answering machine. The

PAO requested a police officer of that district go to the president's home to notify him personally.

At 5:30 A.M., when the PAO again spoke with the chancellor, the chancellor talked about closing the campus but did not want to make that decision until later. The chancellor arrived on campus shortly thereafter. Both the PAO and the chancellor were aware that the police would be rushing the hostage at daylight.

When the crisis ended, the chancellor and the president were immediately surrounded by the press. Both men were deeply concerned for the students and their families.

The Emergency Response Committee wanted to be sure that parents of the students knew what had been happening.

The university was receiving calls from all over. Everyone calling wanted to know how such a thing as the taking of hostages could have happened. The mayor and city officials wanted to know how such a situation could have been allowed to arise and implied that the university was responsible.

One reporter asked the chancellor why the campus had the highest crime rate in the nation. The chancellor said that, in fact, the rate was very low but told the reporter to check with the IO for the statistics. The reporter did not check the statistics and quoted the chancellor's inaccurate statement.

The erroneous quotation in the newspaper led the mayor to conclude that the social problems behind this incident were being attributed to the city. This implication offended the mayor. The PAO and the IO concluded that it would have been better to have made statements in anticipation of the questions the reporters would ask, but there was too little time to plan ahead. The PAO is ever mindful that responses from the university should reflect the unique image and values of the university. The school did not want to be held accountable for an individual's violent act. Within a few days, the mayor and the chancellor had talked together and resolved their differences.

Members of the response team were pleased at how the Emergency Response Committee had taken responsibility for the university reaction to the crisis. The committee appeared to have worked very well. Everyone on the committee played a key role in responding to the tragedy.

The committee again planned a memorial service. Because the family of the victim was well-known, dignitaries from off-campus were asked to speak. Because the mother of the victim worked in the Office of the President of the University system, the planning of the memorial service did not involve students to the same extent as the service for the fire victims.

The PAO is mindful of the fact that whatever happens at this school, whatever is said, will be noted all over the country, possibly even internationally. The PAO is aware that the institution's values must influence everything the university does.

On the Saturday following the hostage incident, Henry's had a ceremonial reopening. Without making any advance statement, the chancellor and his wife attended. That act was appreciated by the university community.

SA—Student Activities Director

The SA, as a member of the command group, coordinated the campus information hotline. Since most of the hostages were from fraternities and sororities, information was being transmitted from the Greek advisor who was standing by the students and finding out from them who was in the bar. The SA was assimilating all information at the command center. As the staff was learning the names of hostages, the staff researched their Greek affiliations so that the university would be ready to serve first those Greek groups most affected.

Because the assailant was an Iranian, the staff had some concern about retaliatory acts against other Iranian students. A meeting was set with the student activities staff and Iranian student leaders.

The Greek advisors coordinated the needs of the different chapters and arranged for a variety of counseling services. Specific members of the student activities staff were assigned to negotiate the academic adjustments for students.

Two of the staff attended the funeral. All of the staff went to the campus memorial service. The following two weeks the SA held two debriefing sessions with staff. CARE visited with staff.

AHD—Assistant Director of Housing and Dining Services

On the day of the hostages were taken, the Assistant Director of Housing and Dining Services (AHD) was called at home about midnight. He used his university emergency personnel identity card to get past the police barriers. A bleeding student had escaped to the residence hall across from Henry's. The residence hall director notified the campus police who alerted the university and summoned an ambulance.

After consultation with the police, the AHD went to each floor, informed students about the hostage situation, and evacuated all of them from their rooms to the hallway where they would sleep to avoid being in any line of fire. The danger was too great to allow any person to enter or leave the building. The residence hall director reportedly felt that he could better inform the students and cause less panic by talking with students floor by floor rather than as one large group.

Four more hostages escaped and later a larger number. The victims had been seriously mistreated and abused. The AHD listened to each victim and tried to help all of them deal with their feelings until they could be taken to the hospital in an ambulance.

The staff of the housing services department made the following suggestions for improving their emergency preparedness:

- There needs to be an after-hours plan for crises. Each unit needs its own plan rather than following a system-wide plan for housing.
- Staff need training with communication radios. Radios need to be left in a central location at night and on weekends.
- Locations where persons will meet during emergencies need call-waiting on phones.
- Staff wanted to be called when crises occur in the middle of the night, even if not in their area, so they would be prepared if needed later.
- Staff suggested they be taught to use the security system to secure a building without changing key cores.
- It would be helpful for management team members to get a basic orientation to dining services facilities including how to make coffee for a large number of people during a crisis.
- During the recent emergencies, the housing staff quickly made signs that were very effective. Also many staff members' answering machines proved helpful in communication.
- Housing staff would like to know how to be more helpful to the university police.
- During the bomb threats, some of the information seemed incomplete about other campus closings.
- Bullhorns are needed for communication with large groups.
- Ready-made signs indicating that a building is closed due to an emergency could be kept on hand.
- Department beeper numbers need to be published and circulated more widely to be useful in emergencies.

The following list of services available, with office locations, was circulated following the tragic events.

University-Wide Services

For hostages, families and friends:

- Individual assessment, support and referral at the University Health Service.
- Academic accommodations.
- Groups for hostages, family and friends by Counseling and Psychiatric Service.
- Calls to parents and families.
- Sexual Assault Group.

For students:

- Open support groups.
- Individual counseling.
- Educational presentations on grief/trauma—to be held in residence halls and Greek houses.
- Handouts distributed.

For faculty and staff:

- Drop-in support groups.
- Groups for offices providing services.
- CARE service.
- Individual support and service.
- Distribution of educational materials.

For all:

- Memorial service.
- Drop-in sexual assault support groups.

For community:

- Services of the city community mental health services.
- Distribution of material.

RM—Risk Manager

Following the tragedy at Henry's, the university failed to inform a family of a student's serious injury. The university had procedures for notifying parents of the death of a student but had not developed a plan for notifying parents of seriously injured students.

DS—Dean of Students

The police dispatcher was unable to reach the DS on the night the hostages were taken. When he heard the news on television at 8:00 A.M., he reported to the Emergency Response Team.

In the case of the fire, the Greek involvement meant that student services had to lead the university response. In the hostage crisis, the police led the response. Student Services provided supporting services for students and families. The whole campus was affected. Parents called, concerned about the safety of their children. Some of the same people affected by the fire were among those held hostage at Henry's. Many students asked for academic accommodations.

There was no guide for how to cope with calls from parents except to be supportive and honest. The night of the events at Henry's, the university instituted a telephone number where callers could obtain information. Student affairs prepared to give victim assistance at various locations, including counseling services in the Greek houses.

After the crisis was over student life staff called the hostages and parents of the hostages to inquire about their needs and concerns. Plans were made to follow up with hostages for the next six months.

In the wake of so much anxiety there was also much distress. As of June 1991, the DS described the university as still reeling from an extraordinarily difficult year. The Greek system had not recovered.

However, some of the sororities and fraternities thought the university's efforts to provide counseling services was an overreaction. They said that rather than services they needed advisors, to help them decide the next steps as opposed to helping them understand their feelings. "The Greeks wanted to act as if the tragedy was not the Greeks' problem."

Follow-Up Activities of the Dean of Students Office

- The dean of students and staff called all hostages to inquire about their needs and concerns. A list of hostages was difficult to get.
- A staff person was assigned to handle academic concerns.
- The chancellor sent a letter to all students and parents.
- A staff member was in charge of contacting all parents of injured students.

- The chancellor visited Greek houses with the dean of students and Greek advisors.
- Student activities staffed the hotline all day until 7:00 P.M.
- A meeting to evaluate progress of the above plans was arranged for two days later.
- The DS asked staff to prepare for students' calling with questions about academic accommodation. Staff were urged not to play "telephone tag." Every effort should be made to communicate directly with students.
- Staff prepared a summary of comments by parents of hostages describing the needs of hostages and families for counseling.
- The Greek advisors coordinated the chancellor's visit to five Greek chapters that were directly affected by the crisis.
- The on-campus memorial service was held on October 2nd.

Health Services

The chancellor called the Mental Health Services when he was preparing a letter for the university community. He wanted to know what the best recommendations would be for the community. He also asked the Mental Health Services to share information with the university.

NP—Emergency Preparedness Officer

The response to the crisis at Henry's was a model of cooperation between the city and the campus and among all the committee members at the command site. All the necessary services were present. The committee had functioned sucessfully in a crisis.

The committee is known beyond the campus borders because the university, through NP, has invited the various disaster relief planning agencies to meet together with the university to create a plan for the whole area.

The committee has recommended, and the university community has agreed, that each faculty member should be asked to read a statement about safety on the first day of class the following fall. The committee wants to be assured that everyone knows that the safety of each student is a concern of the university.

JG—A Student Who Witnessed the Fire and the Hostage Crisis

JG was in her sorority house when she saw the flames in the fraternity house next door. She alerted the other people in the house and was among those evacuated from her building. Although the university housing service offered her sorority alternate housing, she and her friends were able to find a place to stay.

JG and her friends remained at the scene all night and the next day. They watched the firemen retrieve the bodies.

JG made special mention of the admiration that she and the other students had for the chancellor and the top administrators who had all been there helping through the night and into the morning.

JG had just left her friends at Henry's when the hostage crisis occurred. JG's female friends were assaulted during the time they were hostages. JG didn't know what to say to them.

Five of the hostages were in counseling with the others in the sorority, but the victims did not speak of their experiences, and the distance between victims and nonvictims increased. The counselor recommended that each seek individual counseling.

The university gave free meal cards to students who were displaced. JG said that she and the other students were very appreciative.

VC—Vice Chancellor for Undergraduate Affairs

The vice chancellor for undergraduate affairs (VC) circulated a revised student-death policy that identifies which offices are responsible for notifying families of students' deaths in differing situations. The following are named: Health and Counseling Services, Office of International Students, university police, or the senior administrative officer most knowledgeable or closely associated with the situation. Those people are to tell parents the known facts without speculating on them.

Persons responding to a death on campus are to keep an objective account of the event and to inform the specific university offices cited in the communication.

On the following pages are statements released to the community and university after the tragedy at Henry's.

Statement from the Chancellor to the Community
September 27, 1990

The taking of hostages at the Durant Hotel has been a sudden and painful shock to our community and a sad reminder that no place is immune from an act of random and irrational violence.

This is a time for our community to draw together and provide every kind of support for those who were directly involved and for those who were affected. I am making sure that campus services are fully directed toward this need. Beyond that must be the personal caring and comforting of friends and the sharing of our feelings, which I know will be happening in countless ways in the days ahead.

I speak for the campus in expressing our very deep regrets and sympathies to the family and friends of . . . were injured.

We all can be proud and thankful that the students and others held hostage showed such bravery in the face of terrible danger. Both the . . . Police and the U.C. Police showed bravery and the highest levels of professional competence. Campus staff and many others performed far beyond the normal calls of duty. We thank all of them.

A campus gathering for students, faculty, staff, and friends has been set for 5:00 P.M. Monday . . . I will join others in speaking there.

Statement from CARE—Services for Faculty and Staff
Distributed Campuswide—September 27

The Hostage Crisis

The recent hostage situation, that resulted in a fatality and many people physically and emotionally injured, has affected the students, faculty, staff, and others in the campus community. People are feeling the effects of this incident in addition to the post-trauma reactions from the recent fire and deaths in the fraternity house, and the bomb scare. Below is some information on possible post-trauma symptoms as well as the effects of cumulative trauma. Please recognize that experiencing any of these can be normal reactions to trauma, and that, with time, there is a natural healing process which occurs.

Post-Trauma Symptoms

shock, numbness
disbelief, denial
feeling helpless, out of control
feeling vulnerable
disturbing images or memories
feeling unsafe
sadness, crying, depression
sleep disturbances
anxiety, worrying, panic
moodiness, irritability, anger
physical exhaustion
guilt
despair
difficulty concentrating
hypervigilance, jumpiness

Traumatic events can affect everyone, whether or not you have directly experienced the trauma. If you have experienced past traumas, including deaths, losses, fire, sexual or racial assault, violent incidents, and other assaults, you may be experiencing memories and feelings from those events and have increased symptoms now. Freshmen and other people new to the campus may feel more conflicted about their adjustment to this new environment. Parents of college-age children may also be experiencing reactions to this crisis.

Grief/Loss

Some people on campus who knew the students who died recently are actively grieving. In addition, many people are re-experiencing grief for other people in their lives who have died. These symptoms of grief and loss are similar to the post-trauma symptoms listed above.

(Resources previously referred to are listed.)

For all:

Drop-in sexual assault support groups

For the community:

Individual outreach and group services to residents and businesses that were cordoned off

Distribution of educational materials

Cumulative Trauma

Psychologically, we connect traumas; while the actual events may be separate, unrelated and distinct, psychologically we experience them as related—this can intensify the symptoms of trauma and prolong recovery. Recovery from trauma takes time; the cycle of recovery from past traumas has been interrupted by this new trauma.

We relate to trauma with a sense of disbelief, disowning the experience. As a result of multiple traumatic incidents you may experience a greater sense of disconnectedness from yourself, others, and your studies/ work. To counter this, you may create your own "story" explaining the series of traumatic events, promoting a sense of control and order.

What Can You Do?

Experience your feelings—you have the right to have feelings, even if you were not directly affected.

Talk about your feelings, especially to someone who feels safe to you.

Pay attention to your feelings in order to plan for health and safety, including diet, rest, exercise, use of substances (caffeine, nicotine, sugar, alcohol, and drugs).

Spend time with people you care about—ask for emotional support from friends, colleagues, family.

Allow the opportunity to take a brief respite from your surroundings if this would help you feel better.

Remember that each person can experience trauma differently, and that you and others may have different needs at different times; try to be flexible.

Seek support from campus and community resources (see attached list).

If your symptoms persist, cause you excessive discomfort, or increase over time, you may want to seek professional assistance. Of course you should feel permission any time to discuss concerns you have with a professional. In addition to individual help, post-trauma support groups for students, faculty, staff, departments, and other affected organizations are available.

Statement from President of the University System Regarding the Shooting—September 27

Chancellor T. and I visited briefly with some of the hostages immediately upon their release, and we were both impressed with the courage and strength of character they displayed during this very traumatic night.

Chancellor T. is doing everything possible to respond to the emotional implications of this terrible event, not only for the hostages, their families and friends, but also for the campus community in general.

My sympathies go out to the family of . . . . We all hope those injured will fully recover.

My gratitude also goes out to the . . . Police Department and U.C. Police Department for the effective and professional way in which they carried out their duties and the bravery of the officers involved in this action.

Statement by Chancellor—September 28

I have been talking to a number of people on the campus since early yesterday, including students, faculty, and staff members. All are feeling a deep grief over the loss and the pain inflicted on our students in the terrible hostage incident at the Durant Hotel.

For some the grief is simply numbing. For others it is combined with outrage and frustration. The question on all minds is why? Why here? Why now? Why us? The news media have a responsibility to ask those questions as well and to try to find answers. We all want to find answers.

In the case of a random and totally senseless act of violence committed by one person with mental illness, I expect there will be pieces of answers—but nothing that comes clearly and logically together. Our society's shortcomings in the treatment and care of the mentally ill form a piece of an answer. We can also look to the poverty and conditions of our cities . . . at the flood of guns that are easily available . . . at the distrust and hatred that still divide people throughout the world.

But we are still left with a "why" that is close to our own lives and may never be really answered. Such questions remain at other campuses, in other cities, in rural areas . . . at Montreal and Florida . . . at Austin and San Francisco . . . at a school in Stockton, at a hamburger shop in San Diego.

I want to make a special point about the events of Thursday and those aspects that suggest an attack on women. All women feel a special fear because of such things. Our society, our communities, and each of us owe a special obligation to recognize this and do all we can to rid our world of oppression and mistreatment of women. We have strong programs for this purpose at C . . . , but this is a sad reminder that we must continue and strengthen those efforts in every way possible.

I want to make another point. We have many students from Iran and other nations of the Middle East. They are fine students and fine people. It would only deepen the tragedy of yesterday if the sickness of one man were to create ill feelings toward others of the same ethnicity.

Although we cannot answer the "why" of a terrible moment, we must look for the positive and lasting ways we can learn and build. And C . . . has a lot to build upon, because it is a strong and caring place where people share a basic commitment and come together at a time of great need.

I met a student yesterday whose parent was urging him to leave B . . . "I love this place," he told me. "I made my decision to come here, and I am not leaving."

As happened after the tragic fire earlier this month at a fraternity house, there is again a strong sense of coming together and of caring that runs through the campus. It shows in the tremendous dedication, skill, and hard work of support services . . . including health and counseling services, student housing, the Associated Students, the faculty, physical resources, my colleagues in the administration and many others. The suddenness of these two incidents . . . related only by the chance of time and place . . . has demonstrated that C . . . does have the strength and skill to do what is needed, and I doubt any other institution could have done it better. I say that in my way of thanks to everyone.

The individual caring and comforting is another thing that happens in our community. You will see that in a dramatic way, I am sure, when we have a large gathering at 5:00 P.M. next Monday in Faculty Glade.

I want to mention the fine work of both the campus and city of B . . . police departments in the incredibly difficult task of yesterday—and of the fire department and other services that responded to the fraternity fire.

Yesterday's tragedy did not take place on campus. As I said after the incident of the recent fire, our concern has to extend beyond the campus into areas where our students live. We must urge the neighborhood community and the city of B . . . to push harder to solve the underlying problems in the south campus neighborhood. There has been good progress in recent months. . . .

. . . I join with the entire campus in extending our very deep regrets and sympathies to the family and friends of. . . . I have been meeting with students and their families, and in the next few days, I will be sending a letter to the parents of all B . . . students—as well as a letter to all of the students themselves.

When I took the job as chancellor, I said it was the greatest honor for me because of the outstanding excellence of C . . . in its teaching and research. There are no finer students, professors, or staff members at any other campus. Sad events don't change that but only strengthen our resolve to maintain and enhance C. . .'s eminence among the world's great universities . . . and its service to our state, our nation, and the world.

Memo from the Chancellor to Deans, Directors, Department Chairpersons, and Administrative Officers

RE: SUPPORT SERVICES FOR OUR CAMPUS COMMUNITY

The traumatic events this week have touched all members of our campus community, either directly or indirectly. These are difficult times. As we move through them, I wish to remind you that the emotional stress and disruption that some of our students are experiencing as a result of the events at the Durant Hotel may require accommodations in their course work. Those held hostage may experience severe emotional trauma, and even those in adjacent dormitories may feel that they have been through a profoundly disturbing experience. We need to provide support for one another. Please be compassionate in dealing with the academic problems that may arise for affected students, and please be alert for any difficulties that may arise in any courses in your unit. Attached to this memo is an educational handout on trauma, a fact sheet outlining the campus response to the event, and a list of resources available to members of the campus community. Please assist us by disseminating the attached information in order to help our recovery. Chancellor T.

SUMMARY

Each office had, after each of the events, assessed its response to these tragedies. Several assessments were in writing. University employees seemed to want to make sure that credit for good work did not go to them alone. They were dumbfounded by how much tragedy had befallen them but proud of how caring and responsive the members of the university had been.

Many people made reference to the kind things the chancellor had done; the community reported enormous pride in his kindnesses.

On the first-year anniversary of the fire, Greek students held a candlelight vigil in memory of the students who had died in the fire and in the hostage crisis. Approximately three hundred students attended.

COMMENTARY

No campus wants to face such tragedies as UC did, but the experience gained from dealing with them can be valuable. Although the university concluded that they were not fully prepared to respond to the fire, they had informed the community, given solace and care to the victims, and helped the campus to return to its purposes.

The debriefing after the fire enabled a more immediate response to subsequent crises. The work of the previous years' planning was apparent in the command center where necessary staff were present and the needs of the victims, their families and friends, and the rest of the academic community as well as the external community were addressed. The involvement of the entire campus in planning for safety and for crisis had made the response to emergency the business of the whole community.

UC developed its crisis response plan the way it develops all plans, that is, by involving people from each unit in its creation. The ongoing safety committees in each department keep the design current.

The organization and communication scheme UC adopted was responsible for the orderly and rapid evacuation of the campus during the bomb threat. Colleges, like all institutions, need plans for communicating with everyone on campus. The pyramid communication system from central office to building coordinator, to departments, to other employees was effective enough to evacuate 38,000 people within a few hours.

The ID card with emergency information for students and the emergency personnel ID card are ideas worth copying. The information on the student card relates to the residence halls where the students live. This information identifies the responsibility that each person at the residence hall has in an emergency. The focus of the campus plan is that all community members know their responsibilities in an emergency.

The idea to spread information about safety and crisis response through posters and a fair was both unique and attention-getting.

The designated area used for a command center allowed everyone to know where to report. In the hostage situation, the proximity of the command center to the police station made communication much easier.

To provide an agency (CARE) whose exclusive purpose is to respond to employee emotional needs is an exceptional concept. The help they offered people who had been at the front lines of the disasters was uniformly praised and appreciated. To attempt to meet the emotional needs of the people who responded to the crises by having the counselors visit them is a striking idea.

The school has a list of campus organizations. Under each organization is a list of student members. The list of students living in each Greek house allowed for early identification of the missing students from the Greek house.

The information officer's ready access to information about the fraternity allowed him to better inform the media. He anticipated the needs of the press and continually assured the media that the school would keep them informed. With his messages to the media he was also assuring the university community that the school was functioning despite the tragic events.

In each statement the spokesperson defined the limits of the university's authority without saying the university was not assuming responsibility. He issued a copy of the last city-conducted fire safety audit to reinforce that position.

On the morning of the fire, the information officer announced a brief memorial service for the students who had died, which would be held the following Monday. This service offered the people caught in the tragedy of the fire a positive outlet for their emotions.

The chancellor's request for a moment of silence during the service and his announcement that flags would be flown at half mast became important symbols. Researchers on the process of recovery from tragedy have noted the importance of such rituals to the healing of both individuals and for communities. [1]

Nothing can replace the kind acts done by senior administration. Their very presence at the scene of an emergency is a major support to the university community. It was an exceptional mark of compassion for the chancellor to have devoted his attention to the parents and to have told them that alcohol had been a contributing factor to the deaths in the fire. Telling the parents that the media would probably report that information helped to prepare them for the subsequent broadcast of the information.

The chancellor's actions and the president's presence were noted by all the people who responded to the fires. The community identified with the chancellor's many kind gestures. Several people mentioned the thank-you letters he sent to all who worked during the crises. Others mentioned his appearance with his wife at the reopening of the bar, the scene of the hostage crisis. His visit to the police station was mentioned by many people.

In addition, the chancellor's letters to the community that identified which responses to the traumas were normal and which reflected more personal difficulty gave readers a chance to better understand their own needs. These letters helped people understand that shock and grief are normal reactions to a tragedy.

To have university police serve on university committees is an outstanding idea. With such participation, police can better identify with the campus ethos.

The on-the-spot emotional support for police who are facing violence may help avert many serious consequences. The exceptional outreach that had each officer meet with the psychologist whenever an officer was relieved at his or her post helped both morale and healing.

It is important to note that the university had procedures for notifying families when a students dies but no such notification plan when students are seriously injured. Many campuses make this type of omission in their planning.

It was clear in this case study, as it will be in the later case studies, that when a disaster occurs, many want to help and simply need some guidance as to where their contributions will do the most good.

REFERENCE

1. Zinner, E. *Death on Campus*, Jossey Bass Inc., 1985.

CHAPTER
two
* * * * * * * *

Date Rape On-Campus

CU is a doctorate-granting institution located in a metropolitan region. CU has 10,000 students, 9,000 of whom are full-time undergraduates. Fewer than one-fifth of the students live in residence halls and apartments on-campus.

In February, a woman reported that she had been raped on campus at knife-point in her dormitory room by a fellow student. The attack was reported to have taken place some months previous. Other victims of the alleged attacker came forward, two who complained of sexual assault and another who charged rape. Following the expulsion of the accused in May, the local media broke the story.

BACKGROUND

The Special Projects Committee was established soon after a protest group had taken over the offices of the administration to call attention to a long-festering problem of neglected racism. The group apparently found protest the only effective means to effect action. The media gave the protest wide coverage. The administration's investigation of the event revealed that the anger that prompted the protesters to such behavior could have been addressed at a much earlier time, thereby preventing the extreme behavior. The committee was established to prevent explosive needs from arising in the university community and to deal with those needs that did arise in a positive way.

One of the duties of committee members is to report any occurrences on-campus that could lead to extreme behavior or unwanted media attention. When the committee hears of such events, even rumors of them, it contacts the vice president, ZB, who is the president's executive assistant (EAP); she convenes the committee. The committee stays informed and guides the university responses to unusual events.

In addition to ZB, the other members of the Special Projects Committee are the vice president for student affairs, the campus human relations specialist, a representative from the campus police, the information officer, and the VP for administration. ZB keeps the president fully informed.

The committee's task is to get all the facts and to negotiate or reconcile controversial issues. Members make recommendations to the president such as whether he should speak publicly about an issue, state a university position, or take action. The members of the committee regularly relate campus news to ZB.

THE CASE

ACP—Assistant Chief of Police

In February, a woman complained that a student was following her around campus. The assistant chief of police (ACP) spent several hours interviewing her. After a while, she described the man who was following her as the assailant who had held her in her room in handcuffs and raped her at knife-point the previous September. The ACP immediately informed the vice president for student services.

The ACP suspected that the alleged perpetrator might have assaulted other women on the campus. While ACP was investigating this possibility, he called women students whom he believed would know the alleged assailant. He told each women that he was investigating a male student and asked her if she knew him. If she spoke angrily about the student, he followed up with questions about the student's possible offensive behavior. The ACP invited each women to talk with him individually at the police station. Such meetings lasted an average of three hours. These meetings were followed by two or three later meetings. Once these women students began to describe what he concluded to have been rape and sexual assault, they would lose much of their composure and begin to relive the pain they had experienced. The ACP described the victims' retelling of the assaults as a slow process taking many hours.

The ACP asked each woman if she had consented to any sexual acts with the alleged attacker, prior to, during, or after the reported attack. All of the alleged victims said they had not consented to any of the actions they had reported.

At the conclusion of his investigation, two women reported they had each been victims of a sexual assault by the same attacker, and one woman related that she, too, had been handcuffed and raped at knife-point. These later victims described the assaults as having occurred more than a year before.

Each woman was informed about the criminal justice system and the workings of the state's attorney's office. The victims were told they did not have to make the decision to prosecute immediately. The ACP forwarded the reports of the crimes to the state's attorney's office. The state's attorney decided not to prosecute because of insufficient proof and because of the length of time between the crimes and the dates the crimes were reported. The ACP explained that it is easier to get the courts to prosecute on a misdemeanor than on a felony such as rape or sexual assault. The court accepts the misdemeanor charge more readily because it takes less evidence to convict. The campus, however, has the right to hold hearings for any violation of law whether or not the case is prosecuted in court. In this case, the state's attorney concluded that the charges would not meet the court's standard of proof, "beyond a shadow of a doubt," but the university decided to hold judicial hearings anyway.

The ACP gave each victim information about the Rape Crisis Center and the on-campus health and counseling services. The women were urged to contact these offices. The ACP felt that it was important to encourage these women to make their own contacts for help.

Once the women had told the ACP that they had been assaulted, they became impatient to see action taken, and they frequently called to see how the case was progressing.

The ACP helped the women individually to understand what would happen in the campus judicial hearing, what kinds of questions the board members might ask them, how the police investigation is conducted in such matters, and how the campus judicial process works. The ACP insisted that each woman know that the questioners might offend them since the campus judicial system allows questions about prior sexual experience. He told the women that, as the prosecutor, he would be able to object to such questions with the hope that the chair would disallow them.

The ACP presented the case to the Judicial Board with a recommendation that the accused be expelled from school. The ACP was able to arrange for the alleged victims to wait in an office during the hearings rather than in the hallway as is the custom.

The ACP was aware that the alleged victims had turned to a campus women's committee that both supported them and urged the university to take firm action. The ACP urged the students to consider discussing their cases with their parents. Prior to this, the victims had not informed their parents. Later, two of the parents called the ACP.

Another officer in the university police force brought the accused in for questioning immediately after the first alleged victim had related her story. DF, the accused, was advised of his rights. He agreed to speak without an attorney present. At the time, the ACP sat in the room as an observer but asked no questions. The ACP concluded that the alleged assailant was not dangerous because the events had taken place some time before, and because he appeared to be functioning normally.

The accused's parents attempted to call the ACP, but the ACP did not accept the call. The accused was represented by an attorney, and the university lawyer was counsel to the board.

The ACP consulted with the vice president for student services: together they concluded DF was a danger to the resident population. The housing director suspended DF from housing. The accused was allowed to bring his attorney to a hearing to appeal the suspension. The suspension was upheld.

Some of the victims felt intimidated by the accused's presence on campus. One of the victims felt intimidated by his presence in the same academic building where she was taking her classes. The police provided continuous escort service for all victims until resolution of the case. The victims were angry. They perceived the accused as having more freedom than they did. They could not move about spontaneously but DF could.

The ACP informed the Judicial Board that he would be charging the accused with rape. If the victims had chosen not to proceed, the ACP still would have forwarded the case to the Judicial Board for action. Alleged victims do not have a choice about the decision to prosecute within the university judicial system. The ACP tries to get students to be witnesses in such situations. However, if they do not agree to testify, the evidence will be presented from the records of his investigation.

When the press heard of the rape charge, they wanted to interview the alleged victims. Media were referred to university relations.

The judicial hearings ran for many days. Seven people's schedules had to mesh. The first hearing was held March 21st, the second April 18th; then they took place on April 25th, 27th, and all day on May 4th, when the judicial board made a finding of responsibility and recommended a sanction.

Since the time the above complaints were reported, the ACP has negotiated a new procedure. If the complaint of rape is taken immediately following an attack, the victim is taken to a hospital that has a rape crisis service. The hospital provides a support person during all procedures and interviews. When a sexual assault or rape is reported some time after the attack, the ACP will contact personnel at the Rape Crisis Center, who have agreed to send a counselor to be with the victim and to accompany her during the investigation.

IO—Information Officer

The information officer (IO) had already heard rumors about rapes from friends on the campus before April when she learned about the reported rapes from the Special Projects Committee. There was a rumor that a student newspaper reporter attempted to interview the accused student before the hearing. The IO was told it was a community newspaper reporter. The reporter was denied access to the discipline proceedings since special projects was concerned about violation of the Family Privacy Act, which guarantees the privacy of student educational records. Campus behavior records are part of the educational record.

University counsel advised the university that no information about the case should be divulged. Three weeks before, however, after an editor of a student newspaper had sued for access to disciplinary records, a judge in Missouri ruled that the Family Privacy Act was not applicable to university discipline records. The IO was concerned that the press might want to make this a test case in this state.

A different reporter asked the IO about the status of criminal charges, whether victims had been encouraged to initiate proceedings, and whether county police were excluded from the investigation. The IO described the campus judicial process for the press. In late April, the press asked if there was an ongoing judicial hearing for a rape case, and the IO acknowledged that there was. This acknowledgment came on the recommendation of the attorney general's office, responsible for legal interpretations for state universities. When the IO told the press she could not comment because adjudication processes were ongoing, the reporters and editors of that paper became angry with the university. The IO believes the press needed to understand that printing a story could have prejudiced witnesses and the board.

The Judicial Board members were instructed not to discuss the case among themselves or others. Twenty-four hours after the IO's statement that she could not comment, a reporter called and rudely demanded answers, citing the Missouri case. To meet the request, the IO gave information about criminal events reported in the past academic year. The university, she explained, did not want to appear in the national media as another test case. If that occurred, the university would then be responding to many different media requests.

The women on campus were also interested in the information issue, and it was possible that opening the question of who had the right to information in discipline cases, particularly rape and sexual assault, might lead to demonstrations.

The IO responded to questions from the press about criminal charges with information that the ACP had provided about the state's attorney's office's refusal to prosecute. The IO wanted to communicate that the institution took this situation seriously and that it had appropriate university procedures in place to investigate and take action. Further, she made it known that the university was dealing with the case in a timely manner; it had acted within 24 hours to remove the accused from residence. When women complained about delays in the proceedings, the IO wanted the community to know there was an attorney present from the sexual assault clinic to represent the alleged victims.

The IO knew that, had the accused been found innocent, people would have been very angry.

The IO was distressed that the local paper charged the university with "stonewalling" when she knew she had acted forthrightly. The newspaper editor was referred to the attorney general's office. Vice-President ZB, the IO, and the newspaper editor met to discuss the university's position on release of information about student behavior. This topic was picked up by a local television station, but there was not much more interest.

The IO did not provide any information that people could use to influence the results of the disciplinary hearings. The university took the rights of the women seriously but did not want that fervor to deny the rights of the accused.

When the lives of students are in the balance, the university does not divulge information that could be used to harm the students. The university must consider the feelings and rights of both the alleged victims and the alleged perpetrators. The alleged victims were already moving around campus with security escorts. The university felt that the release of information would be a further violation of their privacy.

Usually, in such a disciplinary hearing the university will reveal as many facts as possible. "The newspaper criticism and portrayal of the university as uncooperative was damaging to the process of thinking and planning for the best solution," said the IO. When the reporter and his editor persisted in wanting more information, the IO asked him, on April 24th, to put that request in writing. On May 6th, the IO forwarded the request to the attorney general who decided that the decision of the Missouri judge was not applicable in this state. The university attorney advised that, in order to protect the rights of all parties concerned, the law does not provide for the disclosure of information pending the investigation. Neither is release of information about the internal discipline process mandated.

The IO is the spokesperson for the institution. One of her roles is to respond to daily inquiries for the president. After the inquiries from the newspaper, the IO released a list of the number of victims' reporting sexual assaults and rapes on campus during the academic year and when those events occurred. Four acquaintance rapes and three fourth-degree sexual assaults had been reported.

On May 5th, the IO received a call from the news supervisor at a national network telling the IO a national news team was coming to campus to prepare for the evening news. It was the IO's understanding that the local affiliate had suggested the coverage to the national network. The network team did "man on the street" interviews asking people how they felt about the recent events.

The city newspaper referred to the interviews and described the university as not being open with information. The newspaper lumped together the university concern about student rights in the judicial case with totally unrelated issues that led the press to conclude that the university was not forthcoming with information.

On June 26th, the IO gave the following statement to the media: "This spring, a student was expelled from the university and was banned from the campus as a result of actions which were found to endanger the campus community. Under the provisions set forth by the Buckley Amendment, the university is unable to respond to requests for information pertaining to this case."

May 22—Newspaper Headline
Expulsion is recommended for senior at CU

ZB—Vice President and Executive Assistant to the President

The policy of the senior management team is to attend to issues immediately. The management team's Special Projects Committee meets whenever some issue arises that members of the committee believe can dominate the university community internally, externally, or both.

One job of the Special Projects Committee is to anticipate demonstrations or rallies. They assess whether the issue is of national interest, which may involve a much larger reaction, or a more local one restricted to one unique event. The committee tries to contain the publicly perceived issue to the one at hand.

When the VP for student affairs told the committee that a student had accused a male senior of a rape that allegedly took place eight months previously, the Special Projects Committee decided to oversee the judicial process. Although there had been no news reports, the campus Women's Committee knew about the allegation, presumably from the alleged victim. Other alleged victims of the same perpetrator came forward. The committee was careful to see that all parties were fairly represented and that the judicial procedures were followed. The judicial officer had recently resigned, and the university needed to appoint a replacement. The committee agreed that university counsel would serve as staff to the Judicial Board and be present for all proceedings.

Parents of the alleged victims and the accused were upset. The father of the accused charged the institution with railroading his son. The parents of the alleged victims phoned to insist that charges be handled seriously.

The hearing took longer than expected, requiring additional hearing and meeting days, which were difficult to arrange because of the size of the Judicial Board and the number of witnesses. When one date had to be rescheduled, some women complained that the university was trying to bury the event. There was a charge of "cover-up." Again, alleged victims' parents called.

The institution wanted to maintain neutrality so that the results would be just. The student newspaper ran one article about the case. The institutional newsletter carried no information. However, ZB informed the student government president and the president of the Faculty Council.

The established university procedure calls for the Judicial Board to recommend a sanction to the provost, who may or may not accept it. There is no further appeal within the university. The process is listed in the judicial code. As a result, it was important that the board deliberations in the rape case keep the provost at a distance, to prevent any influencing his decision. When the process had begun in this rape case, ZB kept the attorney general's office informed. The committee worked closely with the police to be sure that all procedures were legal.

The leadership of CU believes that talking together, as they have done in this Special Projects Committee, helps them to address concerns seriously and consistently. It also gives them an opportunity to be clear about where they stand on issues.

When the case was over, an article appeared in a neighborhood paper which accused the school of withholding information and "stonewalling" the press. This article was not picked up by the city newspaper. How the institution did or did not share information was guided by the university counsel's view of the Buckley Amendment.

Although the university did not speak directly to the campus community about this rape, the president had sent a letter to the community urging safety awareness and crime prevention. A rape prevention program is included in the university's orientation program.

PC—Police Chief

The university has modified policies affecting the police. Formerly, the police chief (PC) spoke directly with the press. Later, he communicated only through the information officer. Next year, the police will return to speaking directly to the media. The chief was made aware of all reports sent in by the officer who took the complaint.

When the PC came to the university, the police reported to the vice president for administrative affairs. The PC believed that a closer relationship with student affairs would improve the community services.

VPS—Vice President for Student Affairs

When the vice president for student affairs (VPS) reflects on the alleged rape, she thinks most about the unique role of campus police who respond both to criminal and noncriminal incidents. Unlike his/her counterpart off-campus, the officer may take a noncriminal miscreant to a dean of students' office. The VPS is concerned that the higher education police force's power be properly limited. Student use of the university police is different from that same student's use of police in the community. Students will make complaints to campus police which they would not make at their district police station. They go to institutional police for less serious crimes.

A complainant making a first visit to the university police may not be able to communicate well enough for the officer to understand what he or she wants. The VPS is aware that the first alleged victim complained of harassment; she was afraid of someone who was following her. She eventually said she had been raped. The rape was reported to the VPS immediately and appeared on the police log the next day.

Within several days, the first student, who had reported being raped, had talked to the residence hall director. The residence hall director told the VPS who was now hearing about this same event from both offices. The police officer who had heard the story brought the student to see the VPS, because the VPS and the student knew each other and the VPS would be able to link the victim to services more easily. The VPS was able to explain the steps in the process that would follow. The student called the VPS nightly for a long time even after the case had been adjudicated. The victim's mother also spoke with the VPS. Another of the alleged victims also continued meeting with the VPS for support.

The ACP, the VPS, and the assistant to the VP for student affairs met with the first student victim and her parent and heard the student's clear intention to go forward with the campus judicial process. The VPS first let the victim know that the likelihood of criminal prosecution was slim because the report of the complaint had been made so late.

The director of residence suspended the accused from housing immediately after the victim told him about the attack. The accused unsuccessfully appealed that decision in an administrative conference. The complainant was not invited to attend. Although the campus judicial code permits the presence of lawyers, the VPS prefers that the university communicate with the student and not with his or her lawyer.

The ACP notified the judicial officer that he was charging the accused on behalf of the university. The judicial officer sent a letter charging the alleged perpetrator with violation of the judicial code and informing him about how to obtain assistance for his defense. As the person making the charge, the ACP was responsible for keeping the witnesses informed.

For the accused, the next step in the process was an administrative conference with the judicial officer, the accused's lawyer, and the charging police officer. The accused did not confess to the charges. If he had, all present would have tried to negotiate a sanction. Most cases in the judicial system are resolved at the administrative conference.

If the accused had admitted to the charges, the police officer would have informed the accused of the sanction that the charging authority, the ACP, was requesting. The officer had, together with the VPS, agreed to recommend expulsion of the student from the university. This particular sanction would not have been negotiated because, by this time, there were three additional victims.

The Judicial Board, a committee of five students, a faculty member, and a staff member, deliberated first on the charges and then on the recommended penalty. The board submitted the recommendation to the provost, who made the final decision from which there is no appeal. Formerly, sanctions were imposed by the VP for student affairs. The change allows the VP for student affairs to be more involved in the process.

During the process, friends and acquaintances of one victim called the VPS to learn if the university was planning appropriate action against the accused. Early on, the VPS told the alleged victim, "I get these calls because you are telling these people about your victimization. I can't comment on your behalf."

A fellow student wanted to know what the university was doing about the telephone harassment. One of the victims had complained of being harassed by telephone by the accused. The university did not wish to delay the ongoing judicial process by adding this new charge. Because the accused was scheduled to graduate in late May, it was important to complete the judicial procedures before that time. An additional complaint of telephone harassment could have resulted in the university's bringing additional charges against the accused. The university had the telephone number of that alleged victim changed. The VPS told the caller about the change in the telephone number. Many other callers asked if the administration was aware of what was happening and if it was paying attention to the fact that a crime had taken place.

One victim's mother spent many hours with the VPS talking about the situation. Although this mother was composed, the mother of a later-identified victim of sexual assault in the same case was fiercely angry with the school because of her daughter's experience.

The VPS kept the Special Projects Committee and the president informed at each step of the judicial process. The committee made suggestions to the VPS. (The committee is continually examining the process to assure that it is both fair and administratively responsible.) The Special Projects Committee concluded that the process worked but that it needed some internal improvements. The committee recommended keeping the alleged victims more informed.

Adjustments to the alleged victims' academic records can be made if affected students need an opportunity to repeat courses. So far, none of the victims has left school, although months after the adjudication, one woman considered transferring. The other three continue to attend school. The VPS is in touch with these women.

A neighborhood newspaper had carried a story critical of the university for not giving more information to them. A meeting of the executive staff of the paper and the VPS, the information officer, and the executive assistant to the president was held. The VPS's inability to comment and still respect the privacy rights of the students left her at a disadvantage in the discussions.

At a later date, university counsel, the campus police chief, the VPS, the news director, the state's attorney, and representatives from another state university in the county met to discuss how to release information in a more coordinated manner in any future investigations.

The VPS works to be knowledgeable about concerns that exist on-campus so that the university can address those concerns before rising levels of frustration cause problems to get out of hand. The VPS, with the president and the Special Projects Committee, has worked to develop policies that will decrease the amount of alienation that on-campus students feel.

This past year the university has developed a sexual harassment policy. During orientation, the institution has emphasized safety and stressed students' accountability for their behavior. This fall the university will distribute a safety publication to all community members. The senior staff believe that statistics concerning crime on campus are not complete, and that sharing such information would distort the truth.

The VPS praised the cooperation and communication among the executive staff that enabled all of them to work so constructively together.

The VPS met with the victims after the sanction had been imposed to evaluate the process. The victims felt they had been treated fairly.

PV—Provost

According to the judicial code of CU, a sanction imposed on a student by the Judicial Board may be appealed to the provost. If the sanction recommended is expulsion, only the provost can make the decision. The PV reviewed all records and tapes of the proceedings, as well as attorney's petition on behalf of the accused in which the attorney challenged the fairness of the procedures and the severity of the penalty. The provost also heard complaints from women students because the case did not move rapidly through the system. The PV expelled the student before graduation. The student had been eligible to graduate later that same month. He did not receive his degree.

The PV had no contact with the press. University counsel were concerned that there be no violation of the Buckley Amendment. Therefore the university limited the amount and what information was disseminated.

PR—President

To reflect on the university response to these events, the essential factor that dominated responses was the timing of the complaint, which was eight months after the rape. The first concern in all victim crimes is for the welfare of the victim, that aid and comfort is given, and that the judicial process is initiated.

The judicial process is cumbersome and difficult for all universities. The president pointed out that administration of such processes is not what universities do best. The universities are not well equipped or trained to assure due process. Tension exists between providing a guarantee of due process and being expeditious in the proceeding.

No rules regulate the timing of the proceedings to make the judicial processes more efficient. "All you can do is fall back on the most qualified people, to make sure that the best people implement the system," said the PR.

According to the PR, universities are expected to do things they are not equipped to do in order to satisfy the courts' commitment to due process. The PR sees two areas of accountability, ethical and judicial. In reviewing the institutional response to the rape, he is sure that the moral and ethical challenges were met; he is less sure of the judicial guarantees for due process.

The PR wants the university community to be assured that the university is committed to the safety of its community members and that justice is done. The external community needs assurance that the institution is well managed.

To assure of the university's committment to community safety, the president was in constant communication with all of the people implementing the process. He does not believe in rules or formulas to fulfill the committment, only able, bright individuals.

If they had to go through this again, the president said he would try to educate the press to understand that the school was doing what it thought was legally correct. The press confuses what is in the public interest and what the public finds interesting. It is not in the public interest for an institution's personal tragedies to be widely aired in public. It is in the public interest to know that the institution is well managed and to know about those particular aspects of management that assure fairness.

Although rape has long been a part of the American culture and will not be erased by any immediate programs, the institution conducts rape awareness programs and special safety programs to educate students and to thereby improve the community.

Memorandum to the C University Community from the President
December 1990

The recent reports of rapes and other crimes on college campuses have prompted me to remind our community that personal safety is everyone's responsibility and requires our continued vigilance.

One of the best defenses against crime is precaution. I urge each member of the community to be security conscious and to protect yourself and your property at home, the residence hall, in your office, and in other campus facilities. Please consider the following:

Take extra precautions for your personal safety by walking together. At the end of an evening class find someone who is walking in your direction.

The loop road is great for walking and jogging, but never alone.

Take a minute at the end of an evening class to allow students to find someone who is going in their direction. . . .

It is extremely important that we watch out for each other so our campus is a secure and safe place for each of us. . . .

Signed "from the President"

COMMENTARY

The campus officials' preoccupation with minimizing the press coverage of the rape during the investigative and judicial processes appears to have resulted in the perception that the broader community was not being informed. Although the administration regularly communicated the status of the disciplinary action to the Women's Center, that message may suggest that only the women, and specifically women known to the center, were interested in the incident. If the community is to be intolerant of assault, knowledge of incidents is important for all members of the campus.

With the 1992 change in the application of the Family Educational Rights and Privacy Act (FERPA), schools may reveal information about behavioral difficulties of students while keeping private their academic records. Until that separation of the two records, schools were instructed to include all records of student behavior as part of the academic record, subject to privacy. Under those circumstances the student had to give permission for release of records to anyone who did not have an educational need for the information. With the current state of the law, the campus would not have to withhold the data from the press.

The very long time, more than a month and a half, to complete the judicial process was a major problem for the victims as well as for the university. This prolonged process must have contributed to the press's feeling excluded. The school obviously did not expect to have a judicial hearing of such duration. To prevent long delays, the judicial committee could be appointed before the beginning of the semester. They could plan a schedule for hearings before the semester starts. It may also help to choose alternate board members should any committee member be unable to serve on the board.

The assistant to the police chief served as investigator, prosecutor, and victim support. He also searched for and found other victims of the accused. A conflict of interest appears to exist between the investigative and prosecutorial roles of the ACP. It may be in the best interest of a fair process if the police office presents information without an investment in the consequences of the judicial hearing.

Although the assistant police chief did not find the accused dangerous, the victims were denied considerable freedom. The university could issue an administrative order at the time formal charges were made that instructs the accused to make no contact with any of the accusers. Furthermore, the administrative order could specify the times and locations that an accused person could be on-campus.

The permission to question an alleged victim about her sexual history doesn't have to be a part of the university judicial process. Fair guidelines could limit the hearing to determining if the assault was committed as charged and to excluding questions not relevant to that information.

The involvement of the VPS in supporting the accusers and their parents may have suggested that the institution was partial. Support services offered by the counseling center to all students involved, or support for both the accused and the accusers by the administration, would allow the campus to be more open about the results of the judicial procedures.

CHAPTER
three
✤ ✤ ✤ ✤ ✤ ✤ ✤ ✤

Murder On-Campus

DEAD STUDENT FOUND ON CAMPUS

On September 12, 1990, the body of a student, HM, was discovered in his room. He had been murdered. Another student, HB, attempted suicide on September 14 and died soon thereafter. The police concluded that HB murdered HM.

BACKGROUND

HTU, a state university, located in a rural area in a town of 8,500, has 3,400 students, 1,600 of whom live on-campus. The school employs 200 staff members and 200 faculty members.

PC—Director of Law Enforcement (Police Chief)

On Wednesday, September 12, at 9:20 P.M., the director of Law Enforcement (PC) responded to a call in a dormitory room on the second floor in S Hall and found the decomposed body of a person he presumed to have been dead four to six days. Because of the condition of the body, a positive identification could not be made, although the residence hall director assumed that the dead person had been the student occupant of the room. There was a putrid stench from the decomposition that the PC noticed in the hall before he entered the room. The chief learned later that students attributed the smell to bathroom odors.

The body had a black necktie around the neck with a note attached. The PC's first impression was that this was a death by suicide, but, as he studied the conditions of the death, he thought it might be a homicide and decided a more thorough investigation was needed. He requested that the housing staff evacuate the second floor of the residence hall.

The chief called in the state police, since university police are not authorized to assume responsibility for murder investigations. While waiting for the state police to arrive, the campus police guarded the area so nothing would be touched. The state police decided an investigation was needed, not because the PC had concluded that the death was a result of murder, but because such a possibility needed to be ruled out. Suicide would be the identified cause of death if, after the investigation, murder was ruled out.

The state police interviewed various people, including all the students who had been evacuated from the second floor. HB, later identified as the probable assailant and a known visitor to the victim, was among a number of students questioned by the police that night. On the night HM's body was found, HB came to the room trying to gain access while the police were there. He was visibly upset at not being able to find out what happened. The state police thought his actions strange. At that time, however, the police were not suspicious that HB had a role in the death of HM.

The body could be removed only by order of the coroner, who was not in town. Eventually, an assistant coroner came to campus and authorized the body's removal at 1:28 A.M. The room was secured at 4:28 A.M. by a locksmith. The district attorney, who is legally responsible for releasing information from police investigations, talked to the police but did not release any information until much later. The identity of the victim was not officially released until five days later because of the condition of the body. Identification was made from dental records.

Other students were concerned that they were in danger. University police used basic safety management, which included increased patrols and increased campus lighting.

Early Friday morning, a student, HB, was scheduled to talk to the state police. He was found hanged in his home with a note saying he was sorry and referring to "a loved one gone." At that point, officials did not link the suicide of HB to the death of HM.

When the press came to campus they did not ask to see HM's room. There were articles in newspapers in nearby cities. The story was also aired on three TV stations. Rumors abounded that a mass murderer was at large. Reporters, students, and parents asked if this death was related to recent murders elsewhere in the country.

For a while after the death, the police received calls from some students reporting that roommates had been gone an unexplained length of time.

Six weeks after the death, the case was closed with voluminous circumstantial evidence leading to the conclusion that HB had killed HM. No formal announcement was made, however, to say that the case was closed.

During the investigation, the chief had been meeting several times a day with the VP for Student Affairs to keep her informed about the investigation. In hindsight, he thinks it would have been helpful to have interviewed the rest of the university staff.

The following newspaper reports appeared after the discovery of the body.

Newspaper Report—September 13

A student was found dead on the . . . campus last evening in what officials are describing as a "suspicious death." . . ., University's director of public relations, said the cause of death has not been determined. Details will be released as they become available. We really don't know anything else at this time. We're waiting on a determination from the county coroner's office.

Newspaper Report—September 14

Campus death is called murder. Officials refuse to talk about details. Law enforcement officials have refused to confirm or deny any reports surrounding the death of . . . on the campus of. . . . District Attorney . . . refused to make any comment concerning . . . who was found dead on the . . . University campus Wednesday evening.

State police have also refused to make any comment on the case, instead directing inquiries to the office of the district attorney.

The article continued with the district attorney's refusal to comment on the relationship of HM's death to the attempted suicide of HB that morning. A description of the known friendship between the two men followed.

HD—Residence Hall Director

The residence hall director (HD) has spent many years in similar positions at various other schools and has been present when other suicide victims were discovered on campuses.

HM's mother called the student who lived in the room next to her son on Wednesday evening and asked that the student contact her son. She had been trying to reach him since Saturday and had visited the campus on Sunday to try to find him. She was very worried. HM occupied a single room. The student went to the resident assistant who went to the HD, the hall director, who has a pass key. The HD, in the company of the RA, went to the room where he discovered the body and called the police. The police spent a long time in the room. They asked that the floor be evacuated and that no one enter the room. They said that the decomposition of the body precluded accurate identification. The HD knew who it was because of HM's distinctive red hair, but that would not suffice for official identification.

At about 10:30 P.M., the HD announced to the students that there had been an emergency but did not elaborate except to say that the police requested that the halls be evacuated. Although the RA had been with the HD when he opened the door, they did not discuss what they had seen. It wasn't long before rumors of a suicide were all over the residence hall. HD used the RA and other student workers to clear the floor where 40 male students lived. It was not known when the students would be permitted to return, so they were asked to pack a number of belongings. Students were urged to stay with friends or use the space available in a lounge and in other buildings. A little later a more formal plan was created. An empty room at the field house was opened where the evacuees could stay, dormitory style. The HD had to prevent anyone's entering the residence floor while also evacuating residents. Other residents in the lower floor of the building were permitted to remain. When staff from other residence halls arrived, they helped evacuate students. The HD called the dean of students when he could not contact the VP for student affairs.

The HD knew from prior experience with campus suicides that the amount of time the police were taking and their calling in the state police indicated that they were considering other possibilities than suicide. He said nothing.

Although the HD had known the victim, the victim had habitually spent prolonged periods of time off-campus, one and two weeks at a time. He had not been friendly with people in the hall. HM had taken a two-week holiday from school the year before to "get his head together." When no one saw HM on-campus or at the residence hall, people assumed that he had taken another holiday.

IO—Information Officer

The information officer (IO) received a late night call from the DS. She then called the president. The IO wanted to present the university's viewpoint to counteract newspaper stories that implied that these murders might be the work of a serial killer. Because the known facts could only be released by the district attorney, the IO contacted that office. The DA had released information to the public that had not been given to the school. Reporters and students had asked questions to which the school had unknowingly replied that such information was not available, only to learn that such data had been released by the DA. The president called the DA to request that the institution be informed in advance of the public release of information.

Reporters from all over the country called the IO. Calls inquiring about the two deaths at HTU decreased sharply when national media coverage of murders at another university decreased.

A good relationship with the press depends on the university's communicating with them quickly and forthrightly. It is a matter of maintaining the school's credibility. Each day, the IO gave the media some information.

When the IO first learned of the tragedy, the plan was to share the information. She was to handle press releases outside the university, and student life was to disseminate information internally. The student media could have access to all information; they were not, however, specifically invited to the briefings.

After the suicide attempt by HB on Friday, the university held a press conference to say the police had found a near-lifeless body that had been airlifted to a trauma center. The individual, a male, died four days later.

Official statements issued to the press were given to the press secretary for the university system. The press were invited to witness the support given to the students. They were told about the outreach to students and the care offered to those in shock as a result of these events. The IO asked the media not to enter the residence halls, but they took pictures of the outside of buildings.

The university redistributed written safety policies throughout the campus. At a senior administrative meeting, which the IO did not attend, the decision was to send a letter to parents.

The university did not want to make an event of the closing the investigation. No final statements were issued when the police closed the case, either from the district attorney's office or from the university.

DS—Dean of Students

The police tried to contact the VP for student affairs but did not want to leave the bad news on an answering machine. The HD called the dean of students (DS) and eventually left a message for the VP for student affairs about the apparent suicide. The DS called the VP for student affairs, left a message, and called the assistant VP for student affairs.

The DS, representing the university, gave the deputy coroner permission to enter the room. Since neither the VP nor the president was available, the DS was asked how the university wanted to proceed with the investigation. The police chief asked for the coroner's suggestions.

The police asked the DS for permission to involve the state police. A team of state police arrived and needed formal consent from the DS to investigate. The university police chief gave all information from their investigation to the state police. The state police did not use sirens or bright lights. Everything was done as subtly as possible. At the request of the state police, the DS and the housing director continued to evacuate the floor.

Within an hour and a half, a reporter from a paper 150 miles away was on the campus asking students what happened. The DS felt the reporter was badgering the students. He met with the reporters and could only tell them it was an emergency situation about which the university did not have information.

The VP for student affairs and the assistant VP arrived about 11:00 P.M. Reporters started to arrive in large numbers and to push for information, which the DS could not give out. The DS was helping police locate the students the police wanted to interview. Police wanted to talk to students who had been good friends of the victim.

The overall goal of the university was to take control of the situation in order to see that the public was informed and the student employees were supported. The DS took charge. When he spoke with the university staff, he did not say anything about the death possibly being a homicide.

The police were not willing to say more than that a death had occurred and they would not release the identity of the deceased. The police were attempting to rule out murder as the cause of death. If murder could be ruled out, the death would be called a suicide. The state police recorded everything: who came, who left, and who returned. They were concerned that the room door had been locked from inside and wanted to know where the spare key was.

The DS arranged for the field house to be used as an overflow residence facility for the displaced students. Under his direction, university staff worked with the space available to resettle evacuated students. In the meantime, police used the university staff office to begin a long series of interviews.

When the VP and assistant VP for student affairs arrived, they compared information. Each one learned who had called. They called the information officer and asked that she notify the vice-president for development. The VP for student affairs called the president. They met with the residence directors from 1:00 to 2:00 A.M. Staying within the limits described by the police, the VP explained the situation to the resident directors.

The DS replaced the university's staff's beepers with walkie-talkies, allowing the staff to speak directly to each other.

The people who worked at the SA office gave the students the phone numbers of the residence directors and the university counselors and encouraged students to call. They increased staff visibility on the residence hall floors by having the people who worked in the residence halls work longer days.

By the second day, the victim had not been formally identified but he was generally known to be HM. The DS wrote a report on the situation. Rumors became difficult to control because there was not enough information; the DS found this frustrating.

The students became increasingly resentful of the press. At first the event was a novelty for the students, and they allowed themselves to be interviewed. Then they perceived that their comments were being misinterpreted. The press carried statements that implied that students at the residence hall were sexually promiscuous. When the press came in with lights and cameras, the students avoided them and refused to cooperate.

An additional problem was that the school has only one counselor for 3,200 students. This person, of course, has responsibilities in addition to dealing with crises such as this one.

A state police officer on the investigating team advised the media that he was allowing his daughter to remain in residence on-campus because he did not feel that there was further danger. He considered this death uniquely related to the victim and not to the other students.

Parents and students feared that a death under suspicious circumstances which had occurred so soon after a series of murders attributed to a serial murder in another university, even though over a thousand miles away, was the continued work of that same murderer.

The student affairs staff recognized that they were serving the resident population but needed to do more for commuters.

VPS—Vice President for Student Affairs

When the vice president for student affairs (VPS) arrived, most of the students on the men's floor had left; the identity of the body was in question; the police were investigating but giving out no new information except that identification of the deceased would not be available until after laboratory tests. The father of the deceased called in the early hours of the morning. A student had told him his son was dead. He wanted to know if the student's information was correct. The VPS met with some of the students who were moving out of the dorm. She could only say that police were investigating the death of an unidentified person. Some of the students who had left the building that night were asked to return to be interviewed by the state police, who had taken charge of the investigation.

An immediate problem arose, not of the university's making. The procedure for university police is that any information they collect must be given to the district attorney's office. The district attorney's office is in charge of releasing the information collected by the university police to the police. Since the district attorney did not release information for a long time, and then released it without any notice to the university, it appeared that the university did not want to release information.

The university wanted the media to portray the university staff as they saw themselves, a caring group who were assisting students through a difficult time. At first the local papers represented the university favorably. That impression changed. Soon, the local papers were giving the impression that each student was living with a bureau in front of the door to keep out intruders. The university and state police were sure it was an isolated incident, but the media did not treat it as such. The murder dominated the news. The university, of course, wanted to everyone know that this was an isolated event.

The VPS met with the residence life staff, as well as the assistant and the associate deans, from 2:00 to 3:00 A.M. to create a plan for the next day. It was agreed that Student Affairs would conduct a meeting of all resident assistants at noon, a meeting at 1:00 P.M. with the evacuated residents of S Hall and friends of the deceased, and a meeting at 4:00 P.M. for all students about the death of HM. Starting at 11:00 P.M. and ending at 3:00 A.M. university staff would sponsor a Drop-In for all students concerned about the recent problems on-campus. The VPS publicized the plan in all the residence halls.

Community newspapers were able to give out more information than did the university. Parents were outraged that the identity of the dead student could not be released. The final identification was made almost a week later.

Many parents came to campus. Several reporters called. They were suspicious about the death because no break-in had been reported. The people who worked at the residence halls were exhausted from working long hours. One staff member, who was assigned to two buildings, went back and forth all day since he could not get all the people he was working with together. Some people worked 18 hours straight. When the news of the murder was known widely, parents called with many questions. Most wanted to know if it was safe for their children to remain on-campus. Some university employees who were answering phone calls from concerned parents had children attending the university and living on-campus. These employees were able to share with other parents that their children were continuing to live in the residence halls.

Several university employees remarked that they would have liked to have seen the president when they were working so hard. They were not sure he knew how much effort they were putting forth.

The university staff and students planned a memorial service on-campus for the victim, which the president and a few staff and students attended. The student affairs office was able to have students excused from class for the service.

The VPS and the assistant VP attended both funerals. Some students and university employees questioned the appropriateness of attending the funeral for the alleged assailant, which took place the following week.

The first death occurred less than two weeks after school began. The second death followed the third day after the discovery of the first body; students returned to S Hall residence five days later. It was a disorienting time for everyone. Local media came on-campus and stopped students to ask about rumors, upsetting the students further.

The student affairs office distributed 1,000 pamphlets describing how to deal with grief. The VPS spent time with the RA's to discuss how to deal with the emotional aftereffects of the two deaths. The RA group was invited to a class on self-esteem, which met from October to December. The class was filled.

The university was not aware when the district attorney's office would release police findings. There was no formal report at the time HM's case was closed, or, the report was never shared. There was no discussion about what motives may have led to the two deaths. The VPS commented that no one mentioned the contents of HM's room, which contained an exceptional amount of new clothing and cigarettes. The alleged assailant had previously been arrested and later released on suspicion of stealing the clothes and cigarettes.

The following letter from the VPS was sent to all students.

Letter from VPS to All Students—September 17

To All . . . H University Students:

The events of the past week have touched each one of us in a different way and have brought us closer together as a community. For the friends and families of the students we have lost, we are deeply saddened. All of us continue to search for answers to the questions we have about why the events occurred.

Undoubtedly, there have been many fears about the safety of our living environment. Each one of us wants complete assurance that such events will not ever happen again on or off campus. There has been much discussion about the incidents, and it is thought that they are isolated events.

The university has cooperated with state police who are conducting the extensive investigation. Like you, we have read and watched reports in the newspaper and in the news. This has been frustrating and has raised concerns about what is really happening.

Your patience and trust in the university's staff and systems is most appreciated. Thus far, it is believed that the death of HM is related in some way to the suicide by HB. Both were students at the university.

It is difficult to anticipate when the final determination of the police investigation will occur. Your return to routine activity is very important. Helping each other understand and respond to friends' needs in dealing with their loss will bring our community to safety once again. Talking and sharing your feelings with someone or with a staff member may be one way to regain your sense of security. You are encouraged to speak with staff and friends.

A listing of staff members' telephone numbers and crisis intervention numbers are on the reverse side of this letter. . . .

While the beginning of this semester has been traumatic, I sincerely hope that we will become a stronger community because of our losses. As we put back those parts of our lives that have been disrupted, I hope it will strengthen you and our university.

Sincerely,

VPS
Vice President for Student Affairs

ADS—Assistant Dean of Students

The assistant dean of students (ADS) sent notes to the RA's and paraprofessionals with pictures taken at a staff dinner. She sent warm notes thanking them for all they had done during the crisis.

The student affairs office was careful not to intrude into the academic program. All the people at the university had believed that such a violent tragedy could not happen at their school. The university was a very quiet and peaceful place. Nobody thought a murder/suicide could happen in a small community like this.

Students who did not live on campus were not, as a group, fearful. Off-campus students didn't talk about the deaths in counseling in the same way that resident students did. Staff made no efforts to provide counseling services to the commuters.

At the 4:00 P.M. open meeting, those present, students and university employees, discussed why HM would want to commit suicide. They linked his homosexuality to his alleged suicide. At the time of the meeting, no public information had revealed that the cause of death was murder. Students asked many questions about homosexuality. The meeting went well, but few came because they were grieving; most wanted information. There was a feeling among the students that the institution purposely was not releasing information.

Student services held a workshop for the RA's on sexual orientation. The student workers wanted to know how to handle gays and lesbians on residence floors. The homosexual community on-campus was considered to be a small, close-knit group. Prior to this, when the university had invited student participation in a group for gays and lesbians, students did not respond.

The student service office again reached out to gay and lesbian students, and this time there was a response, mainly from men. Since that time a group has continued with a staff advisor. In the beginning, it was as a support group for men. Over time the group began to attract female students.

From the time HM's body was discovered, the residence life staff worked very long hours. Some people worked 18 hour days. The university employees who worked in the residence halls were trying to be visible to students, and were trying to be supportive of the students who were having a difficult time. The ADS identified which employees had support systems at home or at work and which didn't. She directed her own energies to provide support and time to those who were more alone.

HOM—Head of Maintenance

The HOM is a native of the region and describes the town as very law-abiding. He was first called by the VPS to secure the area. The locks had been checked recently and replaced where appropriate.

The HOM believed the people of the town felt the aftermath more strongly than the students at the college did. The town (population 8,500) is a nice place to raise children, a place where people do not speed or break the law. The town has a high unemployment rate and a low crime rate.

Residence Hall Directors

The employees of the university were not aware that the investigation of HM's death had been completed nor did they know that there was any connection between the two deaths. They observed that students were afraid and talked among themselves about who would be next. Women did not want to walk alone.

Some of the residence hall directors showed up at S Hall the night of the death because they saw police at the building. Of the absent residence hall directors, whose who could be reached by phone were called back to the university. They assumed there had been a suicide. The directors helped the students at S Hall move, although nobody knew what had happened.

Hall directors learned from the student government president, after convocation the next day, that the president had told him that the cause of death was murder. That fact was unknown to the university staff, although the HD, who was the director at S Hall had suspected the death was a murder.

The university never made a statement to the community at large about the death. There was also no closure for the students at the university because no one knew that the person who committed the murder had been identified.

Through none of the events was there any involvement of the faculty. The case was perceived as having nothing to do with the academic side of the school.

The following memo discussing safety regulations was issued in response to the murder.

September 13—Memo to All Students from Student Affairs VP

New safety regulations to be implemented the following day:

Any persons entering a residence hall after midnight will be required to present identification at the front desk.

If the person is a resident of that building, he/she needs to show the appropriate color dot that is affixed to the student identification card.

If the person is not a resident of that building, such visitor will need to call the resident for an escort and the resident will register the visitor.

Any non-resident in a campus residence hall after midnight must have an escort in and out of the building, including non-residents who entered earlier.

Campus Ministers—ND from Newman Center, DR—Protestant

ND learned that a crisis had occurred when, about 10:30 the night of HD's death, several students from S Hall came to the Newman Center. Two students wanted to stay the night. The students were very upset because they knew something was wrong, but they didn't know what.

The students said that they had been asked to find other housing just a short time before. ND felt that there should have been immediate help for the students when they were displaced. The students that she saw were very upset and needed to talk.

ND met with the churches in the community and asked each to adopt a residence hall. The churches were very generous, sent food, flowers and notes, and made special efforts to accommodate students. The people in town wanted to help.

Both ministers felt that the university should have sponsored a drop-in on the night of the death so that students could better understand what was happening and what its impact would be on them. They said that students felt their safe space had been violated. Students wanted to get back to their own rooms.

The "We Care Committee" of the Newman Center met with all the committees of the center and sent notes to the university staff expressing their concern. Through the VP VL, committee members volunteered to patrol the residence halls. ND led the memorial service for the university.

SGA—Student Government President

The student government president (SGA) heard the rumor of a suicide the day after HM died. That same day was the convocation. At the convocation, he spoke with the president, who said it could have been murder.

Little interest in the death was shown by the faculty who, at the time, were involved with a decision about whether or not to go on strike.

Some students called student government to ask what had happened. Around campus it was known that there had been a murder, but the rumor was that the university was trying to keep things quiet. Students also said that someone should have noticed the victim's mail piling up and asked where the student was. The media from a larger campus some distance away provided more information about the death on this campus and its investigation than was provided locally. Students suspected that the second death could have been murder. It was nine months after the deaths when this interview took place, and the SGA said that there was still speculation among the students and staff about what had happened.

As a result of not knowing the facts, the SGA was afraid. When he went home, he made sure all the doors and windows were locked.

SL—Advisor to Student Government

This advisor, though funded by student government, is independent of the institution. There were three reactions among students. Some were blase, some shocked, and a few hysterical. There was a real lack of information; few people knew what had happened. Rumors and speculation abounded.

Incomplete information was given at a general meeting for resident students, but no information whatsoever was forthcoming for off-campus students. The information that was released included reference to the victims' being gay. SL did not see the significance of that fact.

The local media were quiet about the cause of death. The students wanted to hear what happened from the police and the university. They especially wanted to know why it took so long to find the body. Students made jokes about the university's inattention and the decomposition of the body. Students heard that the tie found on the body had been given to HM by the person who murdered him. Students referred to the event as a murder although that aspect was never confirmed.

After the murder/suicide the student government reached out to the gay community on-campus with a Gay Pride week. One of the events during the week featured a lesbian singer-comedienne. The event was funded by the Women's Awareness Group.

PR—President

The president's goal was to support the community as a whole and help it stay calm. His guidelines were to be rational in the midst of frantic people and to be totally honest each step of the way.

Freshman Convocation had been scheduled for the day after the first body was discovered. Although there was no official identification of the victim, PR did not want to pretend that the event had not happened. At convocation, he acknowledged the death of HM and asked for a moment of silence in HM's memory. He further said:

> To bring our community closer together and to reach all those with questions or needs, there will be a meeting for students this afternoon. . . . There will also be a drop-in center for those needing to talk or just be with someone at 11:00 this evening through to 3:00 o'clock tomorrow morning. . . .
>
> As this academic year begins, let all of us renew our commitment to this university community and all its members by reaching out to those who need our friendship, words and consolation.

The police did not criticize the president for releasing the identity of the deceased without clearance from the district attorney's office. PR said that a serious problem exists because the district attorney's office is the only agency that can release information about a murder.

One of the president's concerns was that HM had been dead five or six days before his body was discovered. He needed to explain how the situation occurred to the board of governors. PR requested that the residence hall staff implement a procedure to let the university know when a student has not been seen on campus for 24 hours.

PR was pleased with how well his staff worked with the students from the time this tragedy was discovered. He credited the VP for student affairs for guiding the school's response. She seemed prepared to cope with crisis and in control herself throughout the ordeal.

Five students went to HM's funeral. No students attended HR's funeral. Fourteen people were at the memorial service. The university and town were in shock for at least 24 hours. The realization that a murderer was part of their community caused great concern.

The following letter was sent by the president to all students' parents following the murder.

Letter from PR—September 17

Dear Parent(s):

The recent events at . . . H . . . University have been publicized widely by the media concerning an alleged homicide and attempted suicide. The university is cooperating with state law enforcement officials and the district attorney's office in identifying and investigating all aspects of these incidents. We believe these are isolated occurrences.

In an effort to assure you that your son or daughter remains safe and secure in his or her living environment I am writing to you with confidence that we are providing every mechanism possible. As a reminder, each residence hall is equipped with an alarm system on every door. This system is activated 24 hours a day and is monitored during desk hours at the main desk in each building.

Each residence hall is supervised by a full-time professional hall director who lives in the building. Additionally, every floor has a resident assistant who has been specially trained to work with students. In the event your son or daughter has concerns or is fearful, he or she should make as many contacts as needed with our staff. The student affairs staff is also available to meet with students individually and in groups and would be available to answer your questions at . . .

The student affairs staff has provided a number of meetings for students to share their concerns. Staff met with residents of the second floor of S . . . Hall and personal friends at one meeting, and all students were invited to a later meeting on Thursday. Late that evening, a drop-in center was available from 11:00 P.M. to 3:00 A.M. to assist students in dealing with this loss. Additional meetings are continuing.

> The university remains most concerned for the well-being of all of its students. I hope you will join with me and members of our staff in assisting students through this difficult time for all of us.
>
> Sincerely,
>
>
> PR
> President

COMMENTARY

When events such as this tragedy happen, institutions learn what does and does not work well. The situation where information on murder/suicide could only be released by the district attorney's office, and that the DA might release information without a school's knowledge, may well be a problem waiting to be discovered at many schools.

The proliferation of e-mail and fax should make it easier to inform the university community of a tragedy. The news of the death of a student is information that the entire campus needs to learn because tragic as well as happy events build community spirit among all the members. Also the many people in the university—clergy, faculty, and commuters—may supplement the efforts of overburdened university staff as they did in this school.

In hindsight, the initial request by the police to evacuate the building might have been handled in two steps—starting with an emergency hall meeting with all students to be evacuated so that they would have some idea of what was happening, and then proceeding with the evacuation.

In like manner, inviting the entire campus to some of the open meetings such as the one hosted by the vice president for students may be helpful. No one knows how far the panic travels when suicide and/or murder occur.

The availability and use of walkie-talkies during the first response period was a creative idea worth emulating.

Statements about the current safety of students following a murder or suicide are better made by police and district attorneys' offices than by the university administration. Students will find the police and DA's office more believable.

Resident assistants are very often under stress during such a tragedy. Outreach to them is appropriate after a crisis.

Some consideration should be given as to whether the sexual orientation of the victim should be publicized. Although such a question cannot be answered in advance, it may be wise to have such an item on a checklist. All the information a school plans to release about a victim needs to be looked at line by line to see whether the information is relevant to the situation and is relevant to the interest of the public.

The bureaucratic difficulties of deciding who may remove a body and who may say what happened certainly created more distress in the residence hall and eventually on the campus than was necessary. If the school had the misfortune to go through this event again, the difficulties that they experienced would be repeated because the school has no control of its own information in such a situation. Lack of information increased the stress on the students of S Hall, when they were given no reason that they could not stay the night in their rooms.

The report that the victim's mother had tried in vain to contact her son for several days in advance of the discovery of his body leads us to consider how students could assume responsibility to bring the parent's concern to the attention of the university. Students need to know exactly how to act in a situation where a fellow student seems to be missing.

A dead student, undiscovered for five days, is an unlikely and unhappy event. The question is whether or not institutions are aware of the emotional health of students living alone. There is constant tension between the need for the university to be a caring community and the rights of individual students to autonomy and freedom.

Support services were offered to the students but not to faculty or commuting students. The people who worked at the residence halls offered each other help and compassion.

The letter directed to students and the one to parents were helpful. A final communication might have brought closure when the mystery of the death was solved.

CHAPTER
four

Two Rapes On-Campus

A STUDENT EMPLOYEE RAPED IN RESIDENCE HALL

In July of 1990, during new-student orientation, a student resident assistant (RA) was raped at noon in her room in an upper floor of a residence tower. The assailant was apprehended more than a year later.

BACKGROUND

TSU is a comprehensive university with 10,000 full-time undergraduate students, 3,400 of whom live on campus in residence halls and apartments. Another 5,000 students are enrolled part-time and in graduate school. The campus extends over 306 acres.

PC—Campus Police Chief

At 12:05 P.M., after being raped, C, the victim, left her room to get a friend to call the police, who then summoned an ambulance. Police and the ambulance arrived simultaneously. Their immediate objective was to minister to the victim, then to identify and apprehend the assailant. Officers began questioning the victim as she was receiving emergency medical treatment, and they accompanied the victim to the hospital. Police assumed the perpetrator to be at large; the immediate need was to protect the community from further assaults. Approximately 45 minutes had passed since the attack.

From the time the first call to the chief came in, to the time the officers and the emergency medical team responded, the police chief (PC) was gathering information. The officers on the scene were giving support to the victim, taking her statements, and relaying that information to the PC at the station. In such cases, no statement is released to the community until the PC determines what happened. Although the victim said she had been raped, it was not until she described what had happened that the chief could verify that she had been raped.

Before the PC was sure of his conclusion, he called the director for orientation and told him what he thought had happened, that a student had been raped. The PC wanted to alert orientation as soon as possible, even though he did not have enough information to conclude that a rape had actually occurred.

The PC's not drawing a conclusion about what had taken place until he had enough evidence did not deter the officers from searching for the alleged perpetrator. The PC assigned a sergeant to supervise the investigation, contacted the counseling center for assistance for the victim, and called his superior, the associate vice president for the physical plant. By a previous agreement with the counseling center, a counselor would be on-call to stay with a rape victim through the initial investigation. The PC contacted the county, city, and state police with a description of the suspect. All off-duty officers were called in to help.

Word of the rape became known very quickly because the victim's friend, a residence department employee, called the housing office to tell the other RAs.

It was clear from the beginning that the crime had taken place within the jurisdiction of university police. A prior understanding between the county and campus police was that the university police would be in charge until they determined whether that they needed additional help. The agreement between these two police agencies also allows the university police to use all the resources available to the county officers, including the crime lab.

Officers on the search patrol informed all people they met on the campus that a crime had taken place and that they were searching for the perpetrator, whose description they then circulated. Officers recommended that isolated individuals on-campus return to populated areas.

The PC decided on a spiral search, one that would include both the county and the 306 acres of the campus. A description of the perpetrator was radioed to all university officers, who were then deployed to search for the assailant.

The VP for student services had planned an open meeting for 3:00 P.M. to inform all participants and staff in the scheduled orientation of the rape. She requested that the PC explain what had happened and what he and his staff were doing to improve safety. At that meeting, the PC presented information about the rape, the condition of the victim, a description of the assailant that had been given by the victim, and a description of how the police planned to make the campus a safer place. He immediately increased patrols around the residence halls. The chief suggested to the group how the community could be made safer and offered emergency escort service for anyone on campus that day.

The PC and the orientation director met with faculty and staff who were working in orientation to inform them as well.

That night, the PC received no calls from the press. He was, however, concerned that some information quoted by the media was inaccurate. The county police referred media calls to the University Information Services.

The media reported the rape in the newspapers and on television several times, both the day of the rape and the following day. The PC did not understand why rapes that had happened less than a mile off-campus the week before and two that had occurred at another college in the county had not had any media attention.

VPS—Vice President for Student Services

The vice president for student services (VPS) learned of the rape at 1:45 P.M. The VPS called the housing director and arranged a meeting to take place at a time already set aside for new resident students and their parents to come together. It had been scheduled for 3:00 P.M., and now all new students and their parents were invited to attend. The VPS told the president about the plan. The VPS asked the PC to tell the assembled group what had happened and to allow those in attendance time to ask questions. The VPS informed university relations of the situation. The VPS telephoned the personnel director to request that he inform university staff as well as the dean for continuing studies so that the dean could inform the faculty who would in turn then tell students. The dean was not available that day, and no one sent the message until the next day. The personnel director did not send a message to the community.

The VPS told the 3:00 P.M. assembly of students, parents, and staff members that a rape had occurred. The PC described what had happened and gave a description of the assailant. Some parents made suggestions for improving the security system. One person suggested that a large identification card be made for all program participants. That idea was implemented and the printed cards were ready later that day. The director of the counseling center announced that counseling services were available.

After the meeting, the students were asked to go to another room where they were divided into small groups. Each group met with a facilitator to talk about what had happened and how they were feeling. The parents were also invited to divide up into small groups for the same purpose.

As a result of the rape, four students chose to withdraw from the university. The VPS sent a letter to each of the four students who withdrew. In that letter she told them that if they chose to return to the university at some later date, her offices would assist them in reentry. The VPS also told each student that the university respected his or her right to make such a decision.

The VPS spoke informally several times that day with the parents and the student staff of orientation. One parent was critical of the chief's reference to the race of the assailant. All other comments from parents were supportive of the university's candor. Many parents talked about this tragedy as a part of a societal problem and communicated their understanding that the university was not immune from problems such as rape.

On the following day, the VPS met with the press and was interviewed at two television stations. She presented a picture of a good security system that had been compromised by someone living in the residence hall who left a door open as a temporary convenience.

The VPS gave welcoming remarks to the next group of new students and parents who came for orientation. Since some of the students and their parents had come from other states, the VPS began by telling them that a student worker had been raped in her residence hall on the preceding Thursday. The PC was present to answer questions, but there were none. The president made the same announcement to the last group who came for orientation.

In a review of the events, the VPS and staff agreed that the open meeting had worked well but that employees of the university were entitled to the same open discussion of the event. In consultation with the information officer (IO) and the university relations director, she agreed that the IO should send a message on Friday to all staff informing them of what had happened and inviting them to a meeting on Monday, where the PC would answer questions. Two or three people came; the VPS and the PC spoke with them briefly.

VP—Director of University Relations

Between 1:45 P.M., when the IO learned of the rape, and 3:00 P.M., when the meeting with new students and parents took place, the IO collected information about what the university offices knew and what the history of such events at the university was. He wanted more information than was available to him because he was unable to reach some offices.

The vice president for student services, as already mentioned, had arranged for the PC to speak to an assembly of all new students and their parents. The director of university relations (VP) proposed that the IO should have more properly been the spokesperson reporting the events to that audience. He was concerned that too much detail of the crime had been reported by the PC. The IO would have reported that he/she had learned the facts from the PC. Furthermore, the VP felt a need to determine and then state the purpose for the release of the information. In such cases, is the purpose of the release of information to ensure that all persons on campus are safe or is it to enlist the participation of those being informed in making provision for their own safety? The VP proposes that better monitoring of information would be possible if a decision was made early concerning what information needs to be released beyond what the university is legally bound to give out.

The VP informed the governor's office and the university system's office about the incident and suggested that the president call the chancellor. The VP and his staff planned how and to whom the IO would release information. The VP was especially concerned about protection of the victim's identity. The next day, the VP recalls, there was some difference of opinion between the police and the IO about who would release information. The VP met with his staff to discuss how they would respond and who would be available to answer questions.

The next day, with an update from the police, the VP and the staff escorted the press through the campus. Meanwhile, a reporter, who is a personal friend of the VPs, called to tell him that he, the reporter, had entered the dormitory that morning through an open side door. The VP called the VP for business to register a complaint. The VP's statement to the press was that the university did not have an explanation for the door's being left open other than to say that it should not have happened. The university should have checked all doors to assure that they were locked.

The VP received phone calls all evening the day of the rape from many people who called him personally for information, such as reporters with whom he had worked.

IO—Information Officer

In July, the PC was on the phone with the IO informing her about the rape when a reporter from the metropolitan newspaper called the IO to say that he heard about a rape on campus. The IO acknowledged that she had just learned about it and would return the call shortly. The IO telephoned the reporter a few minutes later with more complete information. She was able to tell what was happening to the victim and what kind of help the victim was getting. The IO described how the university would be informed.

The IO also told the press that there had not been a rape on-campus for a number of years. She did not wish to diminish the tragic nature of the event but, at the same time, she emphasized that rapes can and do occur anywhere, and that a college campus is not immune from crime.

The following day, reporters from three television stations were in her office when she arrived. The reporters wanted to talk to the IO and to students and parents, and to see the scene of the crime.

The IO informed the interviewers about the status of the security system at the university, emphasizing that the residence halls were accessible only by key. She emphasized that security could be breached by students who propped doors open or admitted strangers to the building. She also described the many safety-awareness programs on-campus and the continuing efforts of the university to make students aware of the need to participate in crime prevention. The IO showed the reporters the locked doors and the key-controlled elevators in the residence halls. The message she delivered was that safety was dependent on the residents' not compromising the system. The messages to the campus had been and continued to be that all of the university community needed to work together to maximize safety for everyone.

The IO was interviewed on television. She described what she knew about of the attack and what the school was doing to improve security. She arranged for the VP for student services to be interviewed by two news channels. She gave the press the composite picture of the assailant drawn up by the police department.

The reporters wanted to go to the Student Union to interview students, parents, and staff. The IO hosted their visit. If the media had not contacted her, the IO would have communicated only within the campus. The IO was later told by a reporter that the media did not elect to do any further investigation of the campus because it concluded that the institution was acting in a responsible manner and was not hiding anything.

Press Release—July 26, 1990

On Thursday, July 26th, a TSU student reported that she was raped in Tower A of the GR Residence on the campus at approximately 12 noon. University police were called to the building and, with county police, are continuing to investigate how the suspect entered the building. The residence buildings are locked at all times and a key is needed to open the doors from the outside, as well as to operate the elevator. Approximately 200 people were staying in Tower A for the orientation program.

This is the second incident of a reported rape on the campus in five years. An earlier reported rape was unfounded. The university conducts rape awareness programs throughout the year in residence halls and other campus areas.

TSU administrators and counseling center staff met with students and parents after the incident, and campus security has been increased around the residence halls.

The rape victim was taken to an area hospital and released.

VPB—Vice President for Business and Finance

After receiving information about the rape from the physical plant director to whom the campus police report, the vice president for business and finance (VPB) called the residence department to inquire about the welfare of the victim and to see whether she was receiving all the help that she needed. He also informed the president, the VP for student services, and the university relations director about the rape. He learned that the County Rape Victim Services had made contact with the victim.

The next morning, the VPB learned that a reporter had discovered an unlocked door leading into the residence hall where the crime had occurred. The VPB asked staff begin an investigation to determine if there was sufficient supervision of staff and others who enter the residence halls. He immediately requested that all security policies be reviewed and action taken to ensure the policies were followed.

The VPB asked campus police to increase their patrols of the campus, and he considered ways to increase the visibility of campus police. He also wanted to be assured that all residents in the buildings were receiving sufficient information to enable them to take needed precautions for safety.

A plan to add outside emergency telephones had been drawn up for some time. Some call boxes were placed in each parking garage and in the parking lots for resident students so that students returning to the dormitories at night would be better protected. The VPB provided increased police assistance for resident students at various lots.

DCS—Dean of Continuing Studies

On the day of the rape, the dean of continuing studies was not on campus. The VP for student services asked her office to notify faculty and ask them to tell students about the rape and give them the university's safety suggestions. On the following day, the DCS returned to campus and communicated with the entire faculty by e-mail (electronic mail). The message included a request that faculty urge students to follow the safety rules distributed early in the semester.

The DCS was not sure that the message would be delivered to all faculty by e-mail because many did not have access to e-mail in their offices. It was also possible that others did not read the e-mail on a regular basis. She suggested a combination of e-mail and a pyramid telephone calling system. Secretaries to each dean would call secretaries of departments. This approach would be supplemented with notices for faculty to make appropriate announcements.

CD—Counseling Center Director and Associate Vice President for Student Services

When the counseling center director (CD) returned to his office at 1:45 P.M. the day of the rape, a message from the police chief informing him of the rape was waiting. The CD was present at the open meeting to tell everyone about the services available at the center.

The CD and the HO from housing decided to create small-group discussions. While students, parents, and staff met concerning the rape, the CD and the HO contacted everyone on the staff who had training as group facilitators. Within 20 minutes of the beginning of the meeting, staff were ready to help with small groups. The small groups met for about 45 minutes.

The CD attempted to contact C, the victim, early in the day. He spoke with the officer accompanying her and asked to be told when the victim would be able to meet with him. At 7:00 P.M., the CD met with the victim and her parents at the campus police station. He met with her again on Monday; C continued in counseling into the fall semester. Several weeks after the rape, C began to complain during counseling about the frequent questioning by police.

The morning after the rape, the CD met with student staff to discuss their reactions to the event. Later in the day, he met with parents for his regularly scheduled orientation presentation. A good portion of that time was spent discussing the university response to the rape. Later in the day, he was interviewed by the press.

Ten days later, the president asked the CD, in the absence of the VP, to assemble a group to evaluate how the university had responded to the crisis and to make recommendations for improving the university's response in the future.

Employees and students who reported being worried by the rape used the counseling center during the following few months. The number of requests for help from campus residents and sorority and fraternity members to the counseling center showed an increase.

DO—Director of Orientation

The director of orientation (DO) knew that a student worker who was absent from her job in the orientation program had been taken to the hospital. The PC called to say that a student may have been raped on campus. The DO was unsure about what to do with the information until he received verification; he did not want to start a false rumor.

The DO did not change any aspect of the orientation program. When the rape occurred, student leaders were each in the process of taking groups of about 10 new students on tours of the campus. When student leaders were stopped by campus police and told to return to the Student Union because of an emergency on campus, they became frightened and returned to the DO to get additional information. The police, they said, asked if they had seen a person matching a certain description.

It was after 2:00 P.M. when the student residence department employees came from a meeting where they had learned about the rape. Counselors had been helping them cope with this news. The DO had, by now, been informed that the 3:00 P.M. meeting would include all students and parents. He sent staff to round up groups of students at various locations on the campus and bring them to the meeting. He did not say why. Some groups on tour were not located.

The DO met with his staff following the 3:00 P.M. meeting to discuss their own reactions to the event and to plan for the following day. Everyone was frightened and also concerned for the victim. The DO instructed all leaders to tour campus with two additional groups at a time. All leaders were instructed to know the whereabouts of every group member at all times.

Commuter students who were on the campus only for the orientation program were housed in a separate building. They were further upset by their isolation from the rest of the students in residence. The DO, therefore, spent the night in their building.

Following the open meeting, the DO implemented a new identification process. Large identity cards were printed for all parents and students attending the orientation program. This new method of identification was later abandoned because it was not effective.

The DO planned a meeting for 7:15 A.M. the following morning. The director of the counseling center was invited to attend. Because the campus was empty at that early hour, some of the male orientation staff arranged to meet the women at their cars. (This arrangement continued through the rest of the summer program.) At this meeting, and those that followed, student workers expressed anger and wanted to know why there was not more security including such changes as monitoring TV's and uniformed guards.

At the meeting, the DO prepared students to expect reporters with television cameras who might be on-campus. If student employees chose to speak with the press, he reminded them to speak only for themselves and not for the university.

The DO denied reporters' requests to enter the orientation sessions, but the DO told reporters they could request interviews with whomever they chose. A few students leaders were quite willing to speak with reporters.

Four new students chose to withdraw from enrollment in the university. The names of those students were forwarded to the office of the VP for student services.

The orientation staff met with police and other institutional personnel to plan a comprehensive safety program for the following year, which addressed safety in the garages, the Student Union, and the residence halls.

HO—Housing Orientation Director

At 12:15 P.M., MO, the victim's best friend, told the HO that she had called the police because C had been raped. Meanwhile the ambulance had arrived. The HO notified the housing staff of the rape. He found some of the student staff to be quite distraught.

The police were trying to determine if anyone had seen the assailant before he entered the building.

Without telling the resident assistants (RAs) why, the HO invited them to a meeting immediately after the rape occurred. He told them what had happened to their fellow student. Some began to cry. One of the women revealed that she had been a previous victim of rape. All the residents hugged each other and huddled together. Their first concern was how to help each other. Next they were concerned about who would be able to work and how the orientation program should change in light of the rape.

The group had program responsibilities for 2:00 P.M. The HO suggested that they work that day and get together later that night, which they did. They continued meeting daily for a few days.

When the HO learned that the VP for student services was conducting a meeting for all those who were scheduled for orientation, the HO thought of breaking the large groups into smaller discussion groups. While the program was in progress, the HO was actively recruiting various staff members to be group facilitators.

His own presentation for orientation dealt with community responsibility rather than community development which would have been his topic.

Some students were still upset the day after the rape. Helping those who would themselves be giving help was an important issue for the HO. Student workers were concerned because reference was made to the victim by her first name at the orientation meeting. Students were also angry that details of the attack were given.

HD—Housing Director

The director of housing, the HD, and the VP for student services talked by phone and agreed that the meeting that the HD was to hold for resident students and their parents could be used for a general meeting. After the meeting, many parents congratulated the HD for the institution's handling of the episode.

At 7:30 A.M. the next morning, reporters were on campus. The phones in the housing office rang so incessantly that the staff had to be reassigned to answer phones all day. One of the many callers allegedly learned from the media that one could call the housing office number to recommend how the university could improve security. The HD referred all media calls thereafter to the information office as he was asked to do by information services. This office called back to tell the HD that reporters were on their way to interview housing personnel.

A dispute arose between the housing and the maintenance departments conerning who was responsible for a door to the residence hall being left open and later discovered by a reporter. The HD said that housing had reported previously to maintenance that the door was difficult to close.

In the ensuing weeks and the following semester, many parents called to find out what the university was doing to protect the resident students.

Housing encouraged the RA's to increase the number of security programs in the residence halls during the fall semester. The RA training program that preceded the opening of school subsequently included additional information about safety and security, with presentations by the police, who promised to increase their visibility on campus. Housing offered 58 safety programs within the first few months of school, a sizable increase over previous years. The housing department also made self-defense courses available.

Although many parents called before and after the semester began with questions and concerns about security, neither parents nor students had asked questions about security when students were first moving in for the fall semester. The HD requested that the fall parent newsletter, sent by the alumni office, include information about security.

SGA—Student Government President

Because of the rape, the student government president (SGA) and his colleagues in student government began the fall semester by planning for a big safety campaign with a special safety week that would take place at the beginning of the second semester.

VPP—Associate Vice President for Personnel

At 2:15 P.M., the vice president for student services requested the VPP to communicate with the staff of the university by e-mail that a rape had occurred. She requested that the message include suggestions that people travel on-campus in small groups and that staff members call the police if they saw suspicious-looking persons. The VPP did not send the message. The e-mail had not been used for such messages heretofore. Further, the VPP was not sure it was a concern for the entire university; he saw it as important only for students.

PP—Associate Vice President for the Physical Plant

The associate vice president for the physical plant (PP) is the first person to be informed of a crime on-campus because the police chief reports to him. After the July rape, he immediately asked staff to check doors and he learned that a door had been left propped open to easily admit new students and parents. The situation was not corrected after registration. No fault was found with the door. The PP reported this finding to his vice-president. He instructed his staff not to talk to the press unless so directed by the university relations office. Press requested access to the residence hall, but this request was denied. The PP did not want the police to speak to the press unless it was at the direction of the Office of University Relations.

The PP prepared for the fall opening of school by having the doors checked daily to be sure that they closed and locked without undue effort. That became a part of daily maintenance.

New Crime Prevention Program Added by Police Chief

At peak hours when students are returning to their residence halls, the police now post plain-clothes officers near entrances to discover whether some students will unknowingly admit the officers into their residences. If a student admits an officer, the officer gives the student a "Gotcha" citation and a list of safety tips. Students have reported increased awareness of security issues.

The following memo appeared in the university newsletter on the Wednesday following the crime:

A Memo from the President to the University Community

On Thursday, July 26, we experienced a serious and tragic incident on our campus. A TSU student employee was raped in her room in Tower A of the Glen Residence Complex. This most unfortunate case serves as a reminder to us all that we are not immune from crime on a college campus. While we are statistically "safer" than a metropolitan area of our size, we must continually be aware of our surroundings and work to ensure that security policies and rules are followed. It is only when everyone takes responsibility for campus security that our security measures will be successful. I ask all faculty, staff, and students to be aware of their surroundings at all times and to be sure that security is maintained in their areas. Please report any suspicious individuals to the university police immediately. Doors and windows that are supposed to be locked at all times should be kept closed and locked. Report any broken locks to maintenance staff immediately. Secure your personal property in your office. Follow recommendations for crime prevention published by the university police. The university police will continue to monitor campus security measures and identify areas where security must be increased. I thank you all for your anticipated cooperation. The safety of our community is something we must all work to ensure. If you have any questions about crime prevention, or would like additional information about campus safety, please call the university police, ext. . . .

Thank you.

HS
President

A Review of the Campus Response to Rape—7-26-90

A committee to review the university response included representatives from the following offices: housing, orientation, auxiliary services, faculty, student development, admissions, university relations, university police, counseling center, and information services. President HS requested that the committee review the university response to the event of July 26 and recommend ways to improve that response in the future. President HS observed that the campus had responded well but that "nothing is ever so good as to not have room for improvement." The committee sent the following recommendations:

All communications to the media should come directly from university relations and information services. Should the media contact a staff person, the staff member should first refer the reporter to university relations. University relations should consider sending a guide for media relations to all departments to ensure adherence to the university media policy.

It would be helpful if the university relations staff could be at the scene of the crisis as quickly as possible. The staff would then be more fully informed and more accessible for distribution of information. The committee agreed that this recommendation might be too difficult to implement. They recommended that university relations be equipped with a portable telephone system to allow more flexibility.

The committee recommended that departments who work with affected students help them talk to each other about significant campus events.

ABDUCTION OF A COED FROM A CAMPUS GARAGE AT NOON AND SUBSEQUENT RAPE—ASSAILANT NOT APPREHENDED

On November 1, 1990, at noon on a Thursday when classes were in session at the same TSU campus, a female student was abducted from a garage, taken off campus in her own car, raped, and abandoned; the car was returned to the same garage, presumably by the assailant. Police reported that the rapist was not the same person as in the rape on July 26, 1990. The assailant has not been apprehended.

PC—Campus Police Chief

Following the abduction and rape there was confusion about whether the campus or the county police had jurisdiction over the case. The PC has assumed that, since the rape had taken place off-campus, the county was in charge of the investigation. At 10:30 P.M., seven hours after the crime had been reported, the PC began receiving calls from the media, referred to him by the county police. The callers needed information for the 11:00 P.M. news. The PC called the VP, director of university relations, who said that he could not come to campus to handle questions in time for the reporters' deadline.

The PC and the VP together prepared what the PC would say. The PC answered questions from the media that night and for the next three days. The PC was pleased with the accuracy with which the event was described by the media.

The PC increased patrols in the parking garage where the abduction took place and moved police from regular detail to those places where their presence would give the community more visible assurance of police vigilance. The chief was operating with an understaffed department because of a state budget crisis.

The PC worked with the VP for student services to plan three open meetings, where he could report what his department was doing to increase campus safety. The first meeting was the Monday following the abduction and rape. The PC arranged for a demonstration of K-9 surveillance at one of the open meetings and requested the university's endorsement of his department's acquiring a K-9 dog. A German Shepherd now accompanies a policeman as he patrols the campus.

Before and during the open meetings, women were demanding that the university sell self-protective devices like mace and tear gas. The PC spoke both at the open meetings and with individuals about the best methods of self-protection and discouraged citizens' use of mace and tear gas.

The PC reported at the meeting that a university police aide was patrolling each campus garage daily from 8:00 A.M. to 7:00 P.M., that the university had increased escort service to include the hours from 5:00 P.M. to 2:00 A.M. and was purchasing an additional van for the service. He added that the department was now recruiting additional police to fill all vacancies and that more police aides would be hired to give police a greater presence and higher visibility on campus.

On the following Tuesday, approximately 100 protesting students marched to the president's office demanding more protection for women on campus. Police were present along their route. The PC was present when the marchers confronted the president, and he was a part of a meeting with three representatives of the protesters and senior university administration. One of the agreements reached in that meeting was that the chief would work with the protesters to examine how the campus could be made safer. The PC accompanied the leaders of the protest on a night walk. The purpose of the walk was to examine the campus after dark and recommend ways to improve the safety of the campus.

Within a short time, the community lost interest in how many police were on the staff and in other safety-related behavior on the campus.

The next week, the PC distributed the following University Police Newsletter to every office and every room in the residence halls. Additional copies of the newsletter were available in the Student Union. The student newspaper quoted from the newsletter. Other newsletters followed and are reprinted here.

University Police Newsletter—November 1990

CRIME VICTIM INFORMATION

If you are the victim of a crime such as rape, you have to remember that it was not your fault.

The following information is written to assure you of two important things: that You Are Okay, You Are Not Alone.

A violent crime can happen to anyone. Many victims believe that in some way they provoked or caused it to happen. A crime can be perpetrated on anyone, male and female, young and old, rich and poor. Do not feel guilty.

We experience many different crimes of violence. The most misunderstood and feared crime on a university campus is sexual assault and rape. Anger and hostility motivates your attacker the same as assault and battery. The rape is not perpetrated for sexual gratification but to humiliate, terrify, and degrade you. Most sexual assaults and rapes are perpetrated by people the victim knows, not a total stranger. Don't believe the myth that a male or female cannot be sexually assaulted against his/her will; that is not true.

Although you may feel powerless, overwhelmed, or fearful, you still control your life. You have one important decision to make after you have been raped or sexually assaulted. That is, if you should officially report it to a police agency. The answer is YES! Reporting the incident means you tell the university police or other appropriate agency what happened, when and where it occurred, and what your attacker looked like. You will be asked a series of questions. Do not let this frighten you. They will help in the investigation and possible apprehension of your attacker.

Should You Prosecute?

Prosecuting means you bring formal charges against your attacker. The police will assist you and try to find and arrest your attacker. If he/she is arrested, the courts begin the process of putting your attacker on trial for the charges.

Reporting the crime is strongly suggested. Reporting the crime and prosecuting are two different things. Reporting a crime does not mean that you have to prosecute. If you have questions please call the university police department. If you do not choose to prosecute, your report will help others who may be assaulted in the future or yourself.

A medical examination is mandatory in a rape or sexual assault case. Your examination must be conducted within 72 hours of the initial attack. This is for your safety as well as evidence collection. The hospital personnel are aware and sensitive to your needs. You will also be checked for vaginal diseases, pregnancy, and injuries. The examination is free. Do not bathe, shower, douche, or change your clothes. You must take a change of clothes to the hospital with you.

To Prosecute:

You must tell the police that you wish to do so. You do not need to have a lawyer. The state's attorney's office will represent you free due to the nature of the crime. After the attacker has been charged, it is possible that he may be released on bail. If so, the state's attorney may ask for restrictions to protect you.

REMEMBER THAT THE UNIVERSITY POLICE ARE HERE TO ASSIST YOU IN EVERY WAY POSSIBLE.

University Police Newsletter—December 1990

An excerpt: PARKING GARAGE SAFETY

Even after the abduction and subsequent sexual assault of a female commuter student from the . . . Garage, there are still unsafe practices being observed on the part of some female students. A lone female driver will stop and give a ride to a male who is walking in the garage and take him to his vehicle so that she can take his parking space. These males are not usually known to the females. This usually occurs at or near the garage entrance. The university police ask that this practice be discontinued immediately. We have your safety at heart, and we wish you did also. You ask, is it a crime to give a guy a ride to his car? No it is not, but it could turn out to be one when this guy attacks you. . . .

University Police Newsletter—February 1991

AN EXCERPT: CRIME ON YOUR CAMPUS: 1990 STATISTICS

Because we feel it is very important that the university community be aware of the number and types of crime occurring on campus, we have listed below a breakdown of the types of crime reported to us in 1990. By being aware that crime does occur on our campus, you can take positive measures to prevent yourself from becoming a victim. Making our university as safe as possible must be a shared goal of everyone on campus. Crime prevention should be the concern of our entire community but, ultimately, it must be the responsibility of each individual. If you would like information on how you can help to prevent crime, call the University Police Crime Prevention Section at . . ., talk with any of the police officers you see on campus, or stop by our headquarters. . . .

Crimes listed with their frequency were Arson, Assault, Assault and Battery, Attempted Breaking and Entering, Attempted Theft, Breaking and Entering, Child Abuse, CDS Violation, Credit Card Misuse, Destruction of Property, Disorderly Conduct, Disturbing the Peace, Explosive Device (hoax), False Fire Alarm, Fire Work Violation, Harassment, Indecent Exposure, Malicious Burning, Racial, Religious and Ethnic, Reckless Endangerment, Sex Offense, Rape, Tampering with Auto, Telephone Misuse, Threat against Student, Threat against University Personnel, Theft, Theft of Auto, Trespassing, Unauthorized Use of Vehicle.

VP—Director of University Relations

The VP was with the university president and the business VP when the call came from the police in November 1990 that another rape had occurred. The VP's first understanding was that county police had jurisdiction; therefore, he referred callers to them. However, a television reporter informed him that the university, and not the county police, were responsible for the case. The VP called the PC who stated that to their surprise campus police had just been told that they had been assigned jurisdiction in the case. The VP discussed with the chief what the chief would say to the press. The county police, with whom he had contact, kept asking the VP why the university was assuming responsibility since the rape had occurred off-campus. The VP did not know why. The VP, as well as the news and information staff, worked with the media representatives who came to the next two open meetings. The VP prepared a letter for the president to distribute to the campus acknowledging that the crime had occurred (see p. 92), reporting steps the university was taking to improve safety and urging the community to participate in keeping themselves and the campus safe.

The VP recommended that for any future crisis, those involved in the university response should meet immediately to make up a plan of action.

IO—Information Officer

The IO learned of the second rape at an open campus meeting with press and three VPs. One of the VPs received the call and then shared the information with her. By the time reporters called, the IO had an update on the facts of this latest incident and had formulated a statement of what the university had done to improve security since the time of the July 1990 rape and also what it planned to do now. The IO told reporters about improved security as well as the institution's continued resolve to make the campus safe. That night on the local news, the news anchor reported the rape and what the university was doing to improve safety on the campus. The reporter told of plans to hire more police officers, that campus garage lights would remain on all day as well as night, and that there would be an increase in police patrols of the garage. The message was that TSU had responded swiftly and openly to the incident.

The IO also served as the campus police information officer. In the latter capacity she responded to queries about the status of the investigation.

As plans for the open meetings unfolded, the IO kept the media apprised of them. When camera crews and reporters covered those meetings, she accompanied them.

The IO continually informed the student press. An article about the rape and how the university was improving campus safety was published in the faculty/staff newsletter. Here, too, the community was reminded that safety for all was dependent on everyone. The IO commonly worked 12-hour days for a few days after such crises as the rape.

In order to control rumors, calls from the media had to be answered immediately. A few angry parents also called.

VPS—Vice President for Student Services

When the VPS learned of the rape, she called the VPP, personnel director, to request he inform the community. She asked that he request faculty to make an announcement in their classes to further remind everyone not to walk alone on the campus.

On Friday, the VPS announced by e-mail and by fliers a meeting for Monday at 3:00 P.M., which would be open to everyone, to discuss the rape of the past week. The dean of students (DS) planned the meeting with police and student government officials who agreed to talk about the safety week they had planned. The PC told what he knew of the attack and what university police had done and were doing to increase security on campus. The assistant VP for business talked about the community patrol and requested volunteers to assist with the patrol. The audience was told about increased lighting on the campus and increased security in residence halls where residents would now either be required to use a double key or a magnetic strip ID card to gain entrance. Approximately 150 people, mostly students, attended. The media were present with lights and cameras. Students were angry that a violent act such as rape could happen to a student while on campus, and they demanded more protection. Some students gave suggestions for how the people present could participate in their own safety. The CD from the counseling center reminded the audience of services available at the center. The meeting lasted about one hour and fifteen minutes and was reported on television news that evening. At the end of the gathering, the DS announced another meeting for the following Monday.

On Monday, the VPS learned that a group of students would march on the president's office the next day to demand better protection. The DS notified the president's staff and the police chief. Approximately 100 students, mostly female, marched to the second floor of the administration building and chanted until the president arrived. They demanded more protection. They wanted self-defense courses, items like mace to be sold in the bookstore, and more police protection. After the group had spoken to the president for about 20 minutes, President HS invited the protesters to choose three representatives to meet with him and some others from administration, including the VPS, to discuss how best to proceed.

The VPS invited the three representatives to help plan the next open meeting. One of the presenters at the meeting was a private crime prevention and crime-fighting organization that a student group had invited to attend. The organization wanted to sell its products and training program. (The DS also arranged for a self-defense course to be offered beginning the next week. No one registered for the free course.) About 25 people, mostly students, attended the meeting.

A staff member from the library had come and wanted to talk after the meeting about the fear of the library staff because the building was nearly empty when they left at night. The VPS requested that the police meet with the librarians to plan an escort service for the librarians leaving at night and to plan a shift where students leaving the library late at night could also be escorted to their cars or their residence halls. Since that meeting a special escort service has been organized and is in operation.

Nine people came to the third meeting. Two of those in attendance were students. Staff talked about some particular safety problems that affected them, especially at specific parking lots. The VPS had been meeting regularly with a group of administrators to talk about student safety. The committee was later expanded to include a representative from the personnel department so that the campus safety committee could work for the safety of the total campus community.

CD—Counseling Center Director

When the CD learned of the rape, he called the hospital and visited the student and her parents there. Further counseling was offered to the student. She attended a few sessions at the counseling center but then stopped going. It has been an established procedure for the CD or another staff member to meet with a rape victim as soon as she is able to see anyone. Frequently, the counselor meets the victim at the police station or at the hospital and remains with her, with her permission, through the initial police interview.

VPB—Vice President for Business and Finance

In November, the VPB was with the president and the news director when he learned from police of the abduction and rape. The VPB asked police to increase their patrols; he considered ways to increase their visibility. He also wanted to be assured that all residents in the buildings were receiving safety information.

Although the budget was quite tight, the VPB released funds to increase the number of police aides. He requested police to increase their visibility and their surveillance within the parking garages. The VPB's staff purchased an additional van and expanded the hours of the escort services. He revived the concept of K-9 surveillance that had been proposed some years before. His offices posted signs in the garages warning entrants to be wary because of what had happened there. His staff studied the lighting on-campus and reviewed a number of security devices, including television cameras. He and his staff spent the next staff meeting discussing how to make more effective use of the police. Budget cuts had caused three police positions to be frozen. He arranged for those positions to be filled.

The VPB is planning an identification system for temporary employees who have to enter residence facilities. Those vendors who have permanent service contracts with the university have staff who are known to the community. Other contractors who come to the university for a single task need to be identified. The VPB has asked that such contractors be accompanied by university personnel to the site of their work if the work is to be done in a residence hall. There is no way to check the criminal history of strangers such as exists for employees of the institution.

In a management class that he teaches, the VPB discussed the event and how management could plan for safety without assigning a police guard for each person.

VPP—Associate Vice President for Personnel

When the VP for student services called the VPP to inform him of the rape, the VPP called the police to verify the facts and communicated with all campus offices by e-mail. Because not everyone who receives e-mail reads it regularly, the VPP followed up with a call to the dean for continuing studies to request she read it.

The VPP attended two of the three open meetings, participated in the later-abondoned campus watch program, and agreed to have a representative on the campus safety committee to represent the safety needs of the university staff. As a result of these meetings, the concept of safety changed from student safety to campus safety. The personnel department also increased its safety awareness efforts for staff and faculty.

BFA—Administrator—Business and Finance

The BFA has been with the university for many years and was very angry after the second rape in November. He had been appalled after the first rape. The BFA wanted to create a community response that would emphasize prevention. He proposed a campus watch program, modeled after programs in many communities, with trained citizens enhancing the efforts of local police by patrolling and reporting unusual events and the presence of strangers. Although approximately 100 people agreed to participate, only six came to a meeting. The idea was abandoned.

UC—University Counsel

The UC suggested that the university be careful in public statements to protect the identity of the victim. The use of a full first name or nickname, it was determined, was not sufficiently protective. The UC served as consultant to the Information Office about what information should be shared and cautioned that police reports are confidential until the investigation is complete.

The UC urged the various staff members to keep careful records of what each of them said and did in responding to the crisis.

Because there was confusion over police jurisdiction, the UC drafted a memorandum stating that the university police would have jurisdiction for all crime occurring on campus until they believed they needed to turn the investigation over to the county agency.

HD—Housing Director

After the rape in November, a statement describing the abduction and rape was distributed by the HD to resident students and posted in the dining halls. A more detailed letter followed. Every communication urged students to follow guidelines for safety. The HD called an emergency RA's meeting to talk about increasing awareness and security.

The HD sent letters to all residence building council presidents saying she would meet with any student group to discuss safety. One group responded. Approximately 30 of the 400 students in the residence hall attended. One student wanted to know why the university was treating this episode so "sensationally and glamorously." Another asked why the university would offer protection for adults, some of whom would be recruited to fight in the Middle East.

The HD was getting approximately 15 calls a day from parents but almost no questions from students. Parents insisted on knowing how the university would protect their children. Many of the students seemed unwilling to limit their own freedom and mobility. They continued to prop doors open .

On the day following the rape, television reporters were on-campus. Students were resentful of the press and most would not grant interviews. In the past, when television reporters came to campus, students volunteered and appeared to enjoy being chosen for interviews.

SGA—Student Government President

The SGA was part of the planning group for the three open meetings on-campus. At the meeting, a student government officer presented the student government safety campaign. The group was planning to purchase whistles to distribute during safety week the following semester. When the press described the safety plan, the SGA received a donation of 10,000 whistles and a promise of funds to come from another company.

A student created a "safety map," a guide to the brightest lit walkways on campus. The SGA distributed the maps, 5,000 whistles, and 400 flashlights during "Safety Week" at the beginning of the second semester. During that week, the SGA also sponsored a safety night walk with police, administrators, and physical plant staff to evaluate campus safety factors. As a result of such walks, the lighting on the campus was upgraded and shrubbery was trimmed or removed. Two walks were sponsored within a few months. Forty-two lights were replaced between the first and second walk.

The SGA endorsed the idea of a K-9 dog for the university. The leaders also supported the addition of an escort service for students living off-campus and nearby.

PP—Associate Vice President for the Physical Plant

To help solve the crime, the PP requested that the County Crime Lab study the car which the county had towed at the request of the campus police. The PP assigned police aides to patrol the garages. The PP continued that patrol until the end of the academic year. He hoped that the presence of police would remind people to be careful.

The PP knows that students compromise safety systems when they disengage alarm systems or prop doors open, thereby causing a serious problem for a campus trying to increase its security. He is concerned that there is no way at this time to prevent unauthorized entry by "tailgating" into the residence halls.

The PP plans to increase the number of sodium vapor lights that light up surrounding areas. He added an escort van immediately after the November rape and increased the hours of the escort service.

The PP accompanied the SGA during the night walk and improved areas that students and staff identified as poorly lit. With the permission of the president, he increased the lighting in the parking garage so that lights burn all day as well as all night in both garages.

The PP considers it inappropriate that the news office made the police chief the spokesperson for the university in November. While the assailant was still at large, the media asked for details about the investigation, which the PP believes could have been better handled by the university news office.

When the PP hires new staff he rejects those on the state eligibility list with a criminal record of serious offenses. He believes that doing so is his responsibility to the students. If he hires someone whose record has not yet been cleared, he requires that person to work under direct supervision at all times that he or she is on-campus. He has the same agreement with the contractor for housekeeping services because there is so much turnover in that department. A police record clearance may take four to six weeks. Employees with records are restricted as to the areas where they may work.

The following letter from the president was sent out to students following the incident.

A Letter from the President—On the President's Stationery

November 14, 1990

TO THE UNIVERSITY COMMUNITY

As you know, our university community recently experienced a very serious incident on campus. On November 1, a female commuter student was abducted as she got into her car in a university parking garage, driven off campus, and raped. That followed an incident in July, in which a member of our student orientation staff was raped in her residence hall room by a different attacker.

When someone in the university community is victimized by crime, we are all victimized. Such incidents are shocking and frightening, and they serve as a striking reminder that our campus is not immune from such crimes. The incident in July raised the awareness of our residential students that continuing attention to residence hall security is essential and that everyone must participate to ensure that security is not compromised. These recent incidents have made us realize that crime can occur anywhere, and any time, even at noon on a busy campus.

We believe that T. . . S. . . University is safer than many campuses. However, we know that no place can be completely safe from crime. As a 306 acre community of 15,000 people, located in the midst of a large metropolitan area, the university experiences the same problems as the society at large.

The safety of our students, faculty and staff, is and has been a priority of the administration.

One of our most important deterrents of crime is "awareness." Therefore, when each of these unfortunate incidents occurred, we informed the campus community immediately and urged everyone to be extremely security conscious. We will continue to maintain the heightened awareness through meetings and other special efforts.

T. . . S. . . University has enhanced its security programs by adding a second campus escort van to more efficiently serve students, faculty, and staff who need rides around campus after dark. We now provide constant 24-hour lighting in the campus garages where previously there was lighting only at night and on overcast days. We are also increasing lighting on our campus in those areas that students have identified as too dark at night.

Both campus garages are equipped with emergency phones on each floor, and we are recruiting additional police aides. These additional staff will enable us to increase the frequency of campus patrols, which are made 24 hours a day, 7 days a week.

To enhance security in our residence halls, and in addition to our double-key and card entry systems, we are investigating the use of an ID-checking system. At our students' request, there will be additional safety awareness and self-defense programs. And, of course, we will continue our message of awareness throughout the residence halls and the entire campus.

However, we firmly believe that with everyone's help, awareness, and support we can make our university safe. We ask that you help by doing the following: notify the university police immediately on Extension . . . to report any burned out campus lights, non-working emergency phones, broken door locks, etc., so that the university can correct these problems as soon as possible.

I encourage all of you to take advantage of our crime prevention education programs. If you would like more information or have any questions about security, please contact the university police at Extension . . .

Sincerely,

President

SUMMARY

The campus has modified its safety procedures. Should an emergency again require that the entire campus know of the event, the police will inform the VP for student services and the information officer. Together they will decide if this emergency mandates that the entire community be notified. When they agree that an emergency affects the entire campus, the information officer will inform the community via e-mail. That notification will include special directions for faculty, who will be requested to inform their students. The VP for student services will inform each VP and ask that each VP's office notify all departments in their divisions to check the e-mail. In the academic division, the provost's office will contact the deans' offices, who will contact the department offices where a request will be made for faculty to check the e-mail.

An editorial in the city newspaper late in the spring suggested the university ought to examine its safety policies in view of its having had two rapes on-campus.

COMMENTARY

When campus administrators plan most on-campus services it is with the assumption that only students need support and help. When a dangerous person is at large on-campus, schools need a checklist to remind them that faculty and staff also need information, support, and safety information and services.

Because of the reservation of the police chief, the orientation director did not know what to do with the information that a rapist might be at large. Obviously, in hindsight, the police chief would have said that he had information leading him to suspect that a felony or a rape had occurred and saying that the police were searching the campus for the alleged perpetrator. The chief could have suggested that all of the students and staff stay together.

It is wise when discussing plans for campus response to crises to discuss what the campus should do between the time a crime is committed and then verified. Most campus officers were on the side of added precaution.

Each campus needs a plan for communicating with all its members in the unlikely, but possible, event of imminent danger. Prior to these events, TSU did not have a method for reaching all people in case of an emergency.

The small groups that accompanied the student leaders on orientation tours of campus could have been reached if each leader had been carrying a walkie-talkie. Although such equipment would assure the leader's being notified if necessary, it probably would also aid in communication of less vital information. The approach that the orientation director used of having several groups tour together was a good interim plan.

Universities and malls alike must warn users that garages are frequent sites for crime and that those who park there need both to be aware and to be active in seeing to their own safety. It is a continual challenge to enlist community members in the safety effort by having them recognize and report strangers on-campus. This problem exists in residence halls as well as parking garages.

The question arose as to who should speak for the campus when a crime occurs: the news and information office or the police chief. The arguments in favor of the police chief speaking for the campus include the possible reassurance the community gets from hearing the police state first-hand what they are doing to increase safety. On the other hand the news may be better delivered and more precisely communicated coming from the information officer. Although both arguments have merit, it is ultimately irrelevant who is the spokesperson for the community. What is important is that the decision be made in advance.

Although many details about a crime may not be the business of the public, the suggestion made here by the university relations person is that the information officer doesn't need to be as specific and know as much before relaying information to the media. Limiting information internally, however may not serve the university well. Critics of how campuses share information about crime have charged universities with obfuscating information about campus crime to make themselves more attractive to applicants. They charge the campuses with putting appearances above safety.

It is interesting that although both rapes occurred during the day, students sponsored a night walk to check lighting and shrubbery. Research has shown that although 80 percent of campus crime is committed by students, students typically direct their efforts toward preventing the stranger's entrance at night.[1]

REFERENCE

1. Bausell, Bausell and Siegel, *The Links Among Alcohol, Drugs and Crime*, 1990, Business Publishers, Inc.

CHAPTER
five
* * * * * * * * *

Suicide On-Campus

DEAD STUDENT DISCOVERED

On Sunday, April 8, 1990, at 1:00 P.M., MH, a male undergraduate resident student was found hanging in his room. The cause of death was suicide. The body was discovered by his roommate.

BACKGROUND

University of D, with 19,000 students, 6,000 of whom are in residence, is located in a city of 22,000.

PC—Director of Police Operations (Police Chief)

A student who had returned to his room at 1:00 P.M. called for an ambulance when he discovered his roommate had hanged himself. Police, dispatched when the ambulance was called, arrived a few minutes before the emergency medical team. When the officers could not find signs of life, they called the police dispatcher who then called appropriate university personnel. After the emergency medical team had pronounced the victim dead, police notified the medical examiner's office who arranged to pick up the body. Both housing staff and police assisted in physically removing the body.

The PC was called by the dispatcher as he has been whenever a serious crime or a death occurred on-campus. When the PC arrived at the scene, the officers had completed identification of the body. The PC verified the identification by using the victim's picture on his driver's license. Verifying the identity of the victim is something the PC always does. The medical examiner's office later confirmed the cause of death to be suicide. The medical examiner gave that information to the campus police because they were responsible for informing the family.

Police cordoned off the room to prevent tampering with evidence and thoroughly searched it. Although it was assumed that suicide was the cause of death, they looked for other possibilities, as is customary in such cases.

Students gathered in the hall outside around the room. The PC acknowledged that there had been a death but said very little since the family had not been notified. He told the students that an "unfortunate situation" had taken place. The RA who had tried to help the victim the night before was there, quite upset, as was the victim's former girlfriend, who worried about what part she might have played in his suicide, because she had just broken up with him.

The PC notified the dean of students (DS), who leads the University's Crisis Management Team; the counseling center, which dispatched help immediately; the vice president to whom the police report; and the resident life staff. Continuing according to protocol for suicide in a residence hall, the PC met with students at a floor meeting later that day. The police officer who investigated attended the meeting.

The police discovered a cassette with a suicide message for the young man's family. It was on the telephone answering machine. This message became part of the police file and was kept with all the other evidence.

The PC and the DS went to the home of the deceased to inform the family of the suicide. This visit by the two of them represents a joint decision they made some time ago. Both feel that they are mutually supported and that a team approach to such a visit works better than a visit by either of them alone. Families have appreciated the concern they have shown and the time given to them.

When the PC and the DS found the twin sister of the victim home alone, they were reluctant to relay their message. They visited a fairly long time before feeling coerced into telling her. They then searched the town for the mother. When they found her, they did not tell her the cause of death, but she immediately figured it out.

Both the DS and the PC attended the pre-funeral viewing of the body. By that time, they had come to know the family and felt obliged to attend.

The PC informed some other members of the family about the suicide message but did not want the mother to hear it so soon after her son's death. The university made a printed transcript of the tape for the family. When the mother later requested the actual tape, she was given a copy. Both the DS and the PC wanted to protect the mother for awhile.

The two officers who had responded to the call had no further contact with the case. The PC is aware of the stress that officers experience in such cases, and he works with the officers. He encourages their use of the counseling center.

Residence life staff were responsible for collecting all of the belongings of the victim and returning them to the family.

IO—Information Officer

It is standard procedure for the information officer (IO) to be called immediately when a death occurs on-campus. She observed that all of the officers of the university who responded did so with caring and support. She wanted to communicate the caring and general concern of the university to the internal and external community while she actively guarded the rights of the deceased. In sharing information, the IO finds a constant need to balance the demands of what the community needs to know, what the university wants them to know, and what individuals want them to know.

The IO informed the state's only daily newspaper about the death by suicide. She confirmed the student's status, home address, and parents' names. She sent copies to the student press, as she does with all press releases.

Following a suicide, the information office gets calls from many individuals who want information about the victim or about the circumstances of the death. Those calls are not answered. The IO does not give out information about the grade point average of the student. If the victim was an exceptionally able student, she does inform the press about the student's honors and affiliations such as membership in an honor society.

When the media ask personal questions about why the student may have committed suicide and look for more details about the personal characteristics of the deceased, the IO uses that opportunity to refer reporters to experts on the subject who can discuss suicide or the stresses of college life, alcohol, or whatever may be an appropriate topic. These she describes as second- and third-day stories. She solicits the help of the faculty and counselors in talking to the media.

When an event like this occurs, the IO immediately finds information that will help the media understand the event. In this case, she offered such information as the rate of suicide on American college campuses. By providing such material, she hopes the media will give a fairer perspective of the university. The IO is zealous in protecting the family of the deceased. In the case of this suicide, by the time the media called, the IO had found several articles on the causes of suicide among college-age students that contained comments from noted psychiatrists. She also made information available on behaviors to look for that might indicate someone is considering suicide.

When a female graduate student was killed a few years before, the faculty were eager to speak to the media about how praiseworthy she was. If there are people who are willing to talk to the media about the individual, the IO tells the media when they call. Sometimes faculty want to talk about the student.

Another goal of the IO is to demonstrate to the media how the dean of students and others on campus reach out to people in distress because of the suicide of a fellow student. Generally, the press are surprised by the outreach of the various offices.

University of D is located in a small town with one newspaper. Although the university has a weekly information sheet for its own community, the town newspaper and local radio and television stations are the main source of news and information for the entire academic community. It is not uncommon for reporters to want to speak directly with one of the senior administrators of the university, at which time the IO calls ahead to tell the administrator that the reporter will be calling and generally what kinds of information he or she requires. She may make suggestions to the officers.

Copies of all press releases are sent to the student information desk in the Student Union and posted.

DS—Dean of Students

On the Sunday the body was discovered, after the police dispatcher told the dean about the suicide, the DS called the VP for student affairs who, in turn, contacted the president. DS then turned to his checklist which follows:

- Secure the immediate and secondary areas if a suicide has been completed.
- Staff should direct students to remain in their rooms and out of the way.
- Designated officials should contact resident staff, counseling, medical, and religious persons to come on site to deal with student hysteria and shock.
- Meet with and assist, if appropriate, public investigators.
- Make sure no other student has the same name as the deceased.
- After authorities allow, contact parents.
- Prepare statement for the press.
- Have residence life staff be on the alert for other possible suicidal gestures or acts.
- As soon as possible have counseling personnel on the scene working with groups.
- Clean and vacate the room where the suicide took place as soon as authorities will allow.
- Plan for and provide additional support for residence life staff.
- Plan a memorial service if appropriate.

- Continue to target and monitor potential risks.
- Give special consideration to roommate and close friends who might feel guilty.
- Give special attention to those who may have seen the body.
- Prepare to deal with family of the victim and the roommate's family—one individual should be in charge of dealing with all of the family needs from picking them up at the airport to handling financial aid and billing concerns.
- Send letters and flowers and have an institutional representative at the funeral.
- Provide transportation for students to the funeral but do not make anyone feel obligated to go.
- The institution may wish to assume some costs such as housing and transportation for the family and memorial services expenses.
- Check on the deceased's credit status with the university. If the individual owes any money, eliminate that debt. If the individual has a credit with the university, send a check along with a condolence note. If the individual dies within a session or semester, refund 100 percent of tuition.
- Check to see if the deceased was on financial aid—if the individual had federal loans they will be eliminated—two official death certificates will be needed for this process.
- Make sure all individuals on the notification chain are alerted to the suicide as soon as possible.
- Do a series of "check backs" with the family of the victim over the next 18 months. This demonstrates continuing concern on the part of the university.

The first thing the DS did was to verify the identity of the victim. Although others had done that before he arrived, he is committed to making his own identification. A mistaken identification had been made in the past, and the DS acted on wrong information. After the DS spoke with the RA and the hall director to make sure they were informed, he called the counseling center director who remained available for the next few days.

He and the PC together visited the family to notify them of the death of their son, which they had agreed was best done together. Once, in a previous suicide, when the DS and the PC told the family, the parents had refused to believe what they were hearing. The DS and the PC had the pictures taken by the police, and the PC had to show them to the family before they would accept the truth.

The university does not as a rule hold memorial services. The dean of students office will provide transportation for anyone who wishes to attend the funeral. Although the DS sees that a university representative is present at the funeral, he himself only goes if he has known the student or if the death occured on-campus. In this case, of course, he did attend.

The DS's offices contacts the various offices of the university who need to know that a student has died. Financial aid needs to know of the death and to have a death certificate. The billing office needs to know in order to issue a refund.

Housing, naturally, knows about the death. If the family wishes, the housing staff will pack the victim's belongings. Otherwise, the family may come to do it. Before the family comes, the room is searched for anything that will be detrimental to the good memory the parents have of their child. Items such as pornographic material are removed.

The DS contributes to whatever fund the parents have set up, writes a condolence to them, and also writes a note for the president to send. The DS makes a list of the students who were close to the deceased and are likely to be affected by his or her death.

He also notifies the dean of the college in which the student is enrolled. The dean notifies the student's faculty.

The student services offices ask students who were most likely to be directly affected by the death what help they might need in meeting their course requirements. Some students were not prepared to take their final exams at the posted times.

RL—Residence Life

When the police responded to the call for an ambulance, they also summoned the available residence staff member so he could enter the room with the police. Because of a problem with a beeper, there was a mix-up and the staff member, RL, arrived later. When an emergency requires an officer to enter a dormitory room, the procedure is to have somebody from residence staff accompany him or her. It was not possible in this case. When RL did get there and learned what had happened, he notified his supervisor who made the other appropriate calls within Housing. The supervisor also had a responsibility to tell the VP for student services before 8:00 A.M. the next day. If it had happened during a day when classes were in session, that VP would have been notified immediately.

While the police were investigating, RL contacted the other staff in the building to discuss how and what they would do. Their first efforts were to talk with the roommate and the girlfriend. RL and one of the two responding officers went to inform the girlfriend, who lived in another building.

Staff planned two evening meetings, one on the floor of the residence hall where the deceased lived and one in the dormitory of the girlfriend. Counseling center staff conducted the meetings. There were approximately 35 people on each floor. At the meeting, Housing staff disclosed the facts as they knew them and answered questions. The police officer who had been the first one to respond was there to tell what he knew.

The staff has tried, as a general procedure, in cases such as this to assemble all those concerned with the crisis at a general meeting so that university personnel can answer questions all at once rather than individually. In this particular case the RL did tell the students who were in the immediate area that MH had died.

When police completed their investigation, Housing had custodial staff clean the room.

For the following week or two, hall directors watched students more closely than usual and made referrals to counseling services. There were also some workshops about grieving and about suicide.

Since this death took place less than three weeks before the end of the semester, there was never a return to any really normal dormitory life that semester. University policy at DU is not to maintain the residence communities from year to year but to reassign students at random to rooms all over campus. The same configuration of people who lived with or near the victim or his girlfriend would not live together the following semester.

CD—Counseling Center Director

The counseling center has a staff member available for emergency calls at all times. The center provides help for students and staff in the residence hall when a suicide occurs. They reach out to those who are the immediate survivors within the university community, particularly to roommates, close friends, neighbors, and so forth. They go to the scene within minutes after a body is removed. They focus on the emotional response to the death. Counselors will meet with individuals and with groups, with staff and students together or separately, depending on what appears most helpful at the time.

Counseling center staff met with students at a floor meeting that night to address the crisis. The goal of such intervention is to help people let go of responsibility they may feel for the tragedy. Such guilt is the most common survivor reaction. The counselors do not schedule another floor meeting but do arrange for follow-up with individuals and groups at the center if needed.

The counselors always promise to be back in touch, and the counselor who has been there will call students the next day. The counseling center will honor requests for more floor meetings. Sometimes students request additional meetings immediately before or after the funeral or both.

Part of the center's outreach is to contact those groups to which the victim belonged and ask if any of those students need the counseling center's help.

If a family member of the deceased wishes to come to the center for help, the center staff will meet with him or her for the purpose of helping the family member find an appropriate resource.

RM—Risk Manager

The RM serves on the Risk Management Committee with the vice president for governmental affairs, the dean of students, the manager of plant operations, and the director of the safety department. They routinely discuss all types of dangers that exist on the campus and make recommendations to the president of ways to reduce that risk.

When an accident occurs, they study, then review all the facts and recommend institutional changes if appropriate. They did not choose to review this suicide because they did not see institutional culpability.

COMMENTARY

The dean of student's checklist is a great help. Following such procedures saves pain and confusion and relieves the campus from being dependent on any one person's presence. The checklist also identifies who is responsible for doing what, which makes things much easier in a crisis. The bureaucratic step of notifying the dean of the college who then notifies the faculty is a cumbersome way of informing the community. Sometimes such a procedure deprives the faculty of knowledge of the crisis for a longer period than is appropriate, especially if they wish to inform students in their classes.

The two-person team that visits the family of the deceased is a sound approach. The two members of the team support each other; generally the pair are not as uncomfortable as each would be alone. The only drawback from this approach would be if the community had intepreted the two men's appearance as a sign that tragedy has occurred.

Universities are always tested in situations like these. The staff's stopping its normal routine to spend time with the grieving family and the shocked students is not only important for the recipients of these kindnesses but also for the university. It is hard to know how much influence the university representatives' actions had on the attitudes and experiences of those involved on the campus.

CHAPTER
six

Serial Murders
Off-Campus

FIVE STUDENTS MURDERED AT OFF-CAMPUS APARTMENTS

On Sunday, August 26, 1990, the day before fall classes were to begin, two
coeds were found murdered and mutilated in their off-campus apartment. On
the following day, another murdered coed was found in another off-campus
apartment within a short distance of the first murders. On Tuesday, two more
students, a male and a female, were found dead in a third apartment nearby.
Four of the students went to UF. One was a local community college student.

Three and a half years later the assailant, a drifter from Texas, was found
guilty; the jury recommended the death sentence.

BACKGROUND

UF is a large research university with 28,000 students, 7,000 of whom live on-
campus. The campus has a hospital and a number of professional and graduate
programs. Many of the nonresident students live in privately owned apartments across from the campus where many of the fraternity and sorority houses
are located. It was at these apartments that the murders occurred.

The Crisis Response Team

The vice president for student affairs chaired the committee which he
convened at 8:00 A.M. on Monday following the discovery of the first two
murder victims. The crisis response team, nicknamed by some in the counseling center as "the death squad," had the following members: provost, information officer, housing director, police chief, police representation from the
county and city, director of the student union, associate VP for administration,
campus ministry, student government president, dean of students, director of
the counseling center, director of health services, and a representative from

the County Crisis Center. During the crisis they started each morning with a report from the police.

The team coordinated and directed the university actions, policies, and official responses to the murders. They planned for increased security and deliberated about how and what to communicate to the students, how to control the spread of rumors, and how to help individuals and the community cope with the impact of the tragedies. They recommended extending deadlines for payment of fees and for academic decisions that needed to be made, and also forgiving student absences for the first week of school.

The Community Crisis Coordination Team

The Community Crisis Coordination Team was made up of representatives of the county, the city, the mental health services of the city, the University Counseling Center, the County Crisis Center, the university, the community colleges, the school board, the campus ministry, the United Church of the city, the police department, the county sheriff's office, the university police, Emergency Medical Service, the states attorneys office's Victim Witness Services, the Chamber of Commerce, the Apartment Association, the Red Cross, and the local newspaper and TV station. These groups had been working together in a loosely knit organization until response to this crisis forged a more formal working group. They planned activities to help the community recover. They planned a memorial week from September 16 through 23, distributed white ribbons for people to display, planted trees in memory of the victims, and sponsored a community memorial service.

The Task Force

The Task Force was a committee of city, county, and university police; FBI representatives; and representatives of the sheriff's office. This ad hoc group was responsible for the investigation of the murders.

PC—Chief, University Police Department

The PC was called at home by the chief of police of the town. The PC called the vice-presidents and the president. When the PC learned the nature of the emergency, he assigned an investigator to work with the city and county police, the sheriff, and the FBI as part of the investigative team. The chief was a member of the task force, of the Crisis Response Team, and of the Community Crisis Coordination Team, all of which began working immediately.

The PC made staff assignments and he increased officers' work schedules from eight to twelve-hour shifts so that police presence would be more visible within the community. Three officers were on telephone duty at all times. The twelve-hour shifts continued for three months. The chief's challenge to his officers was to protect the university community.

The PC was concerned with providing immediate support for students. The university was receiving several hundred calls an hour. The media were constantly questioning him, and the PC met with them regularly and frequently. He continued to manage the questions from the media and from the students. Although students repeatedly asked how the assailant gained entry, the PC could only reply with suggestions for increasing apartment security and personal safety. The chief of police for the city, in charge of the investigation, had decided to withhold information about the way the murderer entered the building for fear that release of that information would hinder the investigation. That decision frustrated the students and the press.

The PC encouraged people to use dead-bolt locks. He met with as many students as he could and encouraged his staff to spend time listening to and responding to student concerns. He wanted his staff to remember that callers would be upset and that the officers answering calls would need to be patient.

The Crisis Response Team was called to the scene after the murders and immediately began to serve the distressed students. Victims' assistance services were brought in as part of the Crisis Response Team, and they, together with university staff, provided service to off-campus students through the night and then afterward for many hours.

The university president told the chief, "Do what you have to do to give visible assurance to the community." People left town in the wake of the murder; the town was extremely quiet. The PC increased all escort services. Police were available to enter apartments off-campus, contrary to any previous procedures, to assess for occupants whether the dwellings were safe from entry by intruders. The PC also increased police service around the residence halls.

The PC invited students' parents to ask questions of him and his staff so they could better understand what was happening and what steps the university was taking to make the campus safer. The university police public relations specialist responded for the chief to the media and individual callers. The chief approved communications to the press.

Although the police department had sponsored an ongoing crime prevention program, in the wake of these murders, the best help that could be offered was to try to teach crime prevention agressively to all people on and off the campus. The PC sent crime prevention teams to speak at every opportunity about various types of crime prevention. He and his staff went to apartments off-campus and made suggestions to landlords and residents for improving security.

Vendors were soon selling a variety of self-defense items like mace and tear gas. The PC said he could not recommend them. Many vendors asked for his endorsement of the security devices, but the chief did not have the time to test the claims made for the products.

IO—Information Officer

Called by the vice president for student affairs (VPS), the IO was at the murder scene on Sunday night soon after the first two bodies were discovered. She informed the president, to whom she reports, the provost, and her associate director immediately of the murders.

Media personnel were at the scene when the IO arrived. There was not yet any talk of a serial murderer.

The centerfold of the independent student newspaper, the *Alligator*, was regularly purchased by the information office for the "University Digest," the university newsletter. On Monday, the IO changed Tuesday's "Digest" so that she could publish a list of safety precautions and the names and telephone numbers of various people that students could call on. The university also disseminated information via its university radio station. "Together for a safe campus" became the university's signature when it was issuing safety messages.

The IO clearly stated the university's commitment to the welfare of each member of the community as the guide for all planning and decisions. This goal was to be accomplished regardless of financial or bureaucratic concerns. She found that, while the crisis lasted, offices had, indeed, put aside pettiness and issues of turf to unite as a community to do what was best for its constituency.

From August 27th forward, the IO was part of the Crisis Response Team that met each morning for 10 consecutive days to plan the university response.

At 8:00 A.M. on Monday the 27th, after the first bodies had been found, there were 40 different media representatives, mostly from within the state but a few from the national media. At 10:30 A.M., the police called and said that a third body had been found, and there was reason to believe that these murders were the work of a serial killer. Now the story had become national news; by noon it had been broadcast internationally. Everyone wanted to talk to the president of the university.

The press were angry because the city police were not telling how the attacker entered the apartment. When the IO realized the press were frustrated in their efforts to get information from the city police chief, she arranged a press session for Monday afternoon as an opportunity for the university to respond to questions and for the president (PR) to speak publicly about the incidents.

The IO and the VPS prepared the president by giving him a list of new university initiatives the campus had made to increase community safety.

These included increased bus service on campus, increased lighting, better security in parking garages, and increased escort services.

The IO and her staff organized information about the university's extending deadlines and encouraging students who lived off-campus to move to the campus. The president, in this first communication to the press since the murders, expressed the overwhelming concern the university had for each person and the special care the university was taking to protect everyone. He described the murders as a community tragedy, one shared by all. He told what steps the university had taken to increase safety since the tragedy began, and, further, announced the cancellation of the freshman convocation. There was a well-received question-and-answer period with the media.

On Tuesday morning, when the fourth body was discovered, the following statement by the president was sent to the Associated Press: "The most UF can do is urge its students, faculty and staff, and citizens of Alachua County to look out for their own safety and the safety of others, and get what information the university receives out to the public as quickly as possible to control rumors."[1] Later that day a fifth victim was discovered. The president ordered flags on campus to fly at half-mast.

Over two hundred media people came to the press conference scheduled with the president, the city chief of police, and the county sheriff. After this press conference an open meeting was scheduled in the same location for the purpose of informing the university community about safety on the campus as recommended by the Crisis Response Team. Many students came early for the open meeting and cheered reporters on as they questioned the city police chief, who continued to avoid questions about the murderer's method of entry into the first building. Students were demanding to know, as they had from the time of the first deaths, how the assailant entered the premises, but their further attempts to get information were also frustrated.

Both the president and the president of the student government spoke at the open meeting. The student government representative urged students to stick together and sleep at the homes of friends. The president invited all students who would like to move to campus to do so immediately, without charge. He also invited all students to call home free of charge, and he made a bank of university phones available to them for letting their parents know they were all right. The director of housing talked about safety in the residence halls. Students were able to get more information and also to make suggestions for improving security. Members of the press mixed with the people on-campus. Some members of the state legislature attended the meeting. Some people running for office also came.

On Wednesday morning, the president, together with a senior student, appeared on national television to answer questions. One of the networks announced incorrectly that the university had canceled classes. The university sent corrections, which were not broadcast. Other factual errors were found in several different publications.

The president sent letters to parents, one dated August 28th, and the other September 4th, stating what the university was doing in response to these events.

Because the media were angry about the lack of information given them by the task force, LG invited them to see what the university community was doing to increase safety. The press accompanied staff members and students on a night walk to assess the safety of the campus, while students distributed free whistles. The media mentioned these events in their news coverage.

The IO identified the groups that the university needed to inform: the regents, reporters, chairman of the board, and local leaders.

Until the bodies were identified, families continued to call the university to find out whether their own children were among the victims. One mother said she was wondering about her daughter who was a "very tall, blonde, adorable" woman. The IO had assured her that none of the victims matched that description.

The IO said the university has a policy of treating all issues forthrightly. For example, all media calls were returned in the order in which they were received. The IO had been available morning and night to respond to the media. She believed the credibility that had been established with the press served them well during this time of crisis. She acknowledged to the press, when appropriate, errors made by the university, using the same candor as she used to announce its achievements. Although the media were frustrated that the Task Force had not given them sufficient information, they were very supportive of the university.

The Task Force held press conferences twice daily but gave out limited information about the investigation. They reiterated that it would be detrimental to solving this case.

The IO followed the pace that the press set. For ten days, she responded to the press from 5:00 A.M. to 9:00 P.M. They would call at 5:00 or 5:30 A.M. to be able to prepare for 6:00 A.M. deadlines. The IO felt it was important to keep putting out information to the press indicating that the university was in control. Examples of the university being in control were that classes were continuing and that the university was providing additional protection to students so they could feel safe in attending classes.

Some staff members suggested to the president that he suspend classes. The president, however, simply said he would honor the decisions of those who decided to leave school. When asked if he would close the university if a sixth body were found, he replied, "Then we'll just have to operate under a state of siege."

Women on and around the campus had been very fearful since the first murders. When the fifth victim found was a strong, large male, no one felt safe and everyone was frightened.

The Council of Academic Deans, the provost, and the president didn't want the students to suffer academically or financially because of the tragedy. All academic deadlines were dropped. Students would find the system easier and more flexible. The president invited students to be a part of the safety program.

The president, at first, agreed to appear on television but later refused after realizing that all other programming on the show would be classified as entertainment. He felt it would be wrong to do something for entertainment at the victims' expense. To do so would be a disservice to the students. In a news program, the president was given an opportunity to answer questions and to describe the university responses to the crisis.

The IO kept repeating the message that any student who wanted to live on campus could do so. She continued to give information about the increase in safety measures, including the additional police personnel.

The Task Force announced a special press conference for Friday. It looked as if they might have broken the case, but the press conference was canceled at the last minute. The lack of information from the Task Force made it look as if the university was not forthcoming with the facts, but the university was totally dependent on the Task Force's information.

By the end of the week, the president and the senior administration raised the question as to whether the university should remain open. On Friday, the IO, the APR, the VPS, and the provost called a meeting for the following morning at the president's house. The SGA president was also invited. The purpose of the meeting was to decide whether they should close the school and cancel the fall session. They decided to remain open, on the grounds that if they closed it might appear that the university was being held hostage.

To make that decision known, the IO called a press conference for Sunday, September 2nd, at 2:00 P.M. She faxed invitations to every newspaper in the state, contacted each person who had called her for information, and called every hotel in the region to ask hotel staff to post an announcement for all members of the press. Through the media, the IO planned to reach parents, students, the university staff, and the legislature. It was very important that no media organization be overlooked. At the press conference, the president announced that the school would remain open and he asked the help of the media in getting that message out. In response to a question, the president said that he would allow his daughter to stay on-campus if she were a student at this university.

The committee planned a memorial service for Wednesday, one-and-one-half weeks after the murders began. Although the city was also planning a memorial service to be scheduled for a later date, the university decided that it was important to hold its own service right away. The memorial service would be in honor of all the victims, including the one from a nearby community college.

Invited student speakers delivered a eulogy for each victim. The president's message celebrated the lives of these young people. The memorial service marked the end of the official mourning period. The flags were returned to full mast the next day.

University officials discussed barring the media from the memorial service to keep the service dignified. The IO prevailed on the committee to include them and agreed to take responsibility to see that press did not spoil the atmosphere. In a memo her office sent to the media, the media were informed about what facilities would be available to them so that they could transmit video and audio transcriptions of the ceremony back to their stations by satellite. The media were requested not to use artificial light sources and to remain in their places until the ceremony ended. Media people cooperated.

A football game had been scheduled for the next Saturday. There was no change in schedule. The president and his immediate staff reflected, however, that if that game had been scheduled for the week before they would have canceled it. As part of an agreement with the television station, the university gets thirty seconds of air time. Normally, the time is used for some promotion of the institution. This time the president used the time to thank parents, alumni, and the many others who were so supportive during the crisis.

DS—Dean of Students

The dean of students (DS) was called by the president (PR) on Sunday night, when the first murders were discovered. When he arrived, the PR and the IO were there talking with students and police. The area around the apartments was roped off, and a number of students who lived in the apartments were asking what happened. The DS called his staff and the counseling director (CD) to bring more professional staff to work with a number of distraught people.

Residents wanting more information talked to members of the staff. The county agreed to increase security and to increase the number of police patrols. The County Crisis Team was on its way. The DS asked students who were standing by to get the word out that there would be a meeting of all the students living in the apartments close to campus and that it would be held by the pool area in a private apartment complex. The DS asked students to come together so that so he could assess the needs and determine what the university could do to help. Students were urged to travel together. Members of both the crisis center and the counseling center stayed at the apartment area around the clock that night. The DS and the CD reiterated to all students that many support resources were available.

The police described to the students and parents assembled what had happened and what they knew at the current time. The major question the students wanted answered was, "How did the intruder get in? Was he let in?" The students felt that the answers would help them protect themselves. They did not get answers to those questions, however.

Because it was the evening before the first day of classes, many parents who had transported students to the university were still present. The families of the victims arrived on the scene and learned of their children's death from the police. Police stayed with the families. The DS asked the counseling center staff to be available the next day.

In its first meeting, the Crisis Response Team contemplated how to serve the families of the victims and the residents of the apartment complexes. Also, they thought about how information was to be disseminated; one avenue of communication would be the university newsletter, the *Gator Connection*. The team also discussed how they could best respond to and work with the media and also how they could best support the community.

On Tuesday, at the next meeting, the police speculated that these murders were all connected. They provided support staff for the apartment residents, and again the committee urged all off-campus residents to move on-campus temporarily. Counseling services hours would be expanded to accommodate the needs of students and staff.

The DS and his offices were responding to students and parents calling for advice. Many calls came from parents who had not been able to reach their children. It was the beginning of the semester and not all phones were installed. The DS and staff relayed the request that students call home, and they made a bank of phones available at the development office where students could, between certain hours, call home at no cost. Several parents described their children; the DS reassured parents that nobody of that description was a victim. He felt that it was important to maintain personal contact with callers.

The DS and staff visited the fraternity houses, urging students to stay together and to follow all the safety rules. One of the fraternities volunteered to "adopt" its neighboring sorority house, meaning fraternity members would accompany the women into the house or let them stay in the fraternity house.

The team suggested to the president that the deadline for academic suspension dates be modified so that students would not pay fees for not meeting deadlines. They encouraged students to go home for the Labor Day weekend. Meanwhile, various university offices distributed safety information all over the campus.

The Crisis Response Team recommended turning on the lights on all the playing fields all day. Previously, the lights had gone on at dusk. The escort services were to be beefed up. The number of vans used for the escort service was increased. There was some debate as to whether there should be a memorial service. The public media announced the funeral service for each of the victims.

The student services staff talked to parents of the victims when they came to the campus. They did everything they could to be supportive, including housing the families in hotels without charge.

The university held a press conference so that the president could tell everyone what the university was doing to respond to the crisis and what members of the campus community could do to help. Many students and some faculty and staff attended. The president invited all students interested to stay on the campus. Room would be made for all who wished to do so. The SGA president spoke about what the student government was doing to increase safety; the police reported their efforts first-hand. The audience wanted to know how they could protect themselves.

The neighboring community came forward and opened their homes to students. The university received much public support. Faculty invited students to stay at their homes as well.

The DS got calls from parents saying, "Should I leave my son or daughter at the university?" He felt it was important to tell each parent what the university was doing but not to try to make the decision for the parents. On behalf of the university, the DS offered a full refund to any student who withdrew and gave further assurance that he or she could return to school the following semester.

One of the victims came from a Spanish-speaking family in Miami. The president spoke directly to the family in Spanish. The DS felt that such personal approaches were of tremendous importance to everyone in the community.

Within a few weeks after the murders, people seemed to forget to take precautions and relaxed their vigilance. When students who were leaving the university were interviewed, as is the custom, they reported having felt an unusual degree of tension while on-campus.

The DS observed that male students did not feel threatened until the fifth victim turned out to be a man. In the beginning, the men talked about taking care of the women; after the male victim was discovered, they concentrated their efforts on how to make the fraternity houses safe.

The police believed that many people acquired weapons during the crisis. Since the DS is responsible for judicial affairs, his office let those people know that weapons on the campus were illegal.

Phone calls asking about the latest rumors were a constant distraction. The DS added six telephone lines to be able to respond adequately.

During Parents Day in February, when most attendees are parents of freshmen or first semester transfer students, there were no questions asked about safety or about the murders.

The DS observed that, this past semester, the university had received significantly more reports of harassment of students by students than in years before, which the DS interpreted as a response to the murders.

AVP—Associate Vice President for Student Affairs and VPS— Vice President for Student Affairs

When the VPS was called by the police the night of the first murders, he called the IO (the information officer) and about 15 student affairs staff who were at the scene within 45 minutes. Staff provided services at each of the apartment complexes almost around the clock for the first week.

The large number of media personnel, over 250 at one press conference, with some 120 cameras, presented a real difficulty for the students, even after the initial impact of the crisis began to lessen.

Helping services were available in many places for everyone who needed them, though at first mainly for students. It took a while to realize that sufficient attention was not being given to the vulnerability and safety needs of staff.

The committee planned a memorial service for the five victims, and the president of the community college and the president of the university each spoke. The presidents of each school's student government gave the eulogies. Five wreaths of flowers, on-stage during the ceremony, were later transferred to the center of the campus and allowed to remain there for many days. People commented about how much it meant to have the flower wreaths there on campus.

At the memorial service, the VPS said, "There is a deep sense of loss here, a lot of anguish and anger, a feeling of vulnerability, and yet, a determination to move ahead and not become entirely captured by these terrible events. While I have never seen or experienced such sadness and fear, I have also never seen such genuine caring and reaching out on the part of so many people." Both the DS and the VPS were preoccupied with students' safety. Staff worked long hours without returning home.

Members of the Mortarboard Society, an honor society, held a memorial service during which they planted five trees in an area of the campus that was heavily traveled. A faculty member added a 45-second statement of support for students in his televised lecture.

In the back acreage of the campus, there are several 6 × 10 foot concrete walls where students spray-paint graffiti. Within two weeks, one of these walls was discovered to be painted black, and on this background were clearly written the names of the victims and a red heart. At this writing no other graffiti has been added to the wall.

Since these events, the university has maintained a better relationship with the city police chief, the media, and the mayor than before the crisis.

"The Donahue Show" planned to televise its program from the college and requested that the president and some students participate. By this time the students were not only disinterested, they were also angry with all the media.

Parents, six months after the murders, were pressuring the university for more on-campus housing. Although they lobbied before the murders, after the tragedy interest in additional housing increased substantially.

The AVP and the VPS planned time on the campus to talk with and listen to students wherever they were.

APR—Assistant to the President—Protocol Officer

The protocol officer (APR) was part of the Saturday discussion at the president's house. The university is usually given broadcast time by the radio station during a football game. Customarily the time is used to promote the university, but the APR recommended a different approach. He suggested that the president use the 30 seconds to express his appreciation directly to all the listeners. The president did so and he thanked people for their kind words, letters, and support.

The university did not want to plan a ceremony at the end of the academic year to separate this difficult year from the one coming up. He said that instead it would be nice not to have to relive the tragic events. The press, however, will surely mark the anniversary of the murders and thereby call them to the community's attention once again.

AVPA—Associate Vice President for Administrative Affairs

The staff has a procedure it follows in the event of a natural disaster. The Department for Environmental Health, which reports to the associate vice president for administrative affairs (AVPA), stresses the right of the employees to know about disasters. Immediately following the murders, most of the planners thought of students as the only vulnerable persons, but then they realized that anyone, including staff, could become a victim. For that reason, whatever information he received from the chief of police was distributed immediately throughout the campus.

An administrative affairs newsletter, with a circulation of 1,500 on campus, was one means of providing information to the university community. Additional copies were printed and circulated among the deans and chairs. The newsletters urged staff and students to use the escort service. The police additionally offered individual transportation for those who could not, for any reason, use the escort service. Administrative affairs created banners saying, "TOGETHER FOR A SAFE CAMPUS." They developed posters that were put in heavily trafficked areas and in the bookstore. The crime prevention program of the campus police furnished newsletters and speakers as well.

Campus leadership, meanwhile, was evaluating the impact of canceling school for the semester. Would such an action reduce the anxiety of the community?

The AVPA recently received a letter from a parent who requested a refund after her child had done poorly the first semester, a problem that she associated with disturbance about the murders. He authorized the refund, believing it to be consistent with the university's handling of the difficulties associated with this episode.

In the staff meeting the first week after the murders, a decision was made to be flexible about deadlines, including such deadlines as the last day to pay a bill before late fees are added. The AVPA made extra money available for departments who needed staff to work overtime to increase safety or services.

Morale was surprisingly high among staff, despite long hours of hard work. This was probably because people knew they were actively participating in making the campus safer. Staff were pleased with what the president said in each of his public appearances. Many people received notes from the president that praised their service.

The physical plant kept many lights on 24 hours a day. Extra vans were purchased for the escort service. An all-out effort was made to emphasize employee safety, to make the counseling center services easily available, and to be flexible about deadlines in general.

This office initiated another active safety campaign, stressing that people should not compromise their own safety; the theme was "DON'T FEEL GUILTY." "Call today to see if somebody is there" was another message repeated and printed in the newspaper.

The AVPA arranged for the names of the victims to be pulled from the academic records, from the W-2's, and also from the alumni records. He said that the same name may appear on many different lists, and he wanted to make sure that there was no needless intrusion on the families such as form letters.

In the beginning, the AVPA did not feel the need to supplement the information that was broadcast on television. The TV showed an update almost every 15 minutes. The AVPA directed his efforts toward increasing safety and sending out safety messages. Later, he circulated information sent to him by the police.

DP—Director, Personnel Services

The DP initially heard about the first two murders on the morning news. By the time the staff arrived for work, all the telephones were ringing. Police urged everyone to follow the guidelines in the safety program. He assured staff throughout the campus that police were actively patrolling the area. Some employees were distraught. He arranged for them to get help at the counseling center.

Because of the size of the work force, there may be as many as 7,000 applicants for positions in the university at any given time; some applicants come in person to the personnel offices to apply. Since these applicants are obviously not known to any of the people they may come to see, the DP wanted staff to be especially cautious. The DP arranged a meeting with university police and the VPS to develop the best procedures. The police started a buddy system, urging employees to share space rather than occupy offices alone.

The DP was lenient about absences, allowing administrative leave instead of charging against personal vacation time. When he was off-campus he stayed in touch by phone.

The orientation for new staff now includes a significant amount of safety information. The university police department sends out fliers which the DP distributes. He now requires that an employee working alone inform the police, but he discourages anyone being alone. He wants at least two people in an office at any given time.

The DP initiated a waiver for the police so that the extra time they had earned by working the 12-hour shift would not be lost. They will have a year to use their accumulated time.

All people felt responsible for doing all they could to make the situation better. The university had urged those who lived alone to move in with others on-campus. He discussed these recommendations with staff members. Some people on the staff were afraid to consider moving in with other people. Some moved in for a while until they felt less afraid; then they wanted their privacy again. When staff needed to take time off, he tried to be less demanding of them than he would have been under ordinary circumstances.

Students from the Community Crisis Team distributed white bows to various offices as a remembrance of the victims. One of the bows was on display in the DP's office at the time of this interview.

DPP—Director of the Physical Plant

The director of the physical plant (DPP) learned from the newspaper about the first two murders. He examined all campus lighting to make sure all lamps were functioning properly. The DPP felt compelled to check everything he could think of that might increase safety for people. He patrolled the campus to assess areas where a person might become a target of assault and where shrubbery should be cut back. He urged his staff of 850 to participate in protecting each other and themselves.

He inspected working conditions and suggested ways staff might increase their own security within their work areas.

All staff were urged to report any broken lights so that he could fix them immediately.

CM—Campus Minister

When the university made space available for commuter students to live on-campus, the three religious houses at UF likewise opened their centers and among them housed 72 additional people in the course of the week and provided those students with 24-hour security. There were many offers to house students from the community; the local churches as well as members from other churches and from outlying communities offered food.

The CM attended the news conferences to let students know about the services that the ministry was offering. Several centers offered many types of help during the week. The CM himself stayed on-campus four of the seven nights. To address the needs of his own family, his parents came to stay with his wife and daughter.

As part of the Crisis Response Team, the CM helped plan the memorial service. He thought that such a service would serve to start the healing process. He also thought the timing of the service, one and one-half weeks after the first murders were discovered, was appropriate. The service was a cooperative venture, planned by the community college where one of the victims attended, by the county, and also by the university. The community had suffered from the murders and were ready to end their sense of victimization. The planners agreed that it was important to have this ceremony before the football game, separate from the festive events of the campus community.

The CM feels it will be necessary to do something next year at the anniversary of this tragedy, maybe, at a minimum, placing wreaths on the campus.

He was concerned that students who entered the university this past September will live through the next four years differently because of this event than they would have otherwise.

The CM was questioned by hometown pastors representing parents who wanted to know if students should return to school.

Students returned to more normal behavior after a few weeks. Some seemed to recover. Some turned to substance abuse, and for others the murders seemed to call up past experiences of having been hurt. There was an underlying sense of grief in the community.

The campus residence program took on a fortress mentality. Residents stayed together and felt secure in their unity. Occupants of the apartment complexes were more sensitive to strangers; some changed the locks on their doors. They established more ties with the crisis center in the community.

DUU—Director of the University Union

The director of the University Union (DUU), who has been with the university for six years, was with the University of Evansville when an airplane crash claimed the lives of an entire athletic team. He felt that experience gave him some idea of what the situation would be on-campus after the murders.

He learned of the tragedies on Sunday night when the VPS called him. The VPS told him he needed some people immediately to help students at the scene of the crime. Also, the VPS told him that the Crisis Response Team would meet the next morning. As the single murder became a series of murders, the VPS called the DUU with each new discovery.

The DUU was in a unique position. The day the first murder was discovered, he was notified that his National Guard unit had been called up; he would be leaving for the Middle East within 48 hours. He did not want to have to tell the VPS that he might have to leave. As it turned out, he did not have to leave as soon as he was originally told, but he had to be available to leave on very short notice.

He received calls from friends and family from far away who wanted to know how he was. Some of the calls were to find out whether the news was actually true.

Reporters had gone to Florida State in an effort to see how memories of the Bundy murders compared to what people were seeing happen on this campus. Florida State did not want to relive the events of the past.

The counseling center put a drop-in counseling satellite in the student union for students who wanted to talk. The police also set up an office there for distributing safety information.

The DUU received many calls from vendors who wanted to sell all kinds of safety gadgets.

Since strangers and homeless people continually hang around the union, it is almost impossible to screen people in that area. Many students stayed in the hotel located in the union. University staff encouraged students to stay in the hotel, because it offered maximum security. Some students wanted to sleep in the union, but, because it is so open, the DUU could not provide sufficient security. Instead, he urged the students to stay at the religious centers and other approved emergency housing during the crisis.

The DUU adjusted the night programs so that there were very few classes; people didn't want to come out at night, and the DUU didn't want to pressure people by continuing with a fall schedule of night classes. The union has a number of informal courses taken frequently by students as well as people off-campus. The union decreased the number of these course offerings. The various hobby rooms, normally very popular with students, closed early. Many of these hobby areas also exist in the residence halls. The DUU asked people to help each other and for people to offer rides to those who did not have cars.

Union programming included personal safety seminars and self-defense programs. Someone suggested a program on gun control and gun safety. The DUU rejected any programming about guns.

Many people volunteered services or ideas for making the union safer. Various people tried to sell their safety and self-defense services. The university police patrolled at night. Even before the murders, staff had been escorted to their cars when they left their buildings at night. The DUU was looking for a reasonable balance between paralyzing fear and disregard of danger.

Press conferences were held in the ballroom of the union where the DUU arranged facilities for them. Media people stayed in the union much of the time even when there was no press conference. The DUU was also responsible for coordinating the memorial service.

When unknown persons entered the union, staff scrutinized them. Homeless people who hung around the university, but were not students, tended to leave when there were problems because they wanted to avoid being in places where there was trouble.

Within the community there was an outpouring of goodwill. People were aware of the importance of supporting each staff member and helping him or her to cope with fear. There are 160 student employees, 84 full-time staff, as well as the full-time food service staff of the contractor, all of whom work in the union.

The DUU described the university as enjoying national eminence as an academic institution. He was troubled to see its image changing because of the violence. He was proud of how the university and students supported one another.

The Crisis Response Team debated the best way to conduct the memorial service, whether it should be short or long, simple or ornate. The DUU planned a shorter service, which he hoped would be less likely to offend the diverse populations who might each have a unique way to mourn. He was mindful of not wanting to be offensive to any group of mourners or to the families of the victims.

It was deemed appropriate for the union to return to some normal activities within several weeks of the deaths. The building is used by 19,000 people daily on the average. Among the many planned activities is a film series. The DUU changed the schedule of films to include only nonviolent ones. He mentioned, incidentally, that video stores reported exceptionally high demand for violent films.

Halloween, by tradition, had been an irreverently celebrated day on campus with many people in costume. The committee discussed the possibility of canceling the celebration. After much discussion, the DUU planned a celebration without costumes. He feared that some costumes would mimic either victims or alleged assailants who were being described in the papers. The students saw the celebration of Halloween as a return to normality, and they participated actively.

Each student and each staff member had a different means of getting back to a normal routine. Some people talked about apartments that they had rented and canceled because they didn't want to live alone; others wanted very much to be alone.

Most people did not want to be out at night, although more seemed to venture out for bowling and movies. The DUU could tell by the cash receipts from the food service even six months after the murders that there continued to be lighter use of the union at night. People did come to meetings, however.

SGA—Student Body President

At the time of the murders, the student body president (SGA), elected on a platform emphasizing safety and student participation, had been in office for five months. When he began his tenure, racial tensions were high and his active role in addressing these problems successfully made him a well-known person on campus. He used his presidency to actively promote the university and to support its positive environment. He hosted activities that demonstrated that people could work together. Because of student demonstrations during his tenure, he became very familiar with the university administration.

In late summer, the SGA lived in a fraternity house without a phone and was unable to be reached the night of the first two murders. When, on Monday morning, he realized what had happened, and that "it was not just a murder," he went directly to the VP for student affair's office.

The vice president was meeting with the Crisis Response Team. The SGA was immediately made a member. The team was already discussing a memorial service, but they agreed that at present there was no time to mourn and the service would have to come later. Everyone was sad. The SGA was concerned that physical protection and psychological support be provided for those who might be suffering because this crisis had touched on some previous trauma for them.

The SGA did not go to class for two weeks. During that time, he met with the team, scheduled meetings at the sorority houses, and distributed buttons marked "SNAP," to stand for Student Night Auxiliary Patrol, a student supplemental escort service. After the student government received a donation of several thousand whistles, the SGA and his colleagues distributed them.

On Tuesday, when two more bodies, one male and one female, were found, everything seemed to change. The men on campus had been protecting the women, and now they too were vulnerable. On Monday, one of the sororities had felt safe moving into a fraternity house. On Tuesday, the men felt they could be targets of violence as well as the women.

The information office referred more than one hundred press calls to the SGA. By Tuesday morning he had spoken with reporters from the USA Network, CNN, NBC, and many other media representatives. He tried to respond to all of them. He was in contact as much as possible with the university information office, where telephone lines were so busy it was hard to get through.

In personal interviews with news media, the SGA described life on the campus as more normal than was being described by the media. He felt that the situation was under control because people in the university were doing things to allow campus life to go on as usual.

When the SGA spoke with groups on-campus or to the media, he wanted to make clear that the university was a good place to be. He encouraged people to take appropriate steps to ensure their own safety and peace of mind.

The SGA was a speaker at the open meeting on Tuesday, a meeting to which the university community had all been invited by means of fliers. When he spoke from the platform at that meeting, he said the grades in December would not mean anything unless they, the members of the community, did the right things for themselves in September. He elaborated on the right things by urging students to take care of each other, to have slumber parties, to eat together and stay together. He urged people to use common sense, show some concern for one another, and remember they were all in this together.

The SGA called the president's office on Tuesday and was put through to the president immediately. The SGA's suggestions to the president and to the committee were taken seriously and acted upon. He had urged that students be encouraged to move on-campus to be safe. By the next press conference that afternoon the president relayed that message to students and stated that space would be available even if they had to overfill the residence halls by using the lounges.

The next day, Wednesday, the SGA was on "Good Morning America," which was televised from the campus. The SGA spoke in front of the apartments where victims had been found. On Thursday and Friday, while he and all the staff at the SGA were giving out whistles, he again appeared on national news.

Saturday morning, at the president's house, the SGA participated in the decision about keeping school open. He felt, particularly at that time, that his ideas were regarded with the same seriousness as those of the president and vice-presidents. At that meeting, the consensus was to hold a Sunday press conference; there was some discussion as to whether it should be Sunday or Monday. The SGA supported the Sunday conference because he thought people were less likely to be in transit that day and that it would allow them to return to campus on Monday. If they waited until Monday some families might have already made decisions about whether their children should return to school.

The SGA decided that he was in a position to say things to the campus community that the president couldn't say like, "Welcome back to a safe campus."

The SGA described this experience as a period of loss of innocence for students. They came to college and suddenly faced serious kinds of problems. "It was not a time when others could take care of us . . . we had to take care of each other." The SGA was able to communicate that message everywhere.

At the memorial service he spoke about violence as a national problem and not just a local one.

The football game the following Saturday was an exciting experience. There was a very good turnout, and a lot of cheering. It was definitely a release of the tension under which the students had lived. The SGA was ultimately invited to speak at a student leaders' conference sponsored by the student government at Texas A&M to discuss what had happened and the SGA's role in the university's response.

HD—Director of Housing

Safety, of course, had been an ongoing concern for residence halls before the murders occurred; so much so that the HD was writing a monograph about safety and planning workshops for both on- and off-campus students. The HD had, during the month before these murders, upgraded the housing security program with 24-hour desk coverage. Student workers were hired to sit at a reception desk in the front hall of each residence building to see that only those who had legitimate business in the residence halls could get beyond the entry hall. In such a system, each resident student had to give permission to the front desk staff to admit a guest. The front door to the reception area was open all day and locked at night.

When the VPS called the HD on Sunday evening with news of the tragedy of the two women at the apartment, the VPS wanted to know if the victims had lived on campus before. The HD learned from his records that the two women had each lived in different halls for the second summer session. The HD and his staff located information about the victims' former roommates and immediate neighbors. Those roommates and neighbors who were currently living on-campus were located. The HD requested professional residence staff to inform those former roommates and friends of the tragedy. The radio and television coverage was so immediate that most students knew that bodies had been discovered, but the identity of the victims had been withheld until later in the evening.

The HD told all professional and student staff what he knew at that time. It was particularly important for resident assistants to know all the facts so that rumors would not be started. The housing department has a professional staff of 21; 19 hall directors, who are graduate students; 123 RA's; and many additional students with varying duties, for a total of 600 people. The housing department has its own security staff whose service is augmented by the university police.

On Sunday night, the HD did not upgrade the security system. He considered the buildings to be safe. By Monday, after the third murder was uncovered, the HD ordered the entry doors to be kept closed around the clock. He met with staff from the housing division to plan its response to the crisis.

The attitudes of students changed drastically when the last two bodies were found on Tuesday. The students now had experience with homicide, but these final deaths, including a male victim, seemed to bring very different responses. The HD said that the response to these murders was different from anything he had seen before, even when there was a suicide in the student population. He needed to monitor student reaction. Anything they had been prepared to do in the past to help students seemed inappropriate this time. Staff worked closely with RA's. The challenge was to help staff serve students' emotional needs and their need to feel safe.

The HD wanted to work with the media, but he needed to set limits on their activity so that they did not intrude upon the students' privacy. Media personnel were restricted to the lobby areas in residence halls. Staff monitored the situation.

All staff were busy responding to calls from parents, answering their questions forthrightly, and describing what security measures the university had taken.

The HD increased the lighting in the halls. To change 300 dead bolts in family housing, the university had to send a truck to Jacksonville to buy the locks because all the dead bolts in town had been purchased. More stringent limits were placed on residence hall visitation rights. Normally, each semester began with certain basic rules, and then each floor voted to modify those rules.

Now students were not given the opportunity to make changes. There would be no visitation after midnight. These changes were effective on Monday, the first day of school.

A number of ground-level residence rooms were without air conditioning and students opened their windows. The HD had a device installed on all windows that allowed them to be opened only12 inches. He asked students to place objects in front of the windows so that, if someone were to reach in, the objects would fall and alert them. That was an interim step until the special screens arrived which allowed the windows to remain open but impenetrable.

By Wednesday, after the campus-wide meeting at which the president invited students to move on-campus, housing prepared to accommodate an additional 350 students. Forty students moved in.

The HD urged everyone to alert the staff when there were people in the building whom they did not know. Housing kept stressing the students' role in making the buildings safe. Despite all the warnings, a parent reported that he had walked into a residence hall at 10:00 P.M. and nobody had stopped him.

The HD requested that all of the vending machines be kept filled because he knew that students were sleeping less and would be using the machines more frequently. He asked that snack bars stay open longer hours.

Residence staff continually assessed the safety of buildings, making sure that doors were locked and checking to see that safety procedures were followed. The police also checked the facilities. Police were brought in from other campuses to help.

The general impression was that people felt that it was reasonably safe to live on-campus. Some staff members who lived alone in university apartments moved in with others on-campus.

Parents called continually for three weeks after news of the first murders. Some distressed parents called starting Monday, the first day of school, to request that students come home. The HD had worked with staff to be supportive of such requests and to help students not feel obligated to stay. Many parents called with suggestions for improving safety, including installing individual alarm systems. The HD permitted parents to make some modifications in rooms that housing judged would not be disruptive to the whole system but would increase the safety, or the perception of safety, for those individual students. They even permitted one student to keep a dog.

Housing staff traveled with the director of the counseling center around to the residence halls in teams to provide all kinds of support services. The HD continued to help residence staff stay aware of students who might be in emotional crisis.

Students were angry because spokespeople for the Task Force, the team investigating the murder, continued to avoid describing how the assailant had entered the apartments of the victims.

During the first few weeks of school, students reported much less conflict than they normally did. At the beginning of the school year, it was quite usual for many students to complain about their roommates' habits and behaviors. Previously, many students had requested roommate changes. During this time, students came together as a community and focused much less on individual needs and more on the communal ones. Gradually, however, Housing saw a return to the usual roommate conflicts. During the crisis, residents were more active in student housing governments. Students spent more time with each other. By November, however, they were requesting that the entry doors be left open around the clock.

One of the interesting changes since the murders is the increased number of students who apply to become resident assistants. These positions, once highly sought after, had become less and less popular over the last few years. No particular changes in the salary or duties of the position accounted for the increase.

For some students, the relationships established to ensure safety and to give psychological support in the beginning of the semester made a difference in the long run. Most, however, returned to the more ordinary interactions between roomates including tensions, conflicts, competition, and complaints about each other.

During this period of time, student residence governments were made stronger. Students wanted to be active and to participate more in their own governance. The police officers and the residence staff increased their understanding of how they each perceived the campus. Their continued exchange of information has allowed police and residence staff to become more knowledgeable about what is happening on the campus.

At the time of these murders, the nation was getting ready to go to war. It is hard to tell how this frame of mind affected the university community, but one can be assured that it did.

The theme in summer orientation had been increased security. Housing had stressed in brochures, which were sent to student's homes, that a student can be vulnerable in his or her own dormitory room. The residence department continually provided students with information that would increase their awareness of security issues. The staff plan is to continue emphasizing the need for students to be cautious and aware of safety issues.

Since 80 percent of the students live off-campus, the housing office contacted the apartment association and distributed tips for safer living conditions and security for commuter students. The HD is planning to provide additional safety programs off-campus.

The following are items taken from the HD's list of responses to the crises:

- A meeting was held with staff in housing who answer the telephones about how the phones should be answered during the crisis.
- All residence life staff distributed the flier, "Campus Security," to each room before students moved in.
- Bulletin boards on residence hall campus security were developed in each housing area.
- All entrance door closures and locks to buildings and floor sections/ hallways were checked.
- All entrance doors were checked for presence of security signs.
- Outside telephones were checked.
- Residence staff reviewed exterior lighting and shrubbery to recommend modifications if appropriate.
- Staff conducted door-to-door visits to students in the evenings.
- Rooms that were vacant were checked and secured.
- A flier about security was distributed at off-campus apartment houses.
- Stall stories with messages about personal safety were placed in lavatories in residence halls.
- Hall directors sent letters about security to students in their assigned areas.
- Student residence hall presidents wrote to students in their buildings reminding them of security precautions.
- Messages regarding the student escort service were placed on the university television channel.
- HD sent a letter to housing staff requesting that they report strangers and inform HD of students who are distressed.
- Additional security staff were hired for housing.
- Housing office was open longer hours while off-campus students were moving in.
- More movies were added to the university television programming. Programs were added for Tuesday and Thursday.
- A freeze on room transfer, normally lifted after students have moved in, was extended until all off-campus students who wished to move on campus did so.
- Telephone banks were installed in the temporary housing areas.

- Staff hand-delivered a list of available community services to each student in the off-campus apartments.
- Eight university police officers supplemented the outside surveillance of residence halls by housing security personnel.
- During football weekends, staff were stationed at doors to check and remind students not to allow "tailgaters" in.
- Three fliers were distributed: announcement of the campus grief forum; a copy of the campus weapons policy; and a listing of police and escort service telephone numbers.
- Dormitory air conditioning repairs were given top priority so students would not leave their windows open.
- Maintenance staff was increased to respond to requests for dead bolts.
- The duties of the RA's were increased to include visiting with residents, checking exterior doors, and being increasingly available.
- Residence hall staff coverage was increased to assist students who were not leaving for the weekend.
- Staff added important telephone numbers for students to all the existing safety signs, which declared that "WALKING AT NIGHT MAY BE HAZARDOUS TO YOUR HEALTH."

A flier was developed by housing and police:

Campus Security Flier: Whose Responsibility

On one side it lists the university responsibilities such as having a full service police department; providing security staff all night; providing emergency phones on campus; having a trained residence staff; providing peepholes in student room doors; and providing uniformed housing staff with identification cards.

The other column lists what students are expected to do: Lock the door to their rooms at all times; refrain from propping or disabling automatic door closures; refrain from allowing strangers to enter their rooms, floors, or sections; call police or residence hall staff for assistance when needed; instruct guests or food delivery persons to use outside phones to inform students of their arrival; walk with others or request escort service; report suspicious persons; report crime immediately; take appropriate steps to secure personal property like bikes and cars; participate in security-related programs; remove as many opportunities for crime to occur as possible; report instances of obscene or harassing phone calls immediately.

HEO—Director of Health Services

The director of health services (HEO) was a member of the Crisis Response Team. Immediately after the crisis, use of the health center decreased; it gradually increased again after about four weeks.

By late in the semester it had reached close to the previous year's average.

Late in the semester students began asking to be excused for missing classes. They talked about sleeplessness and other behaviors that the HEO interpreted to be responses to the traumas; he acknowledged the legitimacy of their requests to be excused. Many students had not slept and had not told anyone in authority that they were under stress.

The mental health service increased the number of support groups available to students and staff and became more of an outreach service than was their usual custom.

CD—University Counseling Director

Between 7:00 and 8:00 P.M. on Sunday, August 26th, the CD was informed that he and some additional counselors were needed at the scene of a murder of two freshmen women. When the CD arrived, city and university police, students, television trucks, and reporters were there, and the "students were standing around in small groups talking and looking scared and confused. At one point, the police brought out the bodies in plastic body bags and several TV cameras with bright lights blazing recorded this bizarre scene." [2]

Students were gathered into a group where police told them about the murders. Counseling staff then met with students. Counselors urged students to stay with each other. They met with smaller groups of students to help them with their reactions to the trauma, and to help those students who wanted to plan where they would spend the night.

On Monday, after the discovery of the third victim, students panicked. After the fourth and fifth victims were found, the CD was asked to send six counselors to the murder scene. The CD stayed behind to deploy others, if needed. The counseling center had closed for any regular use and was strictly responding to the trauma.

Being on the campus crisis team, which had previously directed the university's response to murder, rape, and suicide, had given counselors and Student Affairs staff experience which was utilized at the time of the multiple murders.

The counseling center staff, the office of mental health, university police, and the County Crisis Center formed traveling teams to meet with faculty, staff, and students affected by the murders, both off-campus and on. Some of the meetings were initiated by the team, some by those in need of counseling.

The center published and distributed "Emotional Response Fact Sheets" with suggestions for coping with fear and panic. During interviews with a number of reporters and television personnel, the CD stressed that fear was the appropriate response to these events and that, if used well, such fear could result in the individuals being wiser in protecting themselves. The CD urged the community to support one another and to use the resources of the various helping services. He repeated this information on fliers and in radio and newspaper advertisements.

The media wanted to go into groups where people were being counseled. Some waited around to interview distressed students.

Personal counseling was available in person as well as by telephone. The hours of service were extended and an additional center was added in the union.

The staff of the center was experiencing all the fears and panic of the community in addition to working exceptionally long hours. The CD tried to grant them some respite time but the demands of the community allowed little, if any.

Many of the people who came to the center in distress did not attribute their feelings to the murders; many references to the killings came up much later in counseling sessions. Even when the clients did not discuss them, the counselors found these events to be a continuing undercurrent in the lives of the people in distress.

Monday, August 27th, the first day of the fall semester, was also the first day of work for 16 new interns in the counseling center. The center was committed to providing service for everyone and needed the new staff to start immediately. Meanwhile, the center helped interns to make arrangements so that they themselves would be safe. This new staff started working by responding to the families who telephoned the center early that morning.

Students were quick to respond to suggestions for improved safety but may not have understood some of the adjustments it would take. When the strong initial response receded, it was important to help people to continue to be careful.

The biggest question facing students was whether to stay on campus or to go home. Students and parents sometimes were in disagreement, and the role of the counseling center was to help them decide how to work out problems for themselves. Eventually, about 300 of the 28,000 students withdrew. Many of the 300 returned the second semester.

Though no classes were canceled officially, many individual professors did suspend their classes with the understanding that the president would not penalize those who did so.

When the chancellor went on television to communicate with the university community, as well as the external community, his presence on television indicated that the crisis was shared by all.

UC—University Counsel

The UC had no direct impact on the university's response. However, she was concerned, in case the suspects were students of the university, about how much information could be released. In addition to requiring a subpoena for the release of student information, the information would have to be released without telling the student and without changing the student record. The subpoena would need to specify that the record may not contain a notation authorizing the release of information and that the student might not be informed that the data had been released.

As to whether encouraging people to move to campus raised a liability issue, the UC observed that the university had a strong security program, and, therefore, it was reasonable to say that on-campus living constituted a safer alternative. The UC said that the university had acted in accordance with all the standards of its counsel. Students have to made aware that owners of apartment buildings do not have the same duty to their tenants as the university has to its resident students.

PR—University President

The PR attributed the university's good response in crisis to a staff that went to work immediately, understood the environment, and were prepared to go into emergency action while maintaining the values of the institution. He very much appreciated the planning done by the staff and the crisis response team for giving excellent direction.

Following the tragic events, the president wrote a number of letters to parents and the community.

Letter from the President to Parents—August 28, 1990

Dear Parent:

No doubt by now you have seen or heard in the media of the recent tragic deaths of several young people in the Gainesville area. I know you join with us in mourning the senseless loss of these young people. I write to let you know that we at the . . . are doing all we can to protect our students and other members of the university community. Their safety is our primary concern.

We offer a variety of security, psychological, housing, and food services to students and others. Many of those services have been expanded, with increased hours of operation and numerous additional personnel. As just one example of the expanded array of services we are offering, we are providing food and housing on our campus for those of our students who do not wish to remain in off-campus residences. We are encouraging everyone to take advantage of these services.

We have publicly encouraged all UF students who have not called home since the tragic deaths occurred to do so immediately. To make that easier for students, we have established a phone bank at our Office of Development and Alumni Affairs where students can call home for free and let their parents know they are safe.

Our University Police Department is working closely with the Gainesville Police Department, the Alachua County Sheriff's Office and the . . . Department of Law Enforcement to do all we can to mobilize our law enforcement services in the area and provide the best protection and safety possible.

Our Office for Student Services is available to help students at any time. Students who have questions or concerns are encouraged to call the Office of Student Services . . . and they may call the University Police Department . . . 24 hours a day.

We hope you will encourage your child to do everything he or she can to preserve personal safety and to use the services we are providing. We appreciate your thoughtful concern, and assure you that we are mustering the considerable resources available to us to sustain a safe and supportive environment.

Sincerely,

President

Letter from the President to Parents—September 4

Dear Parent:

This past week has been a difficult time for all of us associated with the University of . . . , including you and your son or daughter. We know that you will be making decisions this week about the future academic progress of your student, and I want you to know that we stand ready to do everything we can to work with you and with all of our students and their families to cope with this situation. I have had the opportunity to talk with many of you and want to thank you for the words of encouragement and tell you that we will extend our full support to our students as we move forward in our university activities, both academic and extracurricular.

Classes resumed today with our students present and determined to devote their attention to the usual activities of the fall semester. We are reminding our students that the deadlines to drop and add courses for the semester and to withdraw from the university without financial penalty are this Friday, September 7. The deadline to pay fall term fees is Monday, September 10. As you know, we extended these deadlines to the dates mentioned to accommodate our students and their families. We are determined that the terrible circumstances of the past week not cause permanent disruption to our university.

VPS and I have talked with the deans who, in turn, are talking with faculty members, and we will work carefully to see that no student need suffer academically or financially from this situation. Our faculty will work with students to see they are brought up to speed in their class work. No one will be penalized for lack of class attendance during the time before September 7. We are, of course, encouraging students to work with faculty to ensure they are fulfilling course requirements.

Should your son or daughter experience any difficulties regarding their academic status or their personal reactions to this crisis, we encourage you to have them consult the Office of Student Services . . ., the Office of the Provost . . ., or the University Counseling Center. . . . We will hold a memorial service for the five young people who died last week on Wednesday, September 5, at 4:30P.M. . . ., although that service will likely have taken place by the time you receive this letter. At that service, we will all remember those students and reflect on the meaning of their lives.

In the days that come we will carry on with the work of your university in the positive, meaningful, and sensitive way that is our tradition. We ask that you and your student continue to sustain our pride in the accomplishments of the people of this fine university.

All of us at the University of F. . . value your support and confidence.

Sincerely yours,

President

From the President's Address—Memorial Service

Nothing tests our conviction, nothing challenges our beliefs, and nothing displays our commitment like tragedy. Committed to a civilized society, based on reason and law, and secured by our sense of community . . . we come together to reflect on the lives of . . . .

From the President's Remarks on Television—September 8

I'd like to take the time to publicly thank all of you for your messages, telephone calls . . . .

We will carry on a closer, more concerned community with a renewed commitment to each other . . . .

Letter to Students—August 1, 1991—On President's Stationery

Dear Student:

The fall semester begins in a few weeks with the renewed energy of faculty, students, and staff and the commotion of renewed activity. We welcome you back to this university where we share an enthusiasm for learning and knowledge and a commitment to the quality of our community.

While the first days of a new semester will be filled with the excitement of making new friends, renewing old acquaintances, and managing the details of continuing your academic career, we also will remember that these days mark the anniversary of the tragic events of last fall. Many members of the press will likely remind us of these events, seeking to understand how our community has been able to respond to the tragedies with compassion, caring, and strength. Please be generous with our colleagues from the media who sometimes ask inappropriate questions and seek to identify problems where we know none exist.

You will, I know, be as sensible and careful as you would be if you lived anywhere in America. Lock your doors, know your neighbors, walk with friends, stay in lighted areas, and take advantage of the various campus services such as the Student Night-time Auxiliary Patrol (SNAP) vans. Your parents and families will feel greatly reassured if they hear from you often during the first unsettled days of campus life. You will know that you are fine; you will be impatient with your parents' anxious concern, but please be kind to your family and call home often.

You will find increased security on campus, better outdoor lighting around campus, and much information about safety and services. The Gainesville-Alachua County community has added more police patrols in student sections of town and apartment owners have installed better lighting around their buildings and better locks in the various units along with other security measures. Few communities in America are as committed as we are in the greater Gainesville area to maintaining and enhancing the quality and safety of our environment. We need you to join that effort.

Enclosed is a message from VPS with some additional information.

Please remember, we parents worry a lot, often without reason. We worry because we care about you, and while we may worry too much, please help us by calling home often.

I look forward to seeing you on campus this fall.

Best wishes,

President

Suggestions from the Letter of Vice President Attached to the President's Letter

You can arrange to have your phone service connected in advance.

A phone bank ... will be available. ... This will enable you to call home if your own phone has not been connected yet.

All residence hall area desks are now staffed on a 24-hour per day, 7 day a week basis.

Additional Comments

The respondents expressed admiration for the VPS because he brought people together and stayed on top of the issues. The entire community appreciated his concern for both victims and survivors. I heard uniformly high regard for the Campus Response Team and for the VPS's leadership and dedication. There was praise for his skill in coordinating all the offices and his work with the police external to the campus.

The president's initial speech was described as setting the tone for the university response. Staff said they were proud of the institution's regard for the community. They were pleased that the university appeared to others as the caring place they knew it to be.

During the crisis, those who responded to others in need reported that bureaucratic lines appeared to have dissolved; the focus was on how to make everyone safe. Gradually, things began to return to normal, except that everyone knew that the assailant was still at large.

Every person who mentioned the student body president spoke admiringly about his performance during this time of crisis. Staff members were surprised that a student president's comments could have been so influential in gaining the community's cooperation. His statements, during the first press conference, about all students needing to get together to maintain safety appeared very effective.

The staff who assumed leadership in directing the university's response were people who had worked together a long time; the shortest employment at the university for any of the responders was six years, and many had worked there significantly longer. Before this event these colleagues viewed each other as competent people in an institution that they hold in high esteem.

The president was new to the institution. His reported warmth and candor confirmed for many that he cared deeply for the welfare of the community. Throughout the interviews informants reported the president's charge to be: to do what is right to guarantee the safety and well-being of the people regardless of cost or public image.

Staff, like students, needed to find ways to make their lives and their families' lives safer. They worried about the safety of spouses and about children walking home from school or staying home alone. The staff that I interviewed were, by and large, people whose work hours, particularly during this crisis, were quite long. One man added the same security equipment to the sliding glass doors at home that the police and housing staff recommended for the apartment dwellers.

One man's wife worked where there were security guards who would meet her at the door when she arrived. The man arranged to meet her when she arrived home, which meant leaving work to get her. The HD had his daughter, an apartment dweller, bring her seven apartment-mates home to his house for 10 days. Other people worried about the welfare of their children in different workplaces around town.

The counseling center director wanted to call his son's middle school to see if everything was all right. His son's normal schedule included the boy's being home alone one-half hour after school. He took time from the business of the office to talk with his wife to discuss alternate arrangements for the boy.

The CM felt the campus responded very efficiently and quickly in the crisis, with police working extra time and a task force directing activities. One staff member reported that each staff person felt extraordinary confidence in the leadership.

Some were not happy with the media attention. The approximately 20 TV trucks with their satellites were hard to assign space. Many media personnel demanded to park the trucks right up front on the campus.

Several staff members said that the PR set the style of the university response by stating that the institution would not behave differently because these events occurred off-campus. He said that the university would do whatever was necessary to help, and that the whole campus was affected by these tragedies. He promised that the university would assist everyone with whatever had to be done and that he would work cooperatively with the city.

Another person said that the president's sending letters to students and parents was appreciated not only by the recipients but also by staff whose efforts the president had noted in the letter.

One year later, the Community Crisis Coordination Committee planned a memorial week that included the planting of five trees in memory of each of the victims and a simultaneous ringing of all the bells from campus and community. Flags were flown at half-mast for one week commencing August 26, 1991, the anniversary of the first murders. The university participated in the activities for one day.

August 1991, the president sent a letter to students welcoming them to the fall semester at UF. In that letter, he remembers the past and looks forward to the future.

COMMENTARY

The daily assembling of the crisis committee and their inclusion of the SGA president using the theme, "Together for a Safe Campus," was a clever reminder to the community.

Many things the school did were worthy of emulation: inviting students to move on-campus at no cost, making a bank of phones available so that students could call home to advise their parents they were safe, and adding additional telephone lines to better receive calls.

The university's decision to admit the media to the memorial services while restricting the use of special lighting was meaningful. The president's decision to limit his television appearances to news programs serves as an excellent model in such crises.

The university's request that notices to the media be posted in their hotels was noteworthy.

All those who were interviewed referred to the memorial service as significant in the life of the campus and the town.

The housing director's meeting with residence staff after the first murders was laudatory. Everyone needed to know what was going on as soon as possible to reduce stress. The housing staff's attention to the air conditioning so that students would not need to open the windows was especially considerate.

Small gestures are always appreciated and are meaningful to everyone. Examples are the president's speaking to the family of a victim in their native tongue, his 30-second nationwide comments to thank people and to assure the nation that the school was open, and his urging students to call home often because parents, among whom he counted himself, worry. Some of the Student Affairs people mentioned seeking out students at random to talk with them. So many times in crisis, the focus is only on those students who visit counseling offices. The satellite counseling center made services more available. The Campus Crisis Counseling Team took their services everywhere.

The information given staff about how to answer the telephone during the crisis probably added to the sense of the institution's being in control.

The flexibility of the housing staff to allow parents all types of leeway in increasing their students' safety was an outstanding idea for assuaging some parental anxiety. Housing's extensive campaign to remind students how to be safe appeared to have reached everyone. The people who were on duty following football games to remind students not to allow "tailgaters" in may be one of the most important safety controls.

Outreach of both police and student affairs personnel to the off-campus residents to help them make their homes safe, deal with their anxiety, and to offer general safety tips was important. The crisis committee's work with the community, the residence staff's work with the apartment dwellers and the landlords, and the counselors' work with students off-campus sent a message that the university was concerned about its students wherever they lived.

As was the case in a previous school, when students have been maimed, or as in this case murdered, responders have a tendency to think the danger is only to students. The wisdom of the personnel director to think in terms of the 7,000 strangers who come to them for jobs and to increase safety procedures for the personnel offices is something other schools may want to consider.

Including safety tips in new staff orientation is a fine idea.

Guiding a campus' response to extraordinary and frightening events requires that many of the rules be suspended; doing business as usual is not the most productive way to operate at that time.

REFERENCES

1. Tuggle, Charles, "Media Relations During Crisis Coverage," *Public Relations Quarterly*, Summer 1991.
2. Archer, James, "Campus in Crisis, Coping with Fear and Panic Related to Serial Murders: A Case Study," *Journal of Counseling*, September 1, 1992.

CHAPTER
seven
❀ ❀ ❀ ❀ ❀ ❀ ❀

An Athlete Is the Assailant

AN ATHLETE IS CHARGED WITH FELONIOUS ASSAULT

On October 31, 1992, U of D police charged MS, a varsity athlete from M College, with assault and battery of two female students and with breaking and entering the room of one of the victims. Both victims were released from the hospital the same day. U of D issued a No Trespass Order to MS.

BACKGROUND

M College is a private liberal arts school with undergraduate and graduate programs. Fewer than one-half of the 6,000 full-time undergraduates live in residence. The school is located two miles north of the center of a large city.

The M college policy appears in the student handbook as follows:

> In cases involving student misconduct off campus, the college reserves the right to exercise its discretion in taking disciplinary action. If found responsible, students may be subject to the same sanctions imposed for on campus violations.

The college had previous experience with misconduct off-campus and invoked the policy to take disciplinary action.

VPS—Senior Student Affairs Officer

The U of D police informed the senior student affairs officer (VPS) that they had arrested M College star athlete, MS, for breaking and entering and battering two women. MS had gone to the other campus alone to visit a woman student whom he knew.

When verification of the arrest of MS was received three days later, the VPS staff consulted with the college attorney to verify the appropriateness of the campus's taking judicial action. The assigned judicial officer notified MS in a hand-delivered letter of his being charged with violation of school policy. MS was further informed that he was to move off-campus immediately. Although MS's housing was funded by his athletic scholarship, those moneys did not cover off-campus living.

The VPS decided the college would discipline MS if the judicial officer were to find him responsible. Established procedures would have given the judicial responsibility to the area coordinator for the housing unit where the accused lived, but the VPS decided that the case needed to be assigned to the most experienced student affairs staff member. The multiple factors associated with that decision included the nature and site of the offense, MS's being a well-known minority athlete, and the interest of the press with its consequent impact on the reputation of the athletic department, the team, and the college. The accepted process had been that the person responsible for the hearing also determined the penalty.

Since student affairs issues a summary of the judicial cases and decisions each semester, it does not make public statements about student offenses to the campus community. However, at a press conference, the athletic director announced that MS would not play basketball until the college hearing process was complete. The VPS assumed that the athletic director (AD) had been asked about MS by a reporter.

MS admitted to the charges and did not appeal the one-year suspension that was handed down. The conditions of the one-year suspension included the student's being banned from visiting campus. MS wrote to the judicial officer saying that he planned to return to campus at the end of the year. He added that his criminal charges were dropped after he had made restitution.

The VPS kept the AD and the provost informed at each step of the process. A week later, a member of the board of trustees asked for the results of the judicial proceedings in order to inform the trustees at their next meeting.

MS later wrote again and asked for permission to meet with the AD and to attend the games in the company of the AD. The athletic director sent a letter in support for the request. Permission was granted.

AD—Athletic Director

During a press conference at the beginning of the basketball season, a reporter informed the AD about MS's arrest and asked what the AD was going to do. The AD's position was that once a behavior problem like the one with MS got into the paper, he was obligated to take a strong position. He immediately announced MS's temporary suspension from play until a college hearing had reported its findings. He permitted the student to practice with the team, however, until the college made a final decision.

The press coverage the day of the conference was limited to the sports pages where the writer mentioned the arrest and speculated on the future of the team's standing without MS.

The AD served as MS's advisor both about the college judicial procedures and about how he would use his time away from school. He continued to meet regularly with MS.

When the AD arrived at M College two years ago, he heard unverified stories of MS's abusive behavior to women. On Halloween in 1991, one of the coaches recalled counseling MS not to celebrate, since the year before on Halloween MS had been arrested for assaulting a woman. MS denied any memory of that event because he had been drinking; he reported that he typically blacks out when he drinks and has no memory of what has happened. The charges were later dropped. The coach had helped MS to get into counseling.

Prior to the incident, the AD had observed that MS behaved rudely toward women. The AD had counseled MS about his intrusive and offensive manner.

MS had not attended counseling regularly. The coach had not seen to it that MS did. The AD reported excellent results from counseling with many of his students.

Student Life had not reported MS's presenting any problems. Communication between the two departments was frequent. The AD would have learned of any misbehavior.

The AD talked about the great pressure and abnormality associated with becoming a basketball player. Students as young as the seventh grade have been bribed with expensive shoes and clothes to attend a particular junior high school. The pressure to win is extraordinary. Because of these pressures, students like MS occasionally need some counseling to help them manage their lives.

MS reported to the AD that on the day of his arrest at U of D, he had gone to visit his girlfriend who he thought was having an affair with a lesbian. When MS saw his girlfriend with the woman he thought was a lesbian, he said he lost his temper and behaved improperly. He denied using drugs or alcohol. Everything MS told the AD later appeared in the police report.

The AD said that he didn't like to use punishment to influence behavior but that sometimes he found it most effective. As an example, he had discovered some student athletes were not attending class. They assumed that they would attend summer school to bring their grades up. The AD announced that the subsidy for education did not apply to the summer program.

By the time of the first game, the AD had suspended MS from play, the newspapers had reported the criminal charges, and MS was waiting for the hearing. Without identifying the reasons for the disciplinary hearing except that MS's infraction had nothing to do with playing ball nor with anything that had happened on-campus, the AD announced that MS's future plans were dependent on the college judicial hearing. The suspension from the college took place within eleven days of the incident.

Following MS's suspension, he successfully petitioned the judicial officer to permit him to attend five games in the company of the AD, who had written a letter supporting MS's request. The judicial officer further endorsed MS's visiting the campus to meet with the AD for arranged appointments.

JO—Judicial Officer

The judicial officer (JO) described the coach as taking the infraction very seriously.

When on November 5th, the JO had received documentation of the charges from the university where the assault had occurred, she sent a charge letter telling MS to vacate his room by November 7th and not to return to campus except for the judicial hearing. The letter was hand delivered to MS in his room.

The JO observed that MS took the charges, proceedings, and penalty soberly. She wanted to be sure the student understood how serious the infraction was. MS had also had been involved in a similar incident a year and a half earlier. At that time he was moved from the dormitory he occupied to another so that contact with the aggrieved student would be limited.

PC—Police Chief

The PC's staff investigates all crimes on-campus even though the service is not a certified police force. The PC, a former city police officer, attends classes each semester; he is currently working on a graduate degree and occasionally teaches. The activities give him a better identification with the university.

M College officers do not carry weapons. City police are so busy they do not have time to investigate campus crime. They welcome the campus' investigation of many cases and usually request that the campus officer prepare the case for court.

Because the currently discussed crime occurred on another campus, PC had no direct knowledge of the situation. The response to the assault and the resulting investigation were carried out by the police force at the school where the offense had occurred.

When informed about the assault, he could identify the alleged assailant because the university computer ID records are available to the campus police. He is able to also enforce the student's banishment from the college.

SI—Sports Information Officer

The dean for student life told the sports information officer (SI) that MS had been arrested and charged with assault a few days after the incident. The following day an article appeared in the sports section of the daily paper. Although each office may speak directly to the press, the SI's particular concern is that anyone talking to the press needed to describe how the college was involved in the situation to bring about a positive resolution. The SI wanted to be sure that any specific services provided to the student were mentioned. In the present case, the school arranged for MS to enter counseling.

When the reporter uncovered the story, the athletic director announced the student's temporary suspension. The press assumed that MS's future as a basketball player was over, but the athletic director informed them that judicial hearings had not yet happened. The SI assumed that when a student was involved in the judicial hearings, the campus information officer would be notified. The president had been kept informed at all times.

The athletic director, the sports information director, the basketball coach, the vice president for student affairs, and the academic vice president met to plan what they would say after the judicial hearings was over and to determine who would be the spokesperson. They agreed that the SI would tell the press the story as it unfolded, telling first the results of the judicial hearings and then, if indicated, the length of the suspension. Further, the SI would emphasize that MS would be able to return after the suspension was over.

The college would inform the parents of the involved students both about the suspension and about how the school responded. Information about MS's permanent suspension from campus housing was included.

Until the press report on MS's violation of the law, the athletic staff had not planned to make an announcement. Usually, the dean for student life makes announcements about suspensions. The SI let the press know that MS has two years of eligibility and can return to both the school and the team if he chooses.

The SI notified the press of the suspension from the team and later from the university. Since several reporters wanted to know the impact of MS's suspension on the team spirit, the SI selected the most mature members of the team to be interviewed by the press. The press reporting was accurate; only the sports pages carried the stories and the emphasis of the stories reported there was the team's success.

The SI conferred with the university public information office whose spokesperson advised the SI to continue handling the press about MS because the SI had more knowledge about the situation.

Statements to the press emphasized that college matters are not decided by the athletic department. The college didn't feel its reputation was threatened by the situation with MS. Because of the lack of perceived threat, the college was able to focus on the positive action it takes when a student gets in trouble.

The SI did not know if a paper would assign reporters to study how student athletes, particularly minority student athletes, function in a college environment. If a minority student athlete has any difficulties, the SI is concerned that the press will disproportionately emphasize the problems that minority students experience.

It is generally agreed that if a student athlete does anything that warrants press attention, the sports information person will be the person who talks to the press.

IO—Information Officer

IO knew nothing of the event until he read it in the student newspaper. He was concerned that if he had been called by a reporter he would not have been able to represent the college effectively.

COMMENTARY

When an athlete gets in trouble, the challenges and opportunities for the institution are unique. As the athletic director said, his decision to suspend the student from play was triggered by the newspaper report of the assault. On the other hand, MS's opportunities to redeem himself appeared greater because the athletic director served as his mentor and advisor. Did MS get special privileges or did he get the privileges we would like to extend to all students in trouble?

Moving quickly to preserve the safety of the campus but not moving arbitrarily is a test for any judicial office. Until written confirmation of the off-campus assault, they allowed MS to remain in residence.

Even small schools have problems sharing information as is evident by the information officer's not being aware of the incident, even though the other campus offices involved in the situation assumed he was aware of what was going on.

The amount of attention that college sports receive in the press results in the media asking extensive questions when a player is responsible for an antisocial act. College athletes are known to the community; their misbehavior is more likely to be covered and remembered by the press. Reporters will ask questions about the impact on the team, the school's athletic program, and, more immediately, the plans for the next game. Athletes know that their misdeeds may bring media attention.

Spokespersons for athletics, like all other campus administrators, need to keep university information officers fully informed about student athletes who may get media attention beyond their sporting exploits.

The AD knew about prior problems that MS had with women. Does the AD or coach have a responsibility to inform the student affairs offices or the housing personnel? The close relationship that exists between coach and player may seem to be violated in such a situation, but the relationship of coach to the institution and to the other students may mandate his or her acting for the benefit of the institution.

The decision to remove the student from university housing came a few days after the offense was reported. Although no charges were made about the student's on-campus behavior, his known propensity to violent behavior would make any college move quickly to remove him from housing.

CHAPTER
eight

✷ ✷ ✷ ✷ ✷ ✷ ✷ ✷ ✷

Murders in the Classroom

*N*ewsweek, December 18, 1989:

> A smiling young man who walked in seemed outfitted for a bizarre, end-of-the-term prank: hunting clothes, what looked like a rifle and bandoliers of bullets across his chest. The class laughed as he ordered the women to one side of the room and the men to the other. Then he fired a shot past a student's head . . . . "You're all feminists, and I hate feminists." In four separate locations scattered around three floors of the six-story structure, he gunned down a total of 27 people, leaving 14 of them dead. . . . Most of the injured and all of the dead—except for the gunman himself—were women. He left a note blaming feminists for his failure.

INTRODUCTION

I was asked to share with you how École Polytechnique de Montreal responded to the tragedy which happened on the 6th of December 1989 where, as you probably remember, one female secretary and 13 female students were killed and 12 male and female students were injured.

Our secretary general presented a speech on the same subject at the "Canadian Association of University Solicitors Meeting" where he listed chronologically all the decisions and actions taken with regard to the crisis. So, with his kind permission, I used his paper and rearranged it to this new context.

You will understand that even today, after more than three years, it is still difficult for me to speak about this drama. However, it may be of help to other universities, if not to prevent such an unpredictable barbarity, at least to know how our university officers reacted.

Written by Gilles Gauthier, conseille au secretaire general et ombudsman, École Polytechnique de Montreal.

I hope you will not be disappointed if I do not talk about the tragedy itself or comment on it. I will focus on how Polytechnique managed and on how and why the decisions were taken.

I suggest that we look first at the decisions as they appeared chronologically. This will help you understand the situation we had to face and, perhaps, to share the pressure that was upon us. After that, we will try to consider these decisions through the management process and see if it was indeed a "management of" or a "reaction to" the crisis. Third, I would like to share with you what we learned from the crisis and which security measures have been undertaken since. But first of all, allow me to give you a brief presentation of Ecole Polytechnique. This will set you in the context of the events as a key to better understanding.

ÉCOLE POLYTECHNIQUE

With more than 5,500 students (3,500 at the undergraduate level, 1,000 at the Master level, 250 pursuing a Ph.D., and 700 registered in continuing education), Polytechnique is the largest of the 32 engineering schools or faculties in Canada. École Polytechnique is a French-speaking institution and all the courses are given in French. About 1,000 persons are employed at École, including 240 professors in 11 engineering departments.

December 6, 1989, was the last day of the fall session. There were 32 classes running at the time of the tragedy and around 2,000 students were present. The exams period was scheduled to begin on December 8th.

As all universities, at least in Quebec, Polytechnique has always had an open door policy. At 5 o'clock in the afternoon, people come in and out as usual without being intercepted. It is also frequent that students come during the evenings and weekends and even stay overnight to run their computer programs or work on projects. There are also many gatherings and social activities organized by the students on most weekends.

THE CRISIS MANAGEMENT

Keeping this context in mind, let us examine how the crisis was managed.

It is useful to consider three main periods where we had to act. I will refer to them as the "night after" the tragedy, the "rush days," and the "recovering days."

The Night After

During the shooting, nobody took action. This reaction is explained by the surprise, the fright, and the uncertainty about what was happening. The dean was informed of what was happening by a student who came rushing into his office saying "somebody is shooting in the school." Gunshots were heard in the corridor near the offices of the administration, in the cafeteria right below, and in a classroom right above. They seemed to come from everywhere. It was only after the killer's letter had been read that it was clearly established that his motivation was to shoot women and women only. You may remember that the killer killed himself in the classroom where he had committed part of his horror.

When the police and the ambulance people arrived, things started to get under control. The dean and a couple of colleagues had time just to go over the scene of the shooting and measure the extent of the tragedy in terms of dead and injured persons. The injured were quickly directed to the nearest hospitals. The building of École had already been cordoned.

The police then began the victims' identification procedures and the usual inquiry. This lasted until 2 o'clock in the morning. Although École could not contact the families, many parents came by themselves or were notified by students who knew the victims personally. As the number of parents grew, it was decided to set up a waiting room in the main building of the University of Montréal, a few minutes away from Polytechnique. A telephone service was maintained to answer calls all night because people were calling from everywhere around the world to obtain information and to express sympathy.

At 11:00 P.M., the dean asked his wife and daughter to pay a visit to the injured. A press conference was set up around midnight.

The Rush Days (December 7th–December 13th)

The management of the crisis, as far as École was concerned, really began on Thursday morning, December 7th and, during the following six days, things were going so fast and there was so much to cope with that it is appropriate now to call this period "the rush days."

The director arrived at École around 7:00 in the morning. He decided to limit access to the building only to the top management personnel, the department heads, and persons with authorized access.

Help was offered, and accepted, from many persons.

Psychologists from the University of Montréal and other institutions gave their time to support the students, faculty, and staff. All those people worked on a voluntary basis and their help was really appreciated.

A first meeting was held at 10 o'clock. In attendance were the director, the administrative directors, the department heads, two professors, the public relations director, the building services director, the security officer, the secretary general, the students service director, and three student representatives. The following decisions were made:

- to hold a civic funeral at the Basilica if it was the desire of the families;
- to suggest that a funeral chapel be set up in the Main Hall of the University of Montréal;
- to provide psychological help for the students and staff members;
- to postpone the exam period by one week and to extend it into January;
- to delay for one week the following winter term. This implied that a new calendar had to be prepared;
- to give full exam exemption to the injured, either physically or psychologically;
- to restrain access to the building until the afternoon following the funerals;
- to set up a committee of five people to refer to for decisions. This committee did not function; instead people referred to the administrative directors or directly to the dean.

In the afternoon, a group met with the director of student services to organize psychological aid. It was decided:

- to ask the University of Montréal Psychological Services to receive the requests for help and to channel them to serve as a special group of psychologists on loan to and located at École: for École's students, professors and staff.
- to request The Professional Association of Psychologists to serve the public in general. Note that, at that time, École had only one full-time psychologist on a 9-month per year contract.
- to hold meetings under a psychologist's supervision to allow people to discuss the tragedy. They were divided in groups: students, professors, and support staff.
- to offer immediate help to the injured and to the professors and students who were in the class where the shooting took place.

The remainder of the day was spent contacting the families and visiting the injured.

The day ended with a meeting of the management committee for a review of the situation. By that time, nine families had chosen to set up the funeral chapel at the University of Montréal and opted for a common funeral at the Basilica.

At 10:00 A.M. on Friday, a meeting took place to organize the funeral chapel and the civic funerals.

It was decided:

- to have the funeral service on Monday morning at 10 o'clock at the Basilica;
- to use University of Montréal classrooms to set up private funeral rooms, one for each family. The rooms would be open all day Saturday and Sunday;
- to install a common funeral chapel in the university entrance hall, on Sunday afternoon, open to the public;
- to assign responsibilities for media contacts, for security and access to campus and for the ceremony at the Basilica.

It was also decided to broadcast the ceremony through only one television network and to forbid photographs during the ceremony.

Saturday was spent meeting with the families and visitors. The funeral home was open from 12:00 to 10:00 P.M.

The funeral was held on Monday morning as scheduled.

On Monday afternoon, when the employees returned to work, they were invited to assemble in small groups to discuss the events and to share their feelings.

I have, so far, presented the most significant decisions taken during the days immediately following the tragedy. A few words now about the days following the return to work and to "normal" activities will be helpful.

The Recovering Days

It is easy to imagine that the tragedy continued to obsess students, faculty, and staff.

The real return to work happened on Wednesday, the 13th of December, one full week after the event. The dean and the department heads met in the morning to finalize the exams bylaws:

- injured students (physically and psychologically according to the psychologists) would be exempted;
- students who might think that they were able to pass their exam but once in the classroom were unable to proceed further (within a period of 45 minutes to an hour) would be allowed to leave.

In the afternoon, a meeting conducted by a psychologist was held for all the managing staff, where the following was discussed:

- how people usually react in such circumstances so that they would not be surprised if they themselves or employees revealed such symptoms;
- how the crisis was managed and how decisions were made.

Some psychologists did stay in École for a couple of weeks and people were encouraged to talk to them, if they felt the need to. In fact, more than 40 psychologists were working at École for that time.

The exams began on Thursday, December 14th, as scheduled.

The winter session calendar had been reviewed and the session began on January 15th. The president's and dean's offices sent about 3,000 letters to those who had expressed marks of sympathy.

As you can see, the management of this crisis was not easy. All decisions had to be made mostly under pressure and required fast action. No one could afford to make a mistake. Everything was focused on Polytechnique as the news about the event was rapidly spreading throughout the world. Moreover, as soon as the sexist character of the tragedy became evident, we all felt that we would be closely examined on that aspect. Fortunately, on that particular point, even though no formal decisions were taken, a kind of consensus was reached to act as usual. Students, in particular, did not feel the need for any special action. This was evident when they had to choose their fellow students for the ceremony, or for coffin bearing, or for any other activity that required student representation.

The question now comes to mind: Did we really manage the crisis or did we, instead, "react" to the need for action as required in such circumstances? I will attempt to answer this question now.

MANAGEMENT PROCESS VS. CRISIS MANAGEMENT

You certainly remember that most administration experts think of management as "to plan, to organize, and to control in view of obtaining results." So how did Polytechnique management perform in relation with these concepts?

Planning

Surely no one can plan for an event like the tragedy of December 1989. Like other institutions, of course, École has an emergency plan in case of fire: once a year, employees and students take part in an evacuation exercise. But the tragedy we had to face cannot be compared to a fire drill.

In spite of this, I believe we had some sort of planning, perhaps not a formal one, but at least as far as planning means to set objectives.

Indeed, all along the crisis there were three main objectives guiding all decisions and actions that were, at the very beginning, agreed upon and formulated by the dean:

- to pay attention and to be very respectful to the victims' parents;
- to give adequate support to the students and employees;
- to maintain discretion, moderation, and privacy in all circumstances.

These objectives were very well observed.

Organization

The people most involved in the managing of the crisis were the top management of École. They received valuable help from University of Montréal personnel. During that time, department heads and faculty worked with their own students and staff, and prepared the after crisis healing.

In short, everyone was so imaginative and innovative that immediate action was taken almost instinctively by the right person.

Control

Although the delegation of authority was widely spread among managers, the major decisions were referred to the dean who always kept control of the situation. The meetings scheduled at the end of each day permitted setting the actions to be taken the following day.

Results

Of course, I am not the one who should evaluate whether the crisis management was really adequate. However, the many testimonies and marks of appreciation received from the parents, the students, the professors, and from many people at large confirmed that we acted correctly under the circumstances.

Regarding the exams exemption, our statistics show that only 60 students were totally exempted from their exams while 1,700 others opted for a postponed exam, in the last week of January. A few students did not enroll for the winter session. The enrollment for the next fall session was almost the same as that of the preceding one.

WHAT WE HAVE LEARNED

We have seen which decisions were taken chronologically in managing the tragedy of December 6, 1989. We have considered how these decisions compare with management concepts. In this last section of my presentation, I will point out what we learned from this event.

We Can Benefit from Adverse Situations

The drama deeply wounded both students and staff at Polytechnique. But, with their determination, they quickly regained confidence; they learned to live with the tragedy.

In spite of its initial negative effect, the tragedy actually had a positive impact on the enrollment of women. For many years, the percentage of women enrolling in first year hovered at about 19 percent. In the fall of 1990 and the following, this percentage has increased to almost 25 percent, one of the highest percentages across Canada.

Accuracy of Information

We think that our strategy of keeping students and staff well informed and with precise facts was a good decision. Nobody can claim that we tried to hide information.

Contacts with the Media

I think it is very important to keep good relations with the journalists and other media representatives. Thus, we held many press conferences where we delivered precise information. We asked for their collaboration to be respectful towards the victims' parents, the wounded, and the students. We received their cooperation to minimize the disturbance during the funeral ceremony. On the other hand, we had to be careful in giving access to École to avoid any form of sensationalism. This is why the media was not admitted to visit the classes where the shooting occurred.

In brief, the quality of the relationship established with the media is an indication of the quality of the information they will transmit to the public in the sense that if you deliver true, honest, and clear information, the media will not have to make assumptions or have to interpret it. That is of great importance.

Need of Increased Security on Campus

Finally, we found that there was a real need to increase security on the campus. But it is necessary to keep a good balance between controlled access and wide open access. This is not easy. Universities cannot restrain students from coming in the evening or working overnight. But it is necessary to make sure that whoever is coming has the right to do so. Polytechnique, therefore, reviewed its security system.

A $2.5 million special grant from the Québec Government was spent notably for:

- electronic surveillance using about a hundred cameras in and out of the building;
- a completely new system for keys that cannot be reproduced, except by École's workshop, which is the only one to have the matrix;
- noticeable increase in the number of guards, random patrol in and out of the building, and increased lighting on the campus;
- magnetic identity card system for the evening and weekend entries into the building;
- escort system on the campus during the evenings by students for female students and employees.

CONCLUSION

In conclusion, I wish to consider two alternatives. One is pessimistic; the other is optimistic. The pessimistic alternative: No matter how good or precise is the plan laid out to face emergencies, something will happen that will require you to rethink it. The optimistic alternative: When tragedy occurs, the sense of innovation and the courage of your managers and the devotion of your employees will somehow make things work, as was the case following the tragic events at École Polytechnique.

Thank you very much for your attention.

COMMENTARY

The school's serving as a funeral home must have made it easier for the many mourners to visit with all of the victim families. The school recognized that this misfortune belonged not only to the school but to the entire community who needed to heal.

Unfortunately, an armed, odd-appearing person with a belt of bullets could probably walk through any campus even following this incident and no one would call the police. How can we impress on communities that reporting what one notices may prevent a tragedy as is described here?

The new security devices that École has installed will certainly discourage any intruders but are not likely to prevent a repeat of such a tragedy unless community participation exists or unless the campus becomes a fort with limited and controlled access, certainly no environment for learning.

The immediate announcement that examinations would be postponed and that the following semester would be delayed was a statement of respect for the community. That decision was the first step in victim assistance because the delay recognized the need for the community to react to this horrendous event.

The volunteer psychologists supervised the campus' and community's discussions of the tragedies. Such sharing that allowed faculty, staff, and students to share their reactions had to be a step in the healing of the school. The return to full functioning begins with the recognition of the pain and trauma the community experienced.

The external community knew the school's attention to the trauma was most gracious, especially in view of the great pain on campus.

An extraordinary offer made to the students was to be allowed to withdraw from an exam after taking it. Wisely the administration understood that students may overestimate their readiness to return to the full demands of the university and only discover it when they are overwhelmed. This agreement is predicated on the school's trust in and respect for the students. Campus people must have felt unburdened by these decisions.

The community's failure to turn to the committee preferring instead to turn to administrators for decisions was an interesting observation.

Here as in so many schools where tragedy has occurred, the senior staff held daily meetings to exchange ideas and to plan. Through these sessions the administrators could guide the institutional response and make it responsive to the population. Daily meetings allow the officers of the institution to rethink what they are doing.

PART

2

* * * * * * * * *

INTRODUCTION

❋ ❋ ❋ ❋ ❋ ❋ ❋ ❋ ❋

Hurricane Andrew: Two Schools Respond

The following responses to Hurricane Andrew are included because the institutions involved had to make many adjustments to prevent problems; they had to respond in the most helpful ways to meet the needs of the community; and they had to restore the campuses to normal. The reader should note such preparation as arranging in advance for an 800 telephone number so that the community would have easy access to information. Also worthy of attention is the public safety officer's insistence four days in advance of the hurricane that each officer call in every four hours.

THE HURRICANE

On Monday, August 24, 1992, one of the strongest Atlantic hurricanes of the century, with winds of 150 miles an hour, struck south Florida leaving nine dead, destroying 85,000 homes, and leaving 250,000 people homeless. Commerce was brought to a standstill because electric power and telephone service were out, and most roads were made impassable by uprooted trees and downed power lines. A nightly curfew was imposed. President Bush declared much of south Florida a disaster area, opening the way for federal disaster assistance. The National Guard was activated to safeguard against looting.

Hurricane Andrew had approached the area so quickly and with such ferocity that the first warnings to evacuate had been issued less than 24 hours before it hit. Police announced a curfew from 7:00 P.M. to 7:00 A.M. in anticipation of the strike.

Both schools whose responses follow reported that they had regularly referred to their old manuals to do the yearly preparation for the hurricane season. When they needed to ready their schools for immediate dangers, their manuals were too cumbersome and too outdated to be useful. Although meteorologists had issued many hurricane warnings in the intervening years, the last devastating hurricane had occurred in 1926.

CHAPTER
nine
⬧⬧⬧⬧⬧⬧⬧⬧⬧
FIU Responds to Andrew

BACKGROUND

FIU is a state university with a main campus on 300 acres and a branch campus. There are residence facilities at both sites. On August 24th, FIU was between summer and fall semesters; many employees were on vacation during that two-week period. Three hundred students were living on the main campus, and 150, mainly foreign students, were at the branch campus. Classes were scheduled to begin August 31, 1992.

The county had previously designated the university's administration building as both a regional shelter and a command post for emergencies. Campus personnel prepared the second and third floors for The Red Cross to operate the shelter, the fourth floor for resident students, and the fifth for a police command center. Radio and television announcements urged people in designated areas to go to the shelter. By 6:00 P.M. Sunday, the eve of the storm, 1,700 community people had moved into the building. Four hundred and fifty students were on the fourth floor. By Wednesday, some had returned to their homes, and branch-campus students returned to their own residence hall. Sixteen hundred people continued to live in the building.

As the storm approached, police prevented people from using the elevators so that no one would be trapped in them. At 1:30 A.M., the power failed causing all lights, pumps, air conditioning, and the elevators to stop. When the pumps stopped, the building had no water and no flushing toilets. Emergency generators were operating poorly, and the water supply was very low. The stench in the building grew worse each day.

On Tuesday, August 25th, the president (PR) convened his office staff after the hurricane to learn how they had fared and how they could help one another. He appointed the Hurricane Emergency Task Force, empowered the chair with full decision-making authority, and charged the panel to identify and help employees in distress and to assist those people who could aid the other people who were in need. The task force was further charged to mobilize the faculty to return the institution to its previous state.

PG—Chair, Hurricane Emergency Task Force, Branch Campus Director, Budget Officer

Because North Campus was in the evacuation area, on Sunday PG reluctantly left the secured vacated campus with no attending personnel because of both the curfew and the number of police that would be patrolling the streets. All personnel and students had gone either to private homes or to the main campus shelter.

On Tuesday, the day after Andrew hit, the president appointed PG chair of the Hurricane Emergency Task Force, which PG convened that day and twice daily, morning and late afternoon, and once daily Saturdays and Sundays for two weeks. The committee immediately initiated a program to assess the needs of the employees, creating a well-advertised telephone line so callers could request information and assistance; the committee also created a volunteer program for employees to help one another. The first and abiding concern of the task force, in the spirit of the president's direction, was to care for university employees. The committee created a Housing Task Force to quickly assess workers' needs as well as employees' ability to help others.

To understand the status of the university after the hurricane, they asked all office directors to report immediately the condition of their office equipment, computers, and records and to assess how ready the staff were to return to work. They quickly developed an understanding of how ready the school was to function again.

The task force assigned work to whoever agreed to find a way to accomplish it so they could identify other needs and look for new ways to help. The committee advised the president when the task force felt school could open.

They provided free day care for employees' children to help people return to work. Many people needed money immediately and the committee wanted them to be eligible to get interest-free loans. After a frustrating number of starts, the Task Force was able to negotiate having the Credit Union lend money that was guaranteed by the University Foundation.

DW—Assistant to the Provost for University Long Term Planning and Staff Advisor to President and the President's Council

On behalf of the Housing Task Force, DW devised the following question-naire to be answered by each employee so that the volunteers could match people with resources to people who needed them.

Questionnaire

President M and the administration are concerned about every university employee and will make every effort to support faculty and staff during this time of community crisis. The following information is necessary to assess the needs of our employees so that the university can assist in any way possible.

This information should be immediately completed by the employee or direct supervisor. If the employee is not on campus the supervisor should make every effort to contact each employee to establish the employee's needs.

1. Did you or your immediate family experience a major injury? If yes, please explain.
2. Is your home livable? If no, do you and your family need a place to stay? Please express your housing needs. (Number of people, unique circumstances, etc.)
3. Did any of your immediate family lose their employment? If yes, please briefly explain the circumstances and type of employment.
4. Are there any circumstances the university should be aware of or things the university could do for you?
5. Do you have a place where other university employees and families could stay temporarily? If yes, how many?

DW was a member of the Hurricane Emergency Task Force and chaired the Housing Task Force. In his latter capacity, he convened a corps of volunteers who assessed what housing was still standing in the community. The Housing Task Force planned to offer money to those who might need it. (See report of task force later.)

DW trained volunteers to administer the assessments. Volunteers were also asked to survey the community for available housing. DW recalled that he was prepared to do this work because he had been away during the hurricane. "All those who were in town to experience the hurricane were in shock."

In a summary letter of September 14th, the Housing Task Force reported that they had received 1,688 responses. Four hundred eighteen employees reported major losses. Two hundred fifty-three of that group had either lost their home or sustained so much damage their homes were not livable. Another 70 of them had barely livable homes.

DW sent the following message to the president on September 14th, on behalf of the Housing Task Force:

> . . . we sent a list containing 200 housing opportunities to the 180 employees identified up to that time as having a housing need. This wide distribution of information significantly reduced the number of crisis calls

we were receiving; however, we continue to receive calls or visits from employees needing housing. A second list of over 50 housing opportunities is provided to employees who call or visit. . . .

. . . Considering the many new employees we hire each year, especially new faculty, this service should become a regular function of a university office.

On September 25th, the committee was disbanded because the immediate crisis was over. DW sent the following memo to the university directors. "Most employees have found housing by this time; however, we are still receiving calls for information.

The Housing Task Force was formed to address the housing crisis caused by Hurricane Andrew. Even though the immediate crisis was over, President M had concluded that employee housing information should be provided as a regular service of the university to its faculty and staff. Responsibilities will be transferred to . . . Office of Off-Campus Housing."

VPA—Vice President for Administration, Former Business Department Chair

The Hurricane Emergency Task Force assigned the vice president for administration (VPA) the task of readying the campus for the opening of school. The Wednesday before Hurricane Andrew, the VPA together with the physical plant director, started securing the campus according to guidelines in the existing emergency manual. People were deployed throughout the campus to board up windows and to secure anything the wind could move.

By the time the VPA and his staff left on Friday, the campus had been secured. Supervisors agreed to be available by phone and to be in contact with their staffs after the storm.

On Saturday, when the VPA noted that the hurricane was moving northward with extraordinary speed, he informed the president that he was bringing in an additional 100 employees on Sunday morning to further secure the campus.

They put shutters on all the windows for which they had shutters; they added partitions within buildings to shelter the people; and they covered books near the library windows because that building had no shutters. They covered all the computers with plastic because most employees had not been on campus to take precautions with their equipment.

The VPA met with directors to plan for the protection of the safe and the alarm system. They identified what police were to guard, set up an internal communication system with two-way radios, and arranged to use emergency generators because of anticipated power outages. The VPA released the work force by 4:00P.M. At 9:00P.M., he turned the building over to the chief of police. Two police officers were assigned to each floor.

The VPA arrived on campus at 1:30 P.M. in the afternoon the day of the hurricane. None of his 2,000 employees reported to work on Monday nor did he have a way to reach them. The city had neither electricity nor phone service. One telephone was operating at the university. It was a phone that had been unplugged. Trees were in the middle of the streets; electric lines were down; no street lights or traffic lights were working. Roofs were hanging over buildings. Hundreds of oak trees were uprooted. Four campus buses were all windowless because the wind had pounded gravel against them. The roof of the campus arena was destroyed. Upturned trees and downed power lines prevented walking from one building to the other. By the afternoon, he estimated the damage to be between four and six million dollars. In addition, a million dollars was needed immediately to make the campus accessible.

With no power and with payroll data in computers, the challenge was to see that everyone got paid. Although they were somewhat slow, the VPA was able to get out the pay and to compensate all employees, whether or not they had reported to work.

The VPA and the police set up a command post where they used battery-operated portable radios whose range was limited.

The VPA arranged for all workers to eat free on campus with the evacuees and students. By Tuesday morning, 40 people from the physical plant reported to work. Some of the staff remained on duty for 72 hours. All work had to be planned to allow staff to leave in time to be home before the 5:00 P.M. curfew. To begin to restore the campus to normal conditions required far more people and heavy equipment than they had available. The immediate task was to clear debris from the roads.

Yearly, the VPA selects contractors from those who have won university bids and he then calls on them during the year at the price negotiated. The arrangement allowed the campus to have needed help available during the emergency.

Terrible things were happening to many people. One foreman who had lost his home was crying while directing a work crew because he had not found his daughter. The VPA told him to leave work and marveled at how ordinary people do extraordinary things.

An industrial leader sent a crew of cane cutters, self-equipped with food, water, and heavy equipment. Although the school was well equipped, much of the university machinery required power, which was still out. Florida Atlantic University sent workers to help. Whenever new volunteers arrived, the VPA redeployed his own fatigued staff to the perimeter of the campus and assigned the new people to the bigger challenges.

By Tuesday, August 25th, a vender had set up a food line and the residents had their first hot meal. Everyone on campus was invited to eat. People were encouraged to take food back to hold them while they were working. To avert a severe shortage, the National Guard was asked to transport water to the campus.

DPP—Physical Plant Director

As a part of the annual preparation for the hurricane season, which extends from June 1st to the end of November, the staff of the physical plant follow a maintenance checklist that includes stocking sufficient lumber to cover windows and maintaining an adequate supply of rain gear.

The physical plant director (DPP) listens daily to a weather-watch radio and plots the direction of storms. His designate-in-charge follows the forecast when DPP is away. As a result, although no local warnings had been issued, the DPP convened his staff to ready the campus on Friday. All vehicles were filled with gas and emergency generators were checked to be sure they were operational.

Monday, the day of the hurricane, the water surrounding the DPP's home was three feet deep. The DPP traveled two hours instead of the usual one-half hour to campus. His car had been spared. Most of the vehicles he saw did not have windows.

Part of the roof of the building his family of five occupied had been blown off. His family had huddled together during the worst part of the hurricane in an apartment where water was coming down a hole in the roof and where the remaining section of roof was collapsing under the weight of water.

At the time of this interview, eight months later, the DPP and his family were about to occupy a permanent home. The family had lived in three different homes. During this time, the DPP and his wife had transported their children to and from the schools they attended at the time of the hurricane so that the children did not have to go through yet another change.

In the first days after the storm, the DPP worked 10- and 12-hour days assessing damage and supervising the clearing of roads and walkways. He urged those staff members who needed to be at home not to come to work. Employees were offered advance leave. The physical plant staff helped deliver supplies to their colleagues in need.

Each evening the DPP returned home to repair his house. When the VP for student affairs learned the state of the DPP's personal life and the very long uninterrupted work schedule he followed, the administration sent him home immediately. When the author met with other administrators, sending the DPP home was mentioned as among the exceptionally caring acts that vice president for student affairs had performed.

The DPP stressed how important it had been to be continually available to staff during the time that they were trying to put the campus back into some usable condition. He was personally grateful to the staff as well as to the other institutional personnel who were so caring.

VPS—Vice President for Student Affairs, Member of Hurricane Emergency Task Force

The VPS's charge from the Hurricane Emergency Task Force was generally to assist the students, arrange for food, and provide help for employees who were without housing or food. The VPS had been on vacation but after he called to speak to his fellow vice-presidents on Sunday afternoon, he subsequently returned to campus by 5:30 P.M. That evening he was interviewed by a radio station on the preparations the campus was making for the storm. The VPS felt that most of the population was in massive denial thinking "it can't happen to me."

Although the first meeting of the Hurricane Emergency Task Force was on Tuesday, August 25th, they all realized they should have met before the storm. The first meeting for student affairs was on the following Thursday, but few staff were able to attend. The relief center and the HELPLINE were planned that day. The VPS encouraged all staff to do whatever they could to ease the general stress.

The police and The Red Cross had been announcing all day Sunday which areas were to be evacuated. People living east of Biscayne Boulevard were being instructed to leave and were directed to designated shelters. More than 1,000 evacuees came in all day Sunday. Two Boy Scout troops who had been at Key Largo were brought to the campus.

The VPS worked in the shelter along with volunteer faculty and staff, with some working 24 hours at a time. The first goal was to help people survive by providing for their basic needs. Late Wednesday, on the 27th, telephone service resumed. The next day electricity was turned on again.

At first the adrenaline kept many of the staff and volunteers going, but that soon gave way to exhaustion. The VPS urged employees to take care of themselves.

The devastation the day after the hurricane was unbelievable. There were no street signs, and landmarks had been destroyed. People could not find their way to places that they knew very well.

When his staff had set up the HELPLINE and the Relief Center, the school advertised their availability in the local newspapers and distributed fliers to people all over campus. Three hundred and twenty thousand pounds of donations were received for the relief center. The area suffered additional shortages because stores in the malls were being looted.

The VPS reflected that they had not stockpiled sufficient food and water for the hurricane season.

Three weeks later, early on a Sunday morning, three women were discovered dead in a car on campus. By eleven o'clock that morning, the police chief knew that the murdered women were not students of the university, but they had not as yet identified the killer. The VPS learned from the city police information officer how to make his announcement about the murders: "We have no evidence to conclude that these victims were students. Their car had no parking permit, they had no campus ID, and they had no possessions that would relate them to the campus." By evening, police had arrested the assailant, identified as a member of the National Guard unit that was on emergency duty to help the community.

The VPS joined with the city police to inform the community about the identity of the victims and the subsequent arrest. He, together with housing staff, met with students on-campus that evening to inform them both of what happened and about the capture of the man who was then arrested for the murder. That meeting helped to reassure the campus that the women's death was unrelated to FIU and to control rumors and quell some of the anxiety. In addition, the VPS increased the number of police patrolling the campus.

Many support groups were begun for the FIU community to recover from the traumas they had experienced. The effects of the trauma were even more apparent after a few weeks.

DCP—Director, Career Placement

Thursday, at the first meeting of the student affairs staff after the hurricane, the DCP proposed the creation of a relief center to distribute donated items. She, together with her husband who was a member of the faculty, created and managed the Relief Center which accepted and distributed donations first within the campus community and later to the most devastated areas of the city. The next day she opened the Relief Center for one hour in a room in a residence hall and then in the ballroom of the Union. Contributions had been pouring in even before the center opened; by the end of the first day of operation truckloads of supplies sent from all around the country had been delivered. When people came to the Relief Center, the DCP inquired whether they needed other services.

On Saturday, the DCP and her husband were delivering supplies to faculty and staff who had called the HELPLINE. By Sunday, they were delivering supplies to the hard-hit areas south of the city thereby serving nonuniversity people. They divided duties so that the DCP's husband coordinated the distribution to nonuniversity people and the DCP to campus personnel.

Deliveries were difficult because of street conditions. In addition, allegedly many illegal aliens, afraid to ask for help from any government entity, were stopping trucks to take supplies for themselves, thus creating a dangerous situation for truck drivers.

The center made needed supplies available to all. The items in most demand were supplies for infants and feminine hygiene products.

The DCP's own home community came together and shared the hurricane experience. Although they had not experienced much damage, a neighboring town had sent them supplies. Like many others the DCP said that people in her immediate neighborhood who had not known one another shared food and sought ways to cooperate.

HEO, Health Center Director, and Dr. CD, Counseling Center Director

The Hurricane Emergency Task Force, assembled after the Emergency Task Force had dissolved, was concerned about the varied psychological consequences of the hurricane. The health center and counseling center staffs observed that many more people on-campus were suffering from insomnia, headaches, and abdominal cramps sometime after the hurricane. Staff attributed these to the delayed effects of the trauma. The newly created University Employee Assistance Plan (EAP) had quickly grown from a limited service to a 24-hour a day program in response to the high demand.

The task force sponsored a November post-hurricane conference, "The Aftermath of Hurricane Andrew: What Have We Learned?" The campus and community discussed the impact the storm had on their psychological lives. Another conference was planned. The continuing charge of the panel was to help all survivors understand their own reactions to the trauma and know what would help them to heal.

Dr. CD began each class and meeting by saying, "Let's take time to talk about ourselves." She urged those who were serving others to know what they themselves were experiencing.

The campus was struggling with how much faculty should require from students. Some students complained that faculty were expecting too much. The Task Force learned that the region had experienced an increase in crime and in heroin addiction since the storm.

FUR—Faculty Union Representative

After spending several days fixing up the damage to his own home, the faculty union representative (FUR) formed a caravan with other people who own vans to take food to people in the devastated area. A police escort accompanied them.

The president accepted the FUR's offer to represent the union on the Hurricane Emergency Task Force and also accepted his suggestion for the university to open school two weeks later than scheduled. The administration had announced a one week delay. The FUR suggested that faculty and students needed more time.

The university had two priorities: taking care of the employees and getting the campus back to normal. Everyone continued to be paid. An annual leave bank was proposed. The university functioned as a community; faculty and staff saw one another as colleagues and were mutually helpful. The faculty particularly appreciated the housing relocation services the school arranged. The employees were proud of the university's caring and attention to many details.

The president and provost agreed the university would be flexible by permitting students to register late, to make up missed classes, and to encourage faculty and staff to make every reasonable accommodation. People were working under unique situations; some were living with relatives; some had lost all their possessions. The union proposed and the university agreed to grant a year's extension to those who could not meet tenure requirements. The FUR was able to conclude this agreement amicably.

The state faculty union had advertised that the school was in need, and the FUR was listed as the fund-raiser. He received $3,000 from various efforts: one high school had a dance for FIU's benefit.

After school opened, everyone felt a sense of relief, an affirmation that life would return to normal. The atmosphere in the classroom was different; everyone seemed on edge. Students couldn't be pushed. A faculty member could not say that a paper was due on a particular day.

The hurricane had been no respecter of persons; the provost had lost his home. All the people were in similar situations and "they said nice things to each other."

RD—Residence Director

Overall, staff were treated very well. The outreach to those in distress indicated the institution chose to help the staff. When the student affairs vice president came to the shelter to help, he demonstrated the attitude of the institutional leadership.

The residence director (RD) was the only employee living on-campus before, during, and after the storm. When hurricane alerts were broadcast, the housing maintenance staff prepared the residence building and the RD contacted the director for public safety to know if and when to evacuate. On the Saturday night before the storm, she and her staff advised the 300 resident students to go home or, if they remained, to move to the residents' shelter on

Sunday. They communicated this message by having the resident assistants (RAs) go to each student's door. Because forecasters had issued few warnings about the hurricane before Sunday, it was difficult to convince students that the danger was real. Foreign students with limited English skills had difficulty understanding that they had to evacuate the building.

Students were advised to take blankets, canned food, and important documents with them. Some resident students wanted to go surfing. Any staff that were not officially on-duty could stay in the Red Cross shelter. On Sunday, about 300 students were evacuated from the residence halls and moved into the Administration Building. Later the RD returned with the public safety officer to the residence hall to discover a student hurricane party where students were planning to wait out the storm. Public safety convinced them to evacuate the building. Another 150 students came from the other campus.

At first they could not assure students that they would not have to pay for food after the first two days which is all they had promised. The RD reported the students' concern to the VP for student affairs, and he soon assured them the food would be free for as long as they had to stay. Students later reflected that they had been treated well during the crisis.

The contingency planners had not conceived of the emergency's lasting for longer than two days so no provision was made for feeding people for a longer period. On Tuesday, August 26th, a full buffet, the first hot meal, was served to all the building occupants who along with staff ate free. Some food was donated by local companies.

The usual protocol of chain of command was not operative. The RD dealt directly with people in the president's office.

No resident students or staff were alone during the storm. During the hurricane, the rain was so hard that the windows vibrated and appeared as if they would break from the force. The president called in the morning to see how everyone had fared.

The RD kept the students informed as fully as she herself was since no other means of communication was available. For the first few days, people worked around the clock without feeling exhausted. Community evacuees were becoming more irritable and small disagreements were escalating. Whole families were living in small spaces with no electric power, intense heat, no plumbing facilities, and a growing stench. Resident students had a delayed reaction with more irritable behavior beginning some time later.

After a few days, the RD was able to wangle permission for the students to shower in the athletic complex while she found a shower in the police station.

Students went to the county shelter to talk to some displaced persons. The RA's stayed on duty the entire time they were in the shelter. The RD stressed the need for staff to attend to their own needs. The branch campus students returned to their own dorms on Tuesday, although 20 of them came back to the shelter.

With the power outage, the RD arranged for a sewage removal company to remove the waste from the building. The conditions under which people were living were difficult. Some people were troublesome. Some students got very drunk.

When the RD looked outside for the first time, what she saw reminded her of a war zone with debris everywhere; all the car windows had been broken by the flying debris, and many other cars were totally flattened. Walking was impossible because of broken power lines and upturned trees. When students returned from areas that had been harder hit, they were dazed by the tragedy of homelessness, devastation, and total disorder.

The RD returned with the students to the residence hall on Thursday. People appeared to be irritable, ready to quarrel and fight. Some people talked about their homes having lost roofs, and they were deeply affected by what they had seen and endured.

The university community provided various supportive meetings including a hurricane support group. Since the storm, people have been behaving somewhat differently. They engaged in more roommate conflicts during the second semester and consumed more alcohol.

Two weeks after the hurricane, a student who had been involved in a fight with another student that had racial overtones went to his car, brought a gun into the residence hall, and waved it at the RA. Campus officials expelled him from school. The RD sponsored an open meeting with students to allow them to discuss the episode.

On the following Sunday when three women's bodies were found in a car on campus at 7:00 A.M., everyone was upset. Reporters were all over campus stopping students, asking their reactions, which appeared to heighten the tension. More than 600 students attended the open meeting that evening where the vice president for student affairs together with police were able to report that the assailant had been put in jail, and the murders were not in any way connected to the school.

BCH—Director of Branch Campus Housing, Director of HELPLINE

The BCH needed to evacuate the residents to the main campus; she called the main campus for busses but learned that the bus shuttle contract had been canceled at the beginning of the year. She asked students to arrange rides. Meanwhile, the business office had arranged for drivers to use the athletic vans. The evacuation procedures needed to be completed by early afternoon to get students settled. By the time the busses came, few students remained. They had gotten to the main campus shelter on their own.

FIU had no means of communicating with the faculty, staff, and students. The vice president for student affairs asked the BCH to start a telephone answering service. She created HELPLINE, an information telephone service, which was operated by volunteers working together at a university phone bank. The BCH informed the university media staff who then advertised the following message on television, in the newspaper, and in circulars:

Hurricane Aftermath Information

FIU Information HELPLINE

During this time of loss and hardship, we at FIU are committed to helping our students, faculty, and staff and their families in every way we can. As part of this commitment, FIU is providing the following services to our students and employees to assist them through this crisis:

- Relief supplies (food, water, clothing, etc.) for students and university employees
- Special financial aid assistance for students
- Emergency personal loans to university employees
- Free counseling services available for university employees and students
- Free on-campus child care is available during normal working hours for university employees in (room location identified)
- Important Student Information
- Fall semester classes have been delayed and will begin (date)
- Registration date
- No phone registration
- Orientation (new dates given)
- Deadline for tuition and drop-add
- Important Employee Information
- All FIU employees who are able should report to work

FIU employees who are unable to report to work should contact their supervisor as soon as possible.

For additional information call: On Campus Student Housing, Financial Aid Office

---

Most of the help offered to employees came from the HELPLINE responses. By the end of the week, the calls to HELPLINE were less about crisis and more about registration. Since other information sources were now available, the service was ended after seven days.

PS—Director of Public Safety

The director of public safety (PS) described his department as a respected and effective campus police force. He stated that a measure of that respect is that he reports to a vice-president. That recognition allows him to make decisions that permit his staff to function professionally and successfully. Police can shrug off the demeaning references to them as guards and security if they have institutional esteem.

Four days in advance of the hurricane, the PS put his 35 sworn officers on notice to call the public safety office every four hours. This level of preparedness enabled him to staff the university when the hurricane hit.

The PS was charged to care for the people in the shelter. He set aside space in the Administration Building for the families of the officers to live and eat on-campus. A few families came. "The disaster plan required that people be there to implement it." All officers reported for duty.

The PS had to coordinate the needs of the many different groups on-campus and set priorities for the officers' assignments. Someone needed to be in the command center to make decisions.

The staffing needs included two to three officers and a dispatcher in the command post. Two officers for each housing floor and officers to serve as protectors of special areas were the requirements.

Officers had to staff the shelter, patrol the area, and secure the facility. More people had come to the shelter than had been anticipated.

The priority had to be the safety of people who were housed on-campus. Officers, eight of whom lost their homes, were on-campus for 36 hours straight responding to immediate needs. The very presence of the officers helped ensure the safety of the community. For two or three days bureaucracy disappeared; everyone did what had to be done. Bureaucratic rules were suspended, and the university offices could make necessary purchases without delays and approvals. The PS believed that the university and all offices needed to stay in an emergency status for a full week.

When the president established the Hurricane Emergency Task Force, public safety was given a high profile. The first group was small and worked well with their daily meetings. The committee later grew to 10 or 11 and became less effective. No ongoing committee was established to further address crises.

Three weeks after the hurricane, on a Sunday, when three bodies were discovered in a car on-campus, it was essential to solve the case quickly because everyone was so upset. The bodies had been discovered in the early morning. By 11:00 A.M., they had established that the victims were not students. The perpetrator was identified as one of the National Guardmen who was assigned to live in a compound next to the campus. By that evening, the PS was able to announce to campus administrators and the press, and they in turn to the campus and the community, that the murders were not related to the campus. That announcement stopped the rumors. The PS joined with the city police in making an announcement about the solution of the case and the arrest of the perpetrator.

COMMENTARY

The president's charge to his newly appointed Hurricane Emergency Task Force was to attend to the needs of the employees and to restore the university to normal. His first priority was the employees. Assigning full decision-making authority to the committee chair, allowed for maximum efficiency. The faculty union appreciated the priorities given to helping the work force and the president's accommodating their request to further delay the opening of school; they in turn responded with more amiable approaches to campus dilemmas.

No one knew how to do the things they found necessary to do. They all learned in the process of doing them. Institutional leaders immediately set out to help employees with housing and interest-free loans. The survey conducted by volunteers enabled the university to identify needs and available resources that they may not have uncovered so quickly otherwise. This work resulted in recognizing that employees would benefit from a permanent housing office.

The emergency HELPLINE stopped operating after seven days when the callers were asking the normal questions concerning the opening of school. The decision to end special help appeared wise.

The recovery of the campus was probably facilitated by the yearly contracts that the business office negotiated for anticipated labor needs. By having locked into that arrangement both for availability of personnel and agreed price, the university was able to proceed with repairs immediately.

The chief of public safety's arrangement with the police officers to call in every four hours allowed the campus to have total police coverage when it was needed. The extras of inviting officers to move in with their families also helped.

Such decisions as providing food free for staff as well as for students gave needed encouragement to people who were working under much personal hardship.

Students, with their "hurricane party," were disbelieving of possible danger from the hurricane. They evacuated the residence hall only after the insistence of the Task Force.

Everyone in the community regardless of who they were was in need of help and suffered the effects of the hurricane.

CHAPTER
ten
* * * * * * * * * *

University of Miami's Response to Hurricane Andrew

BACKGROUND

After the ordeal of Hurricane Andrew, Edward Foote II, president of University of Miami, requested campus administrators share with him their experiences in the aftermath of the storm. Included are President Foote's own reflections of the time. He has graciously allowed the author to use the communications as they have been written with the hope that others may profit.

(Author's note: I have taken the liberty of eliminating notes that writers included about the particular hardships they endured. Some of the writers described how they lost their homes and their struggle to find accommodations. They all described their successful efforts to find their staffs, some after many days.)

PRESIDENT

FROM: Edward T. Foote II

      President

RE: Hurricane Andrew, August 24, 1992

This memorandum, written in the weeks following Hurricane Andrew's devastation of Greater Miami, summarizes my activities and impressions during and following that terrible storm. It is intended to supplement the similar reflections I have requested of my senior colleagues, all so that we may remember and learn from what is proclaimed as the worst natural catastrophe in the history of the United States.

As the hurricane gathered force a thousand miles to the east of Miami, Saturday, August 22nd, Bosey and I were at our home in Captiva, preparing it for what was increasingly sure to be a significant storm. (As it developed, the hurricane passed well south of Captiva where there were only strong winds; we are told that one large branch fell on our house but did little damage.) Listening to the radio as we worked around our property, we realized that we should return to Miami as quickly as possible. We left early Sunday morning and drove fast east across the Everglades.

As we approached the Miami metropolitan area, we found the community in obvious turmoil. Traffic was thick. Grocery and hardware stores were packed with people seeking emergency supplies. We stopped at a Winn-Dixie west of the interstate, saw the crowds, and decided to drive on. It was a mistake. The closer we got to our home, the bigger were the crowds. We were regrettably ill-prepared for what was to come.

Arriving home in the early afternoon, I came immediately to the university, as Bosey joined the work crew gathered to secure the university's house, our residence, at 8565 Old Cutler Road. In my absence, my colleagues at the university had already gone through the hurricane emergency drill, reviewed procedures, gathered key officers and others to compare notes and make preliminary decisions. By the time I arrived, preparations were well underway. Spirits were high. Everyone listened to the radio or watched television. Every indication showed the gathering of a major storm. But as neither Bosey nor I, nor most of us at the university, had ever been through a hurricane, we did not know what to expect.

The hurricane was approaching on the first day of new student orientation! Approximately 3,000 students, mostly freshmen, were on the campus. They were accompanied by many hundreds of parents and hundreds of others—faculty, staff, people stranded, workers—for a total of approximately 5,000. This was the community that came together in fear but mutual support the next 72 harrowing hours.

That Sunday night, August 23rd, was to have been the happy occasion of our welcoming parents of new students to a reception at the Lowe Art Museum. As the danger of a direct hit by a major hurricane escalated, we decided to cancel that and other orientation functions. We concentrated instead on securing the residential colleges and apartments especially, as that would be where people would ride out the storm, and all other buildings on this and the other five campuses. That occupied everyone's time with frantic activity until well into the evening. I checked on the School of Medicine and the Rosenstiel School of Marine and Atmospheric Science campuses, and, as best I could, on the South campus, although information about that part of the university came secondhand through Robert (Bob) W. Rubin, vice provost for research and deputy dean for research and graduate studies, School of Medicine. For obvious reasons of location, we were most concerned about the Rosenstiel campus, perched as it is a few feet above the water at the tip of Virginia Key, about as exposed as any institution could be. All campuses were prepared and secured.

In the late afternoon, I returned to our house to work with Bosey in preparing for the storm. We took a quick trip to South Miami but were only able to purchase a little food. The workmen were still attaching the aluminum and galvanized steel shutters to the expanse of large windows which faced directly into the path of the approaching storm. We greatly appreciated their help and hoped they would finish the job by the time the sun went down. They did, but just barely.

In the meantime, I had returned to the campus to visit the residential colleges, cafeterias (which were packed), the public safety headquarters, and the building and grounds headquarters. Everywhere, people were busy work-ing—and enjoying each other. People were animated and friendly, but there was a growing apprehension that something terrible that we didn't under-stand was soon to happen. The masters of the colleges, the housing staff, the residence coordinators and resident assistants, the police officers, and other members of the faculty and staff were everywhere helping, explaining, prepar-ing, and calming nervous students and parents. I was proud of them.

Authorities urged people to return home by nightfall, which I did, believ-ing preparations at the university to be adequate and my colleagues in leadership in good control of a difficult situation.

Like millions of others during the late evening hours of August 23rd, Bosey and I listened to the radio and watched television, tracking the storm which seemed, as it did to everyone else in town, to be bearing down directly on our house. We went to sleep in our bedroom at 11:00 P.M. By 1:00 A.M., the wind was so strong that we became concerned about flying glass. Warned to avoid being near windows, which are plentiful in our house, we slept (at least I did, but not much) in the hall on the first floor. Although our house was technically in an evacuation area, we had decided that it was high enough on the ridge and built strongly enough that we would be safe there, including from storm surges. We wandered around the house, checking windows, and, the wind now howling, worried whether preparations had been sufficient. Power disappeared sometime during the rising winds. For the rest of the night, Bosey and I crept around with flashlights.

The wind and the noise built slowly for the next hour or so. By 3:00 A.M., the hurricane was swelling to full blast in a howling, incredible concentration of force. Although instructed not to do so, I did open the front (west) door to see what was going on. The sight was terrifying. Huge trees were whipping back and forth as if they were flowers. Debris of all kinds shot through the air.

At about 3:30 A.M., the winds attained such force (ultimately measured by the National Hurricane Center at 164 m.p.h. in our neighborhood) that trees, huge trees, were toppling and snapping like match sticks. The sound of this destruction reminded me of nothing more than the big guns of the Marine Corps.

For hours Bosey and I lay under a quilt on the rug wondering whether the house would last, and whether we would. Bosey, in retrospect, believed the worst sound of all was made by the huge live oak in our backyard near the house next to the swimming pool. With a diameter of maybe four feet at the base, that tree was probably 50 years old. A huge burst of wind knocked it toward the house, which it hit, scraping down the east wall, damaging the gutters and ripping off the aluminum hurricane shutters. Thus, for the first time, we could see into the backyard.

Again against advice, we went to Willy's (our son's) window on the second floor and looked out. I did not recognize my own backyard. There was no backyard. The storm surge had lifted the water approximately ten feet, and instead of a yard there was a lake that stretched east from our swimming pool and north around the bend toward Armando Codina's house. The only part of my backyard above the lake were the tops of the two large hills. (The next morning we noted a ring of leaves within six inches or so of the top of each hill, indicating where the surge had crested.) Our small sailboat and two others tied in the slip were wildly tugging at the lines, which instead of angling down into the slip, which was by then under ten feet of water, were angling up. The surge stopped perhaps three inches from our swimming pool, which is the level of our basement. It subsided quickly. When I looked out again half an hour later, the water was rapidly receding. By dawn, it was settling back into the slip and canal, but the yard remained unrecognizable.

By 6:30 A.M., the peak of the storm in our neighborhood had passed. We learned later that the eye missed us by just a few miles. The high wind continued into the morning, but as dawn broke the worst was over.

Bosey and I went outside and could not believe what we saw. The house had withstood the hurricane well. The roof held. Even after the falling oak tree knocked off the aluminum hurricane shutters, the windows did not shatter. Later that day, however, we noticed that the large bank of windows in the living room had pulled several inches away from the wall. Probably one more big blast would have shattered it, opening the house to the kind of terrible damage that afflicted so many of our friends and neighbors. We were lucky in that respect. The force of the wind also jammed several wall-mounted air conditioners a foot or so into the house.

But outside the sight was sickening, especially to Bosey who had devoted so many countless hours helping to landscape those beautiful 5 acres, as well as the 260 acres on the main Coral Gables campus. Trees were uprooted and broken everywhere. It was nearly impossible to walk down the driveway from the front to the backyard. Bosey worked side by side with our colleagues from Physical Plant and the independent contractors we hired.

As the sun rose, I began to learn about a problem that would plague us for many days, the lack of normal systems of communication. Our telephone didn't work. Our electricity was gone. I tried the cellular telephone without success, because the transmitting towers had been damaged. My police radio just barely reached public safety headquarters in Coral Gables. The quality of transmission varied greatly depending on atmospheric conditions, strength of batteries, etc.

By 9:00 A.M. or so, I was able to contact the campus police. I learned that the hurricane had hit hard, but as far as the dispatcher knew there had been no deaths or serious injuries. I asked the dispatcher to send a police car to get me, believing that civilian vehicles might have a more difficult time getting through security checkpoints, which I heard were being established in the chaotic aftermath of the hurricane. At approximately 9:30 A.M., Eric Shoemaker, director of public safety, and Alan J. Fish, assistant vice president, business services, somehow arrived at my house. We drove back together along Old Cutler Road, which was nearly impassable because of countless large trees strewn everywhere. We were barely able to navigate over people's yards, backtracking, frequently abusing the small police car, but finally arriving at the campus.

Again, I could not recognize the place where I had worked for nearly 12 years. Trees were down everywhere. There were no traffic lights. Power lines and telephone wires dangled from leaning poles. The Ponce Building at the intersection of Ponce and Hurricane Drive was ripped wide open, and all of the first floor windows blown out. Papers from the university advancement office were everywhere. I asked that a security guard be posted there as soon as possible to avoid looting and loss of valuable documents. That was done.

Here is a summary of how Hurricane Andrew damaged the University of Miami (at least as we know it as of this writing):

- The Coral Gables campus was hardest hit. The hurricane flattened 3,000 trees (of which 700 are now righted); smashed approximately 800 windows; damaged 50 roofs, many buildings and offices, and much equipment. Only one office, that of university advancement, has been temporarily relocated because of storm damage. The rest are now functioning normally.

- The School of Medicine sustained relatively minor physical damage, but a serious loss of patient care income, because people are delaying treatment.

- The Rosenstiel School of Marine and Atmospheric Science sustained relatively minor physical damage, but significant losses in research projects.
- The South Campus sustained significant damage, but none structural.
- The Knight and Koubek Centers were relatively undamaged.
- The early estimate of the physical damage and cleanup costs on all campuses is approximately $13 million. About two-thirds of this total should be covered by insurance, and another third by the Federal Emergency Management Agency (FEMA). (This does not include lost revenues, the value of lost research, and increased financial aid needs of students.)

As would become my custom for the next three weeks or so, I stopped first at public safety to get a quick summary of how the night had passed, then went next door to the physical plant headquarters which was already a busy center of activity. It was there that emergency supplies and building materials, etc., were distributed. Elsewhere in the building, Alan J. Fish, Victor J. Atherton, assistant vice president for facilities administration, D. Michael White, director of our physical plant, Alan M. Weber, landscape manager, and many others were already making plans to clean up the debris, repair the roofs and windows, and return the campus as quickly as possible to normal. After physical plant, I would typically visit both cafeterias, then make the rounds of the five residential colleges, talking with masters, residence coordinators, resident assistants, parents, and students.

Most of the campus was without electricity (and, therefore, air conditioning), water, and telephones. The health center, provided immediately with emergency power, was an exception. Dr. Frederick A. Kam, Jr., director of student health services, presided over an oasis of help. Fortunately, none was needed for major medical emergencies—only cuts, stomach problems from drinking contaminated water, etc. In the residential colleges, students, parents, and others milled around on the first floor. Many were still sleeping in the halls. People had sleepless, stricken looks on their faces, but generally the mood was positive. Because of the danger outside, especially including fallen power lines, we encouraged everyone to remain inside. I was impressed again with my colleagues' cool professionalism and the courage already demonstrated during the hours when the hurricane rocked those buildings. Especially visible and helpful were the masters, and Robert (Bob) J. Redick, director of residence halls, and Patricia (Pat) A. Whitely, associate director for residence life and staff development.

Among many decisions made rapidly those first few days, the most important was to delay the opening of the university by two-and-a-half weeks. We were running out of food and potable water for an emergency community of several thousand. The people from Marriott, who cater our food service, were doing an outstanding job, but until Wednesday their suppliers could not break through the wreckage that clogged so much of our community. Toilets wouldn't flush. My resourceful colleagues somehow acquired 80 portable toilets. Under those circumstances, we encouraged all students who could to return home, and we helped them by contributing toward the cost of this extra and unanticipated trip. By the end of the week, the population in the residential colleges and apartments had fallen from approximately 5,000 to 350, tremendously relieving the pressure on our facilities and all concerned with caring for those good people.

During the first two days after the hurricane, few besides those in the central administration were on the campus. By midweek, as the students were leaving for home, members of the faculty and academic administration began to return, checking their offices (many of which were a shambles), comparing personal stories, and generally beginning to understand the enormity of the storm and its aftermath. As my colleagues did return, I made a point of visiting every academic division on the Coral Gables Campus, many at the Medical and Rosenstiel schools, and twice at the South Campus. To get around during those first few days, I chartered helicopters, and with others, including a professional photographer to document the damage for insurance purposes, visited all six campuses, which would not have been possible until much later because of the impassable roads. From the air and on the ground, we photographed the destruction on every campus.

The campus police worked uncommonly hard, all on 12-hour shifts for much of the first two weeks. We were already stretched thin when Coral Gables exercised its apparently legal right to commandeer half of our police officers—a serious blow to public safety and security, and one that remains to this day inexplicable. (I will be meeting with H. C. (Jack) Eads, Coral Gables city manager, sometime soon to try to understand what happened.) Charles B. Reed, chancellor of the state university system, generously offered eight police officers from public universities elsewhere in the state. Those officers, however, fully trained and licensed elsewhere, were not able to begin service to our campus for two days, while the bureaucratic process turned slowly.

We hired many undeputized guards, posting them at key places around the campus. For many days, we simply secured the campus to all but those who had a good reason to enter. During the first three weeks we had two armed robberies and a little pilferage. One fellow, caught riding a bicycle and carrying another, had an implausible explanation, but in the confusion of those first few days he was released without charge.

To facilitate communication, on the second day I began gathering the university's leaders daily for an hour or so of sharing information, announcing and/or making decisions, contingency planning, dealing with emergencies, and generally supporting each other. These daily meetings proved extremely effective, indeed essential, to our crisis management. We continued them until September 9th when we were able to return to our normal systems of communication. We established a hurricane bulletin, ably published by Susan Bonnett, associate vice president for university relations, Jerry Lewis, editorial director for publications, and others. That bulletin was widely distributed on the campuses. The medical school produced a similar bulletin.

To communicate with the broader public, including members of our own university family, the faculty, administration, and staff, the media relations staff helped me get on as many broadcasts as possible, with some success. Conchita Ruiz-Topinka, director of media relations, who worked hard those first few days, got me on local and some national radio and television stations. We tried especially to communicate with our students in the northeast through the media there, and she was able to get me on one Chicago radio station. We wanted to explain to our students, alumni, and others interested that the university had been hit hard but was rapidly recovering, that classes had been postponed for two-and-a-half weeks but would begin September 14th, and that they should telephone to obtain further information. The *Miami Herald* ran occasional articles on local educational institutions, the impact on them by the hurricane, and emerging plans.

Attached to this memorandum are the various communications that we used during the crisis, copies of the hurricane bulletins, our letters to students, my letters to the university family and to the board of trustees. Dorothy M. Ball, assistant secretary of the university, sent all of these communications on a nearly daily basis to the board of trustees throughout the emergency. Beginning on the day of the hurricane, I was in touch with Charles (Chuck) E. Cobb, Jr., chairman of our board of trustees, daily or nearly so. The first few days, I had to navigate a massive barrier of trees in my 4WD Suburban to reach the Cobb's residence in Cocoplum, or their boat (where they lived for a while as their roof was being repaired). At my invitation, Mr. Cobb attended two of our crisis management meetings. His presence was much appreciated by those on the front lines.

As the enormity of the damage became clear during the first day or so, we systematically began searching for our people, all 7,000 of them. Under the direction of Roy J. Nirschel, Jr., vice president for university advancement, and David Poole, associate director of Admissions, we created a 40-person volunteer phone bank in the alumni office. Those good friends placed telephone calls to all 7,000 employees and reached 4,600. The telephones of the others did not work. The purpose was to determine who needed help and how badly, and who was willing and able to help. Accordingly, we learned quickly who out there was in real trouble. And we put together quickly a cadre of wonderful volunteers.

By September 2nd, we had located all but two members of the University of Miami family, either by telephone or through communications within the various divisions of the university. Those last two were finally found by our police officers. No one had been killed or injured by the storm, although sadly two members of the faculty, William J. Harrington, of our School of Medicine, and James A. Sawyer, of our School of Business, died of heart attacks, post-Andrew, but apparently related to the crisis. We found that 419 members of the university family were homeless or had suffered extreme damage to their homes.

Through the good offices of Roosevelt Thomas, Jr., associate vice president for human resources and affirmative action, we set up a system of assistance to our employees. We helped find homes and apartments, dealt with immediate financial or other personal emergencies, sent teams from physical plant to do emergency repair on roofs, established an emergency day care center (operated by Susan A. Rosendahl, director, University of Miami/Canterbury Preschool).

One of the first major challenges was getting the paychecks cut and delivered on time. Through extraordinary efforts of Alan V. Matthews, associate treasurer, treasury operations, among others, this was accomplished, alleviating what would have been much immediate fiscal anguish.

Somehow, David A. Lieberman, senior vice president, Victor J. Atherton, and their talented associates were able to assemble a vast crew of workers to clean up the campus. Within the first few days, chain saws and huge trucks were everywhere. I learned for the first time about "Bobcats," small tractors designed to move a lot around in restricted spaces. They were everywhere, scraping, pushing, and lifting refuse and branches into piles or trucks. Then arrived the two largest pieces of mobile equipment I think I have ever seen, boxcar-size shredders. They devoured every branch and piece of wood, up to huge logs, spewing the shredded results 40 or 50 feet into growing piles of mulch—one in front of the Lowe Art Museum reached dimensions of perhaps 60 feet long by 30 feet wide by 20 feet high. It turned out that mulch like that is used by the sugar industry. We telephoned our trustee Alfonso (Alfy) Fanjul, who sent his own trucks the next morning. The mountain of mulch disappeared.

Within a day or so, all of Dade County was crawling with visiting woodsmen, roofers, construction crews, teenage boys who had just invested in their first chain saw, not to mention a growing entrepreneurial army that would sell anything from gas generators to hot coffee. Within 24 hours after the storm, I noticed generators sold at Cocoplum Circle. The university was able to contract with sufficient people to get a big head start on much of the rest of the county. We had to move fast in order to be ready for our returning students by the promised deferred opening day, September 14th.

Little by little, the campus returned to its original condition, but minus those 3,000 trees. Within a day or so, all shattered windows were boarded up. Repair of windows and damaged roofs began almost immediately and continues to this writing. Sprinkler systems were crushed. Huge pieces of construction equipment chewed beautiful lawns into mud lakes. The cleanup began with the roads, restoring access. It moved next to the major interior malls and open spaces. Slowly, what had been a nearly impenetrable mass of fallen trees and branches disappeared amidst the diesel smoke of huge machines.

Many of these workers, plus 200 FPL employees, slept in the Lane Center gymnasium. The contractors apparently had hired many migrant workers from the central part of the state, so much of Central America was represented in our work crews, not to mention Georgia, Alabama, and points north and west. These workers ate in our cafeterias.

As for hundreds of thousands of others, life at home wasn't much fun. For several days, a sundown curfew was in effect. In the early evenings, we would sit on our front porch watching, for the first time in our 11-½ years here, the sun actually set. Until then, there had been far too many trees in our yard and across Old Cutler Road to see anything but heavily filtered light. The tap water was contaminated, so we drank only bottled or canned water or drinks. Cooking was reduced to the basics. For many days, we cooked with sterno, later graduated to the luxury of a generator-powered stove. As darkness came, we would turn on our kerosene lamp. We would try to read for a while. It wasn't easy. We usually went to bed shortly after dark and spent many hot, uncomfortable nights.

For several days, there was no water pressure and the toilets didn't work. We had filled up two bathtubs with water, as instructed, and we used it to make the toilets function and to bathe. When the water was turned on, approximately a week after the hurricane, there was no hot water for many additional days. We did not wash any clothes for a long time. The telephone lines were dead for days. We used the portable phones when we could get through the cellular system, which wasn't easy. From dusk to dawn, excepting emergencies when I would use the police radio, we were essentially out of communication with anyone for many days.

As the campus began returning to normal, and as the immediate crisis for those 419 members of the university's family subsided, we began turning our attention to the needs of the broader community. Those needs were and remain staggering. By helicopter, I witnessed in the south part of the county almost unbelievable devastation. Entire neighborhoods were simply flattened. I once counted a dozen blocks of what had been mobile homes, with not one standing anymore. The media reported looting. When the U.S. Army arrived, security returned to most of the area, but even with the National Guard and the 82nd Airborne patrolling the streets, some lawlessness prevailed. Authorities quickly set up emergency medical care, and food and clothing at distribution points. They established tent cities, which I visited during my trips to the clinics established by our Schools of Medicine and Nursing. Without electricity, water, or telephones, life in Homestead and Florida City quickly descended to the most basic of issues. I was proud that my colleagues in the Schools of Medicine and Nursing had so quickly responded to the emergency.

The volunteers working the telephone bank called thousands of our alumni seeking those who were willing and able to work in rebuilding the community. Simultaneously, Carrie A. Edmondson, coordinator, Volunteer Services Center, reopened her offices to coordinate the volunteer efforts of the several hundred students who remained on the campus. In all, probably 300–500 University of Miami employees or students were out in the community working within the first few days following the storm. Members of the School of Architecture and College of Engineering faculties immediately volunteered their professional services. Several engineering professors began working with their colleagues at the Citadel to coordinate a national volunteer engineering initiative to help assess the damage and its causes. Members of the law faculty began organizing emergency seminars and services on legal and insurance issues arising from the destruction.

James K. Batten, chairman and chief executive officer of Knight-Ridder, and our trustee, invited community leaders to a meeting in his offices on the Sunday following the hurricane. Present were approximately a dozen or so corporate and civic leaders. Jack Kemp, secretary of Housing and Urban Development, arrived. So did Senators Bob Graham and Connie Mack. For a couple of hours, we discussed how to organize the private sector into an effective partnership to work with public officials. President George Bush was scheduled to visit Dade County later that week, and we wanted to be ready with a community-wide response team. We discussed the mission, composition, and organization of such a private-sector effort. We agreed to meet again the following day after further thought, which we did.

Within the next few days, we had organized "We Will Rebuild," chaired by retired Knight-Ridder Chief Executive Officer, Alvah H. Chapman, Jr., a friend and political associate of President Bush. R. Ray Goode, former chairman of the University of Miami Board of Trustees, was named president. When President Bush arrived in our community, he gave instant national visibility to "We Will Rebuild" by announcing its existence and urging people all over the country to send money and other assistance. The University of Miami is significantly represented on the several task forces of "We Will Rebuild." In addition to Mr. Goode, Luis Glaser, executive vice president and provost, Bernard (Bernie) J. Fogel, senior vice president for medical affairs and dean of our School of Medicine, Pedro J. (Jose) Greer, medical director, Camillus Health Concern, and I serve on the board of directors, and I serve on the executive committee.

As this is being typed, "We Will Rebuild" has organized itself into 17 different task forces, raised $18.5 million, and become a huge and busy enterprise. Increasingly, we who live in this stricken place are coming to believe that from such terrible devastation we can build an even better community. People joke that it may have taken the worst natural catastrophe in the history of the country to unify beleaguered and divided Greater Miami in the late twentieth century. Time will tell, but there is no question about the level of spirit, cooperation, and mutual support that now exists here. Everywhere one hears stories of neighbors meeting neighbors for the first time, and helping each other as never before. Rebuilding efforts have been remarkably free of the kind of racial and ethnic bickering that has characterized so much public discourse in Dade County. Certainly the level of national support and concern, including but not limited to the $9-plus billion federal relief commitment, is unprecedented.

We are concentrating especially on the health committee as the medical school is such an important pillar of health care in our community. Admiral Frank E. Young, M.D., deputy assistant secretary for Health/Science and Environment, U.S. Department of Health and Human Services, has been working with this health committee. He invited Bernie Fogel, Dave Lieberman, and me to join him in a helicopter tour of the most devastated areas. With us for part of the ride were representative Mike Abrams and Dr. Gwen Wurm of our medical school faculty, who also serves as medical coordinator for state government. In a Blackhawk helicopter, we visited a ruined migrant worker camp so far south into the Everglades that it did not even show up on a Dade County map, and the south Dade County headquarters doubling as the headquarters also of the 82nd Airborne division. Running out of time on the way back, the good admiral arranged to drop me off in a park downtown, so that I could attend a meeting.

As damaged as the University of Miami is, I am absolutely convinced that we will emerge from this ordeal a stronger, better institution. In my nearly 12 years here, I have never seen such cooperation and mutual respect and assistance within the university family. People are expressing not only genuine concern for each other but also offering to translate that concern into help. They are opening their houses to those who need shelter. Without complaint, faculty members are covering for each other to teach classes and otherwise serve our students when personal crisis has interrupted colleagues' plans. Praise for all concerned in the crisis management and cleanup phase has been widespread. With limitless gratitude, I pay my respects to Luis Glaser, Dave Lieberman, Bernie Fogel, the other vice presidents, and all concerned for great leadership during the crisis.

We are back in business, teaching, doing research, and again building a great American university.

Snapshots of hurricane memories:

- Retired Professor Julia Morton, whose house was destroyed, living in her office and proudly refusing any and all offers of assistance.

- A Bobcat operator working furiously in a driving thunderstorm, totally oblivious to lightning striking all around, who, when I suggested it might be safer to wait a few minutes, said he had work to do and didn't believe in rest breaks.

- My wife, Bosey, standing by the swimming pool soaking wet when I returned from the campus. She had volunteered to jump in the pool to help the crew of laborers remove the huge oak tree that had slammed against our house on the way down.

- The looks of shock and pain in the faces of countless colleagues and strangers.

- The continuing disorientation of losing so many landmarks in our own neighborhood so long taken for granted; during the first week following the storm, I drove right by my own driveway several times, so unrecognizable was it.

- The accumulating fatigue that burdened everyone following so many nights of fitful rest.

- The roar of portable generators before electricity returned, and the devil's alternatives our own presented each morning at approximately 2:00 A.M. when its gasoline ran out: either get hot (and it was very hot) as the air conditioning ended and therefore sleep poorly; or get up and spend 15 minutes increasingly wide awake putting gasoline in the generator and therefore sleep poorly. At first we got up, but later opted just to stay hot.

- The absolute frustration of being unable to communicate with friends and colleagues. I tried and rejected five or six portable telephones until I found one that worked reasonably well.
- Fear of looters as the sun went down and the only light anywhere around was a kerosene lantern or a flashlight, and the moon and stars.
- The comfort of noting troops stationed in our neighborhood, and especially half a block away at the intersection of Kendall Drive and Old Cutler Road.
- The extraordinary commitment and genuine bravery I saw uncommonly displayed by so many of my associates.

SENIOR VICE PRESIDENT

FROM: David A. Lieberman
Senior Vice President
Friday, August 21, 1992

Facilities Administration

Preliminary hurricane preparations began.
Alerted physical plant personnel of a possible call-back for the hurricane.
Verified supply of plywood, plastic, sandbags, etc.
Took inventory of hurricane supplies and inspected pumps and generators.
Topped off fuel in vehicles.
Notified building contractors of the storm threat and put them on notice to clean up sites in preparation for a hurricane.

Saturday, August 22, and Sunday, August 23

Facilities Administration

Vic Atherton, returning from Australia, learned at 9:00 P.M. Saturday we were going to have a hurricane. Earlier the same day, Mike White notified Physical Plant crews to come in at 7:00 A.M. Sunday and begin full-scale boarding up and securing of facilities.

Contacted members of Hurricane Advisory Committee to discuss preparation and alerted them of the Sunday morning meeting.

Hurricane Advisory Committee emergency meeting convened at 10:00 A.M. and discussed the preparation procedures department by department, to make sure responsibilities were understood.

Physical plant crew boarded up: Pick Music Library, University Center, Student Health Services, Centrex Building, Richter Library, Ungar Building,

President's residence, and Physical Plant Service Desk (finished at midnight Sunday).

Physical plant crews sandbagged: Cox Science Center, Centrex Building, Merrick Building, President's residence, James L. Knight Center, Lane Recreation Center, and Engineering.

Cleaned up construction sites and loose debris.

Checked roofs, windows, weather-proofed electric vaults.

Secured elevators.

Powered down utility plants.

Readied generators at various locations and stationed portable pumps.

Stayed in constant touch with all other departments to assist them with their needs.

Preparations continued through the night.

Physical Plant families arrived for shelter.

Towards the end of the storm, while still dark, sealed with plywood three windows that blew out.

Information Resources

Reviewed with Coral Gables City officials the availability of city gas supply to the generator located at Centrex Building.

Reviewed, via phone, the emergency procedures with managers and supervisors.

Requested from Florida Radio Rental, 12 hand-held radios for emergency communications, to be ready on Sunday.

Continued to support orientation and registration.

Ordered from AT&T the 1-800 number for emergency information.

Installed two additional lines for Dade County Metro Police in the RSMAS Campus Switch Room.

Released the 1-800-227-0354 number to the Hurricane Preparedness Committee at 9:00 A.M. meeting. Public affairs requested the number be steered to Public Safety.

Requested sand bags for Ungar Computer Center and Centrex Equipment door.

Requested Centrex's lobby and ingress-egress door be boarded up.

Requested installation of hurricane shutters in Ungar Building.

Started emergency air conditioning (62 degrees) in the Centrex Building. This was done to lower the temperature in the equipment room in the event the gas supply to our generator was cut off. With proper temperature, the uninterrupted power supply batteries could provide an additional two hours of telephone services.

Tested generator. (This generator is normally tested every Wednesday.)
Picked up emergency radios from Florida Radio Rental.

Called every university emergency telephone installed for verification. Ninety-two percent of the phones were staffed.

Brought down the computer system, backed up data storage, and secured the computer room according to the emergency procedures. Power-off and hurricane alert procedures were implemented.

Computer center generated two back-up files in each system. One to be delivered to critical files off-site storage, and the other was placed in a secure area on the second floor of Ungar.

Installed an amateur radio station in the Centrex Building, and checked in the Dade County Emergency Operation Center at 9:00 P.M.

Stayed in Centrex Building during the storm.

About 11:00 P.M., noted an immense amount of water running between the Centrex Building and the Studio. Discovered that the emergency air conditioning runs on city water for cooling. Wasteful.

Installed additional EXXEX Times for Medical Security.

Business Services

Public safety finalized shift configuration, obtained emergency supplies, fueled vehicles, and assisted physical plant in locating and securing all outside items that could become flying debris. Public safety also assisted student services personnel in placing and securing families here for freshmen orientation. Volunteers from uniformed patrol unit, "Adopt a Cop," were placed in each residential college. Placed public safety personnel on "Alpha-Bravo" shifts.

Material Management opened the warehouse for distribution of supplies.

Treasurer-Controller-Operations

Contacted employees to let them know of the expected seriousness of the storm and to develop list of past-storm critical operations.

Determined what the probable effect of the storm would be on the registration process.

Determined how best to handle the cash management functions.

Contacted consultant to assure that pending financing transactions would proceed.

Registered students and established Cane Card accounts until 3:00 P.M., Saturday.

Worked with physical plant in the interior of the cafeterias to disconnect and disassemble, cover, and store all computer equipment.

Prepared all private offices within the student account services for the storm.

Monday, August 24, 1992

Facilities Administration

Learned that the generator powering physical plant and public safety was not generating adequate power. Hooked up another one, still inadequate.

Toured Coral Gables campus at 7:15 A.M. and made the first report of damages. Established priorities for beginning the clean-up and further assessing mechanical and structural damage. Worst-hit buildings were Ponce, McCarther, and Ashe, due mainly to blown out windows.

Borrowed contractors heavy equipment from construction sites and cleaned roadways along San Amaro, Ponce, and the interior drives.

Activated generators at the lift stations. Stayed in touch with Florida Power and Light's Coral Gables Emergency Command Center.

Physical plant crews spent the day boarding up broken windows and doors, making other emergency repairs, and checking mechanical equipment and assessing damages. Physical plant managers conducted site-by-site inspections of facilities and conditions.

Worked closely with residence halls to obtain essential services for students: portable toilets and potable water.

Information Resources

Water and debris was coming in through the front and equipment room doors at the Centrex Building. Situation corrected.

Used the Amateur Radio Emergency Network to serve the community:

At 3:50 A.M., a Florida Highway Patrol trooper was injured by flying debris. Call came through amateur radio and was relayed to UM Public Safety Department which in turn radioed it to Coral Cables Emergency Operations.

Publix lost its roof and sent distress call. Information relayed to UM Public Safety Department and in turn to Coral Gables Emergency Net.

At 4:15 A.M., checked with Temares in the Ungar Building, Atherton in Facilities Administration, and with Caesar Ferreiro and Paul Dalba in the Medical Campus's telephone room.

Checked entire Centrex Building for leaks or water incursion. With the exception of the front and equipment room doors, found none. All emergency equipment working properly.

Problem noted with telephone switch. Reported malfunction to AT&T. Unsuccessfully attempted to clear the problem through software.

At 6:00 A.M., preliminary inspection of the building indicates no damage but parking lot blocked by fallen trees.

10:00 A.M., tested the DEC VAX System.

Noted low water pressure in air conditioning system.

Inspected Ungar Building, noted no damages to Computer Room. Brought in additional telephone operators, activated all communications links to the public switching network.

Hurricane Preparedness Committee meeting scheduled for 5:00 P.M. Monday canceled and rescheduled for Tuesday at 10:00 A.M.

Preliminary assessment of the satellite switches in North and South, Women's Center, and RSMAD indicates they were down due to lack of commercial power.

Continued to provide university telephone operator services around the clock.

Noted data backbone facility was damaged by uprooted trees.

Business Services

Public safety secured and sealed off the university to outsiders to protect people on-campus and to prevent looting.

Environmental health and safety personnel inspected all chemical storage areas on all campuses except RSMAS (personnel were denied access to the Causeway to Virginia Key); no damage or chemical spills were found. While on South Campus, staff helped Division of Veterinary Resources clean up and catch monkeys that had escaped.

Risk management contacted insurance carriers. The Risk Management Department was designated the university's focal point to submit Hurricane Andrew damage reports.

Materials management opened the warehouse facilities at noon on Monday.

Tuesday, August 25th

Facilities Administration

Contacted contractors (electrical, roofers, general contractors, landscaping, and debris removal) to assist with restoration. Retained Jack Niebel of West Palm Beach as project manager. He began assembling crews.

Received limited electrical service from FPL.

Continued to assess damages.

Plumbers worked to restore lift stations.

HVAC personnel worked to restore utility plants. (We suffered from lost water pressure and fluctuating voltage.)

Worked with public safety in establishing ID security system for contract personnel on campus, to distinguish potential looters from those hired to be on campus.

Physical plant worked to temporarily dry roofs.

Established physical plant crews to assist university personnel at their damaged homes.

Assessed elevator damages.

Met at 8:00 A.M. with department heads at facilities administration to stay updated on the progress of damage repairs.

Alan Weber made arrangements to acquire portable toilets and water, and to secure trash pick-up.

Met at 4:00 P.M. with contractors to stay abreast of progress on cleanup and debris removal.

Information Resources

Computer Center recovery team placed on standby. The computer is water cooled but the water pressure was very low; Centrex Building running on emergency power; and low city water pressure is creating shutdowns of the air conditioning unit every 30 minutes. This was critical to communications links, almost a crisis mode.

Checked computer production schedule for potential problems. Payroll scheduled to run.

Telecommunications staff on-site manned the university's information number.

Water and food for the staff on-duty became a problem. Staff living in Broward County started to buy and transport food and water.

Requested Southern Bell to forward president's residence phone calls to UM office; routed phone trunks to give RSMAS outside phone service.

Business Services

Public Safety Director Shoemaker's request to Coral Gables Police to swear in Virginia Tech certified campus police officers to supplement the university force is denied.

Purchasing department became operational, focused on key projects.

Obtained 30 portable phones from cellular vendors for loan to key administrators; also got beepers.

Automated faxing information through the university. Faxed claims, information, contractors' lists, hurricane newsletter, etc.

Facilitated acquisition of water tanker and water in jugs.

Obtained additional security guards.

Worked with real estate and employee benefits to obtain housing for employees/faculty who had lost their homes.

Negotiated bus service for volunteers.

Helped to expedite payments to vendors.

Treasury Operations

Analyzed the effects of the storm on the banking system and our ability to produce a payroll.

Set up revised registration calendar .

Collectors began working with admissions personnel to make contact with students to determine the hurricane's effect on enrollment.

Assessed damage to student accounts, payroll, accounts payable, and collection offices.

Made calls to ascertain the status of the department's 75 employees.

Human Resources

Became coordinator for homeless UM employees and began the effort of matching employees who lost the use of their homes with those who had space to house an employee or family.

Attended 10:00 A.M. meeting of expanded Long Range Planning Committee.

Wednesday, August 26th

Facilities Administration

Started Ungar Building air conditioning to allow computer center to come on line.

Worked with Florida Power and Light to systematically restore power, worked with City Gas to restore gas service.

Extensive contract manpower fully on site removing debris.

Established plan to complete roofs drying-in process, using contractor personnel.

Physical plant crews assisted 70 plus University of Miami personnel at their damaged homes.

Began assisting residence halls in damage assessment and repair of roofing and broken windows.

Developed a lighting damage report and restoration plan.

Instituted 8:00 A.M. daily meetings, which continued for two weeks, seven days a week, to assess progress and make short-term operational and priority decisions.

Information Resources

11:30 A.M., necessary water pressure attained and IBM central facility came on line. An initial program load with Power on Resent was performed to ensure that 11 related memory modules were loaded with the proper microcode.

Contacted Barnett Bank in Jacksonville to test the online Lock Box transmission. Test successful.

Loaded all subsystems data successfully.

Several computer operations personnel on duty including payroll system programmers.

Prepared and installed lines, sets and data lines for U. S. Department of Education representatives.

Directed 1-800 emergency information to regular telephone.

Activated the Alumni House phone bank.

Provided a line for Student Union Volunteer Desk.

Installed two lines for Ogden Allied in purchasing conference room.

Surveyed security blue lights phones, nineteen are damaged.

Requested additional help from outside vendor, International Network Systems, to assist on the data backbone cable problem.

Business Services

Real estate office began assisting human resources to identify potential apartments and houses for displaced university employees. Rented 24 apartments plus several homes and townhouses. The tenants will reimburse the university through payroll deduction.

Purchasing department was back to full staff.

Materials management was back to full staff and open daily from 7:30 A.M. to 7:00 P.M. or later.

Public safety continued on "Alpha-Bravo" shifts securing the campus from possible looting.

Environmental health and safety staff assigned to take care of the feeding and housing needs of the contractors on campus.

Treasury Operations

Developed policy for student travel funds.

Preparations made for emergency check cashing for students and staff at residential colleges. Preparations were made for check cashing and employee emergency assistance at the Medical School.

Preparations made for temporary check distribution at the Max Grovitz Building.

Accounts payable system processing began. Checks were run at night by Information Resources.

Payroll management began working on the month-end payroll with information resources.

Human Resources

Phone number announced in various news media to inform UM employees of the university's efforts to assist.

Four administrative staff spent the day planning strategy, receiving phone calls, and sharing information with anyone who called about assistance in any way.

Coordinated placement of homeless UM personnel in temporary and not-so-temporary residences, using listings obtained from a variety of sources.

Contacted more human resources staff and asked them to report to work on Thursday, August 27th.

Thursday, August 27, 1992

Facilities Administration

Spent considerable time with roofing contractors.

Worked with general contractors to rebuild fences and board up windows. Continued debris removal.

Established record keeping procedures for contractors.

Started compiling comprehensive documentation of damages in a database format.

Began to hear complaints about the behavior of contractor personnel being fed and housed on campus. Tempers flared, minor damage was done to Lane Center exercise equipment.

Trash service, although spotty, resumed.

Information Services

International Network Systems staff arrives on campus to help with the data network problem.

Successfully completed 30 payroll jobs including the monthly, bi-weekly, and student payrolls. Ran students' labels requested by provost's office.

Business Services

Sent three police officers to work under direction of city of Coral Gables for the "B" shift and for both "A" and "B" shifts daily hereafter, for the next five days, through September 2nd.

Treasury Operations

Opened check cashing at residential colleges and Orovitz from 10:00 A.M. until 3:00 P.M.

Worked from 9:00 A.M. until 4:00 P.M. answering phone calls and assisting parents with registration issues.

Accounts Payable staff processed invoices for purchases of essential and emergency services; check distribution prepared accounts payable checks for distribution.

Payroll completed the direct deposit payroll and coordinated banking transfers.

Emergency checks were issued for deposits for leases on apartments re-served for UM faculty, administrators, and staff.

These activities continued each day thereafter.

Human Resources

Coordinated leasing of houses and rental units, working closely with real estate and purchasing departments. That effort led to a full-time job of finding rental units in Dade County for UM employees as needed. Received numer-ous calls.

Assisted residence halls staff in finding temporary homes for students stranded on campus. Continued this for the following week.

Friday, August 28, 1992

Facilities Administration

Continued roof and fence repairs, and debris removal.

Received a water tanker (from Indiana, refilled daily in Hollywood) and empty water containers for student use.

Set up outdoor showers for contractor personnel.

Business Services

Again, requested and were denied approval by city of Coral Gables for swearing in Virginia Tech police officers.

Human Resources

Shared housing list with HR Medical Office. Received many phone calls both from the homeless and those with temporary space to share; matchings occurred.

Leased "Laurels" apartments in Plantation and "Vencino Del Mar" apartments located in Miami Shores, and began leasing to employees.

Saturday, August 29, and Sunday, August 30

Information Resources

Restored data network backbone.

Executed accounts payable, purchasing, and check writing systems.

Initiated UM CAN (Caring About Neighbors) Relief Drive in Ibis Cafeteria to receive donation of food and supplies from August 30 to September 9, 1992.

Business Services

Convenience store opened on Saturday and Sunday, 8:00 A.M. to 5:00 P.M.

Six officers from University of South Florida and four from Florida Atlantic University arrived and were put into service, August 30th. They stayed until September 6th, when Coral Gables released remaining UM officers.

Treasury Operations

Check distribution prepared payroll checks and direct deposit receipts for distribution.

Monday, August 31, 1992

Business Services

Notified that city of Coral Gables executed agreement for SUS police to have Coral Gables police powers.

Human Resources

Learned that 58 business and finance staff either lost their homes or suffered extreme damage.

As a result of university advancement calling every university employee received an extremely high volume of calls from alumni and students looking for housing.

Staff Development Office set up Hurricane Assistance information sessions on three issues: insurance, selecting and dealing with contractors, and home renovation loans.

On and after Tuesday, September 1, 1992

Human Resources
Distributed fliers soliciting rental space for commuter students, to all 700 employees.
Staffed the office all three days over Labor Day Weekend.

Some Lessons Learned
Centrex needs a stand alone emergency air conditioning unit to mitigate the chilled water pressure from the city supply.
The computer center needs a closed loop chilled water unit.
Centrex gas generator needs to be augmented to support diesel as well as gas supply.
Public Safety Department Key Station unit is not hooked up to the emergency generator. Therefore, when commercial power is out the officers cannot see which incoming line is ringing.
The university was not prepared to house families of those employees working during and after the emergency.
Food and water supply can be improved.
Telecommunications route diversity is needed to RSMAD campus.
Plan needed for operational staff to be in communication with cellular or radio connection.

DIRECTOR OF PUBLIC SAFETY

FROM: Eric Shoemaker

Director of Public Safety

August 22, 1992
University of Miami police officers placed on a 12-hour on, 12-hour off schedule ("Alpha-Bravo" configuration).

August 27, 1992
Invoking provisions of the university-city contract, 6 officers were pressed into service by the Coral Gables Police. Appeals for reconsideration refused.

August 29, 1992
Advised by the provost that help was coming from Florida Atlantic
University and The University of South Florida. Work began . . . to execute
a mutual aid agreement with the city of Coral Gables and the universities
sending police officers.

August 30, 1992
six officers from USF, and four from FAU arrived and put into service.
During that week, Coral Gables reduced their requirement by two officers.

September 6, 1992
Additional officers depart for home. Coral Gables releases remaining
University of Miami officers.

DIRECTOR OF RESIDENCE HALLS

FROM: Dr. Robert J. Redick

                   Director of Residence Halls

DATE: October 9, 1992

SUBJECT: President's Request for Hurricane Chronicle

The Department of Residence Halls hurricane actions were as follows:

Friday, August 21st

- closely monitored weather information
- reviewed departmental and university hurricane procedures

Saturday, August 22nd

- closely monitored weather information
- prepared hurricane supplies for distribution
- fueled all departmental vehicles

Sunday, August 23rd

- closely monitored weather information
- attended a meeting with university senior administration
- held a meeting of residence coordinators and residential college masters
- each residence coordinator held a meeting with his/her resident assistants
- every resident assistant held a meeting with his/her residents and parents who were available to attend

- each resident assistant took his residents and the residents' parents to dinner in the dining halls; in addition to dinner, everyone received a bag containing food for breakfast the next morning; parents and relatives were fed at no charge
- held meetings with maintenance staff
- held meetings with secretarial and administrative staff
- secured buildings with storm shutters and plywood
- distributed hurricane supplies, i.e., flashlights, water containers, first aid kits
- held meetings with Marriott to plan pre- and post-hurricane meal service
- held meetings with Ogden to finalize pre-, during, and post-hurricane housekeeping services
- answered telephone questions from parents, students, and media throughout the country
- opened the Residence Halls Office at 7:00 A.M. and continued operations throughout the night
- shut off elevators when winds began increasing in intensity
- maintained communications with residential colleges and apartment area, including during the storm
- evacuated floors 7 through 12 in Hecht and Stanford residential colleges and relocated these students on floors 1 through 6
- evacuated students from their rooms into hallways in Pearson, Mahoney, and Eaton residential colleges
- mopped water during storm
- monitored residential college lobbies to deter anyone from leaving the buildings during the storm
- resident assistants, residence coordinators, and residential college faculty sat with students and their parents throughout the storm and provided a calming influence

Monday, August 24

- cleaned up water and broken glass
- relocated students whose rooms were uninhabitable
- identified safe paths to Hecht/Stanford dining hall
- met with Marriott staff on several occasions regarding Monday and Tuesday meal service

- answered telephone questions from parents, students and media each day
- maintained continuous, 24-hour operation of the Residence Halls Office
- wrote and distributed a newsletter to all staff and faculty in the residential colleges and apartment area regarding post-hurricane operations
- got water from health center well and purified and delivered it to the Hecht/Stanford dining hall
- instructed resident students, staff, and faculty on how to flush toilets with buckets of lake water when there is no water pressure
- talked with the uncle of a resident student about the possibility of his supplying drinkable water to the campus
- fed two meals to everyone on campus at no extra charge, i.e., students, parents, guests, faculty, staff, and faculty and staff family

Tuesday, August 25

- maintained continuous, 24 hours a day operation of the Residence Halls Office
- cleaned up water and broken glass
- worked on securing envelopes of buildings
- participated in President Foote's post-hurricane meeting
- wrote and distributed a newsletter to all staff and faculty in the residential colleges and apartment area regarding postponement of the beginning of classes and university support of student travel home
- every resident assistant held a meeting with his/her residents and the residents' parents regarding the delay of the start of school
- met with Marriott management
- met with purchasing regarding the purchase of drinking water by jug, contracting with a bulk water carrier to supply drinking water, and renting of portable toilets
- met with Ogden regarding housekeeping of buildings
- purchased generators
- fed two meals to everyone on campus at no extra charge, i.e., students, parents, guests, faculty, staff, and faculty and staff family
- got, purified, and delivered water from health center well to Hecht/Stanford cafeteria and to residential college and apartment area offices

Wednesday, August 26

- met with contractors and physical plant management regarding cleanup and repair
- participated in President Foote's post-hurricane meeting
- wrote and distributed a newsletter to all staff and faculty in the residential college and apartment area
- maintained continuous, 24-hour a day operation of Residence Halls Office
- continued to clean up water and glass
- continued to work on securing envelopes of buildings
- each residence coordinator held a meeting with his/her resident assistants
- met with Marriott management
- fed two meals to everyone on campus at no charge
- pursued, purified, and delivered water from health center well to Hecht/Stanford dining hall and residential college and apartment area offices
- met with Ogden housekeeping management

Thursday, August 27–Sunday, August 30

- same activities as on Wednesday, August 26

Monday, August 31–Wednesday, September 9

- continued cleaning and repair of facilities
- prepared for return of students
- served three meals a day to those living on campus
- communicated with students and parents around the country
- accepted housing applications from and moved into university housing immediately those students whose off-campus housing was destroyed or damaged

DIRECTOR OF VOLUNTEER SERVICES

FROM: Carrie Austin Edmondson

Director of Volunteer Services

RE: Hurricane Relief: Volunteer Services Center

The Volunteer Services Center began a job/volunteer placement program which operated from the university center information desk on Thursday, August 27th. The program had two primary purposes: to help faculty and staff repair personal damages to their homes; and to create jobs and volunteer opportunities on campus and in the community for approximately 300 students remaining on campus. We began this operation with more volunteers than jobs, though the reverse soon became true.

During the two weeks following the hurricane, we placed many students, faculty, alumni, and staff in hurricane relief projects. Some of these included phone work for the information hot lines established for UM students and parents, phone work for the admissions office, on-campus cleanup with physical plant, phone work for the Lowe Art Museum, and the UM-CAN (UM Cares about Neighbors) program.

We also organized nine trips to the South Dade area, using buses donated by Club Limousine. The trips were to Homestead and Leisure City, and many students and staff members participated. Students participated in food distribution, community needs assessment, roofing repairs, and other worthwhile projects. Most of the students were extremely interested in volunteering directly with the people most affected by the hurricane.

When the students returned to class, we began scheduling trips on each Saturday and Sunday after Orientation Weekend. A group of students who had volunteered expressed interest in forming a student committee to organize relief projects. We worked with the students to form the Hurricane Relief Committee. The students help organize weekend trips, volunteer to be site leaders for the student groups, and help with needs assessment in the South Dade area. The students are currently seeking a long-term project in conjunction with Dade County Public Schools.

The Volunteer Services Center has also been arranging logistics for groups of student volunteers visiting from other colleges and universities as well. In October, students from Warren Wilson College and Guilford College in North Carolina came to volunteer. A large group from a consortium of West Virginia schools is expected during the week of Thanksgiving. A part-time hurricane "relief coordinator" has been hired to organize the efforts of UM students and visiting students.

Finally, the Volunteer Services Center continues to emphasize long-term efforts in community service. We are hosting a regional conference in conjunction with Florida's Office for Campus Volunteers on October 24th. The conference will feature a "hurricane relief" panel discussion, with representatives from United Way, We Will Rebuild, Habitat for Humanity, and UMCOR (United Methodist Committee on Relief). Also, the hurricane has served as a catalyst for integrating the concept of "service-learning" into the UM curriculum. The Volunteer Services Center will co-sponsor a workshop entitled "Service Learning: A Powerful Pedagogy" on November 6th.

DEAN OF STUDENTS

FROM: William W. Sandler, Jr.

Dean of Students

RE: Hurricane Andrew Procedures

Listed below is a chronicle, day by day, of the Office of the Dean of Students preparation for the hurricane, the impact of the storm, and what occurred after it hit.

Thursday, August 20, 1992

Hurricane procedures for the fraternity row area were distributed to the fraternity graduate advisors during their annual orientation.

Sunday, August 23, 1992

The Office of the Dean of Students staff prepared building 21-H and 21-E for the hurricane.

Hurricane procedures were delivered to each fraternity house and each fraternity made preparations for the hurricane. Pi Kappa Alpha and Zeta Beta Tau made the decision not to allow anyone to remain in the house during the hurricane.

Dean Walker and Dean Abrahamson were available to answer questions and phone calls from students and parents regarding the school closing for the hurricane.

Monday, August 24, 1992

Dean Sandler and Dean Walker came to campus to assess any damage to the office (21-H and 21-E) and to check on the fraternity houses.

Tuesday, August 25, 1992

The fraternity graduate advisor staff were contacted and a meeting scheduled for Wednesday, August 26, 1992, to assess the damage to the fraternity houses.

Provost Glaser, Dr. Butler, and Dean Sandler met with the residence halls staff to discuss long-range preparations for the feeding of students and staff.

Dean Walker and Dean Abrahamson began to attempt to contact all of the Dean of Students staff to determine that they were safe, the condition of their homes, and what their needs were.

Wednesday, August 26, 1992

Dean Sandler, Dean Walker, and Dean Abrahamson attended the student affairs staff meeting regarding Hurricane Andrew.

Dean Sandler, Dean Walker, and Dean Abrahamson attended the president's Hurricane Andrew update meeting.

A meeting was held with the fraternity graduate advisor staff to inform them of the university's clean-up effort and to assess the damage to each fraternity house. Dean Walker began to work with the staff and the house corporations in the area of repairs.

Thursday, August 27, 1992

Dean Walker and Dean Abrahamson attended the president's Hurricane Andrew update meeting.

Dean Walker contacted the Pi Kappa Alpha national fraternity concerning the severe damage to the Pi Kappa Alpha fraternity house located at 5800 San Amaro Drive. The university recommended to the national fraternity that the house be closed until the extent of the damages could be properly assessed. The national fraternity issued a letter authorizing the immediate evacuation of the house.

Vic Atherton and the physical plant agreed to assist the fraternity area with the removal of the debris.

The students living in the fraternity area were allowed to begin eating meals in the cafeteria.

Friday, August 28, 1992

Dean Abrahamson met with the residential college security assistants and scheduled 24-hour security in all residential areas through Wednesday, September 9, 1992.

Dean Abrahamson coordinated campus-wide programs/ activities for all residential students.

Dean Walker held an update meeting with the fraternity graduate advisor staff.

Dean Walker began working with physical plant to restore electricity to the fraternity area. (This was not achieved for at least another week.)

Drinking water was made available to the fraternity row area.

Monday, August 31, 1992

The dean of students staff began to make plans for the changes in the university calendar and to revise the dates for the previously scheduled programs (i.e., rush, orientation, etc.).

Dean Abrahamson recruited student volunteers to circulate a newsletter to faculty and staff. (August 31–September 7, 1992)

Dean Abrahamson coordinated relief/vacation schedule for residence coordinator staff. (August 31– September 7, 1992)

Tuesday, September 1, 1992

Dean Walker held an update meeting with the fraternity graduate advisor staff.

Dean Walker met with Sid Dunn, executive director of Alpha Epsilon Pi, to survey the damage to the fraternity house and to begin to set priorities for needed repairs.

A letter was sent via facsimile to all of the national headquarters of all of the fraternities and sororities informing them of the damage done by the hurricane, the changes in university calendar and the changes in the fraternity and sorority rush schedules.

Dean Abrahamson made preparations for an appreciation dinner/social for all residential college and apartment area staffs. (September 1–9, 1992)

Friday, September 4, 1992

It was determined that the Pi Kappa Alpha fraternity house would have to close the rooms on the second floor for the fall semester. Dean Walker worked with Jim Smart in residence halls to secure on-campus housing for the members of the fraternity who were displaced as a result of the hurricane damage to the fraternity house.

Dean Walker and Dr. Fred Kam toured the occupied fraternity houses to check the health and well-being of the students.

Saturday, September 5–Sunday, September 6, 1992

Dean Abrahamson provided assistance to the UM-CAN program in delivering food to the Homestead/Perrine areas. In addition, Dean Abrahamson coordinated student groups to work with volunteer services in clean-up efforts.

Tuesday, September 8–Wednesday, September 9, 1992

Final preparations were made for the arrival of the students on Thursday, September 10, 1992.

Repairs to the fraternity houses continued.

Throughout the entire two weeks following Hurricane Andrew, the Office of the Dean of Students was covered by available staff members to answer the telephones and assist with the relief effort. Dean Walker was on-call via a beeper throughout the hurricane relief efforts. Work is continuing on the repairs to the fraternity houses.

DIRECTOR OF COUNSELING CENTER

FROM: Malcolm Kahn

Director, Counseling Center

In regard to the counseling center, I had previously prepared a letter for you describing the literature that we have been disseminating to help university staff and students cope with Hurricane Andrew. That packet is enclosed.

You also need to be aware of the counseling center's efforts to help the campus community in the face of Hurricane Andrew. We were very fortunate to have on our staff Dr. Pam Deroian, a psychologist who had gained expertise through her involvement in Hurricane Hugo in Charleston, South Carolina. Dr. Deroian prepared handouts for the students on campus and the residence halls staff on the day following the hurricane. She joined two psychologists from the Medical School in meeting with the residence halls staff who had performed so valiantly during the hurricane. This group of psychologists, who were able to reach the campus soon after the storm, provided immediate crisis intervention on behalf of the residence halls' staff. After that session, Dr. Deroian continued to work alone, although she was in touch by telephone with the rest of the counseling center staff, whenever possible, until we were able to reach the university.

By the week of August 31st, all five psychologists were running stress management workshops to help university employees and their families, as psychologists from the Employee Assistance Program were not then available for consultation. These workshops were conducted on a daily basis for approximately two weeks until classes began and have been held with less frequency in the past few weeks.

During orientation and since the students have returned, we have regularly run similar workshops and rap sessions for students regarding their emotional reactions to the storm. It has been somewhat surprising that students who were on campus during the hurricane have not finished dealing with their feelings about that extraordinary evening. We had thought that once classes began that they would be able to get past that event and start focusing on some of the regular frustrations and demands of being college students.

Additionally, we are finding that many of our individual clients have emotional problems that have either been directly or indirectly impacted by the events of the hurricane. Some of them do not recognize that relationship. We also have noted, though, that the group that is continuing to suffer the most is the staff and faculty. We will continue to have various types of group interventions to aid students in coping with conflicts and problems related to Hurricane Andrew throughout the semester and probably the year.

Finally, I should note that our staff intends to conduct a study to assess the emotional effects of Andrew on our students. It is our plan to seek grant money to support this research.

DIRECTOR, CAREER PLANNING AND PLACEMENT

FROM: Elina Artigas
Director, Career Planning and Placement

SUBJECT: Request from President Foote for a Chronicle of Hurricane Andrew Preparations and Impact

For others, the major impact came as a result of a loved one's loss of her home and personal property, as was the case with my mother.

Operational Impact on Career Planning and Placement

On-campus recruiters, originally scheduled to start interviews on September 28, 1992, were called and rescheduled for the week of October 5 to allow time for our students to sign up and get ready for the interviews.

Career Fair was rescheduled from October 14, 1992, to February 17, 1993, to allow time to promote the event and because of a lack of hotel accommodations in the area (some of the participating employers are from out of town).

Approximately 60 job listings, mostly from small local businesses, were closed out due to the economic hardships sustained by the businesses. Anticipating that a boom in retail will occur, and to counteract the loss of these job openings, the director made personal contact with various store managers to offer our placement services. The response was very positive, and we are well positioned to receive those listings.

Assistance to University and Community Efforts

Members of our staff were "loaned" to development and spent hours calling undergraduates, ensuring that they and their families were okay, letting them know that the university cared and was there to help.

In the community, our staff worked to help others who were in greater need by volunteering in various ways and also by taking in individuals who had lost their homes as house guests.

A Note of Appreciation

Career planning and placement's staff members have taken advantage of the various workshops sponsored by staff development. The sections on working with contractors, on working with insurance adjusters, and the session facilitated by Pam Deroian were all informative and supportive and much appreciated.

A Pledge of Support

Our staff members will continue to support the university's assistance to the needy by giving blood at next week's blood drive, assisting at the Orange Bowl, and by donating baby needs for the kickoff of United Way.

DIVISION OF STUDENT AFFAIRS/COMMUTER STUDENT AFFAIRS

DIVISION OF STUDENT AFFAIRS
COMMUTER STUDENT AFFAIRS
Hurricane Response Strategies
August 1992

After Hurricane Andrew, the Department of Commuter Student Affairs implemented a number of strategies to assist commuter students with their housing needs.

1. Information on off-campus housing options was collected from various sources, including human resources (vacant apartment list) and residence halls (computerized list of vacant apartments and roommates wanted) and made available to students in the DCSA. These lists were updated daily.
2. Housing information (private listings) posted in the DCSA prior to the hurricane was checked for availability.
3. Alternative housing options were researched including local hotels, the Biltmore Hotel, the Lane Recreation Center, the fraternity houses, and the residential colleges. Strategies were developed to address the potential emergency housing needs of commuters.
4. Extensive marketing efforts were implemented to find rooms available to rent (or offered free of charge) in private homes. A letter from Dr. Butler was sent to all UM employees with this request, announce-

ments were made in the president's crisis management meetings, and an ad was placed in the Thurs./Sun. Coral Gables Neighbors section of the *Herald*. Additionally, the local CNN station (via Dynamic Cable) addressed this housing need on their English and Spanish channels.

5. A card catalog system was implemented in the DCSA to organize room-for-rent offers. Standard information collected included contact name, address, and phone; rent amount and length of rental availability; smoking/gender/pet preferences; and access to public transportation. The DCSA also collected information from students looking for housing in order to contact them should housing become available after their visit.

6. Student visits to the DCSA were counted as accurately as possible to assess student housing needs.

7. The DCSA was publicized as the housing resource center for commuter students in Dr. Butler's letter, at the president's crisis management meetings, and in an advertisement in the campus newspaper.

8. "Guide for Renting to Students" was developed for staff and faculty who were considering housing a student, but unfamiliar with the rental process. The DCSA offered additional informal consulting to all employees regarding the rental process, and advertised this service in Dr. Butler's letter, and in the president's crisis management meetings.

DIRECTOR, STUDENT HEALTH SERVICE

FROM: Frederick A. Kam, Jr., M.D.
             Director, Student Health Service

SUBJECT: Hurricane Andrew

Saturday, August 22

Hurricane Watch
8:30 A.M.–12:00 Noon—International Orientation
3:00 P.M.–5:00 P.M.—Black Student Orientation
Gilbert Arias and I reviewed the university's policy on hurricane preparedness and discussed our own plan of action including staffing, supplies and the health center's role in the event of a hurricane.
9:00 P.M.—Dr. Kam received a call at home to attend a meeting at 9:00 A.M. with committee.
9:10 P.M.—Gilbert Arias was called to activate our plan of staffing.

Sunday, August 23

10:00 A.M.—Hurricane Warning
Several members of the staff came in to assist with preparing the building.

The disaster kits were personally checked prior to their distribution to the residential colleges by physical plant.

The generators and water pump were verified to be in good working condition. Exam and treatment rooms were prepared and fully stocked with supplies from warehouse.

We obtained a radio transmitter from public safety.

2:00 P.M.—Dr. Kam met with the president and others to discuss plans.

Evening—Dr. Kam and wife, Charlene, Elizabeth Astorga and family, James Spall and friend, Sandra Thomas and husband, Gilbert Arias, and Dr. Gardner and family spent the night at the Health Center to secure the building and be available for students throughout and after the hurricane.

Power was lost for only a few hours.

Monday, August 24

10:00 A.M.—Hurricane shutters were lifted and the health center opened its doors.

Besides uprooted trees, the health center did not sustain any damage as a result of the hurricane.

The health center began to see students, parents, faculty, staff, and hurricane clean-up crews with minor bruises, viral infections, and stress-related disorders.

By noon on Monday, all health center staff were accounted for and were in fairly good condition.

Dr. Kam began calling hospitals and the School of Medicine asking for medical supplies in order to be able to perform certain medical procedures in house, such as suturing, and not to have to send patients to already crowded emergency rooms. Several hospitals, including Health South Doctors' and University Departments, sent several supplies.

The pharmacy ordered extra emergency supplies such as tetanus shots and pediatric medications.

The health center water well became the major provider of water for the entire university including the residential colleges. Every couple of hours there was someone operating the pump to the water well to fill 20–25 five gallon jugs at one time.

Dr. Kam gave instructions on how to treat the water with bleach to make it drinkable.

Dr. Kam participated daily in many meetings to help coordinate recovery efforts in the Coral Gables Campus.

The health center remained open for 24 hours a day for the week following the hurricane.

Although the university was closed for business, the health center was operating with almost a full staff every day for that week following the hurricane, including Saturday and Sunday. Our hours of operation were 9:00 A.M.–5:00 P.M. and after 5:00 P.M. and throughout the night we were accessible by telephone and in person, if necessary. Two or more staff members spent the night each night. Dr. Kam and wife, Charlene, remained in the health center for six nights and seven days before returning home.

DIRECTOR, CAMPUS SPORTS AND RECREATION

FROM: Norman C. Parsons, Jr.
             Director, Campus Sports and Recreation

SUBJECT: Hurricane Andrew

Per President Foote's request please find below a brief chronological summary of Campus Sports and Recreation Department's involvement with Hurricane Andrew.

Friday, August 21–Sunday, August 23

Departmental preparation for the anticipated arrival of the hurricane. Securing of all outdoor facilities to include sailing club boats and trailers, soccer goals, removal of tennis court wind screens, wrapping of the tennis nets, preparation of sandbags for Lane Recreation Center, and overall evaluation of campus sports' facilities to minimize damage.

Tuesday, August 25

The Lane Recreation Center gymnasium underwent a transformation into a "residential college" for a variety of workers who were in town serving both the University of Miami and the local community in hurricane relief. Dr. Redick coordinated the move of 250 mattresses from residence halls' storage into the Lane Center gymnasium. Linen and towels were provided to the workers with campus sports personnel doing the laundry as well as cleaning the gymnasium each day. An average of 95 individuals resided in the Lane Center gymnasium through the two weeks the facility was utilized by the workers.

Wednesday, August 26

The Lane Center opened with a skeleton staff between noon and 5:00 P.M. and the hours were continued until normal operation began approximately 10 days later.

Thursday, August 27

CSR delivered sand volleyball kits, frisbees, footballs, and basketballs to each of the residential colleges and the apartment area for their use for the next two weeks. The department assisted in organizing events as requested by the RCs.

The department gathered used sports equipment and donated it to the United Way/Red Cross of Homestead. The equipment was to be used for children's programs.

All departmental facilities were repaired, as necessary, in time for opening on September 10th. Outdoor lights at the basketball courts, tennis courts, and fields have not been replaced and/or repaired to 100 percent but are functioning for the university community.

All insurance claims were submitted to the risk manager by the requested date. Overall cost to campus sports facilities is minimal. The largest loss was suffered by the sailing club with approximately $5,000 damage to two boats.

VICE PROVOST AND DEAN OF ENROLLMENTS

FROM: Deborah Triol Perry
         Vice Provost and Dean of Enrollments

RE: Hurricane Andrew Chronicle

I. A Chronicle of the Division of Enrollments Activities

Saturday, August 22

Enrollments staff, in midst of fall registration and orientation, assumed that normal orientation schedule would be followed.

Discussion and rumors abound that Hurricane Andrew will hit farther north.

Sunday, August 23

9:00 A.M.: Registration arena opens for registration (as scheduled). Members of the enrollments staff who were not prepared for the hurricane were visibly worried, some panic-stricken; nevertheless, they felt bound to fulfill their obligations to the university.

1:00 P.M.: Enrollments staff along with . . . meet in the Rathskeller to discuss hurricane preparedness and modifications in the orientation schedule.

2:00–4:00 P.M.: Efforts made to secure enrollments offices and registration areas: computers and other valuables moved away from windows; files in Admissions covered; phone answering messages changed; telephone "calling trees" developed.

By 3:00 P.M., most staff had gone home; managers remained until 4:30 P.M. to finish hurricane preparations.

Monday, August 24

Communication systems lost.

Tuesday, August 25

10:00 A.M.: Meeting in Law School auditorium; first expanded LRPC meeting held. Plans were discussed and made to send students home and to offer a travel refund. Discussion to make efforts to contact staff.

Afternoon: Staff called . . . Sign-up sheet placed on the outside of the Ashe Building for students and staff to provide enrollments with their location. Financial assistance staff attempts to locate all staff.

Evening: Admissions officers staff the 800 telephone number; Rob Pritchard assists in the residence halls by answering phones.

Throughout the week, Rizzi, Mullin, Pritchard, and Poole assist in the residence halls by giving relief to overworked residence halls staff.

Decision made to meet daily for updates, discussions, and decisions.

Wednesday, August 26

9:00 A.M.: Provost initiates and holds a pre-LRPC meeting with enroll-ments, residence halls, health center, and student affairs staff, as well as residential masters and associate masters. Discussion of student phone cam-paign to reach all students.

10:00 A.M.: LRPC meeting. Discussion of when to reopen the university. Plans made to send students home with a refund travel policy in place.

Richard Ritzman assesses damage to financial aid operation. Ana Villeverde and family take supplies to families in need who work in Office of Financial Assistance Services.

Thursday–Sunday, August 27–30

9:00 A.M.: Daily meetings with the provost and his staff (Perry, Ullmann, Masterson), David Lieberman, and admissions, residence halls, student affairs, and health center staffs prior to LRPC meetings. On Thursday, discussion of student phone campaign.

Thursday: Monica Morris (receptionist in enrollment services) attempts to reach all staff in Office of Enrollment Services.

Monday, August 31

Student phone campaign begins and continues through September 6. Difficulties encountered in getting personnel to assist. Professors in the School of Business Administration, enrollments staff, and residence halls staff are especially helpful in making calls. Mary Sapp and Jerry Nichols provided an updated listing of students. Phoning priority: first, new freshmen, then new transfers, then non-Dade students, and finally, Dade students.

(Dade County is where UM is located—Author's note)

Enrollment staff (as many as can) return to work; about 70 percent of staff return. Attempts made to assist staff affected by the hurricane.

Federal officials arrive to offer assistance. On Monday, Tuesday, and Wednesday, they are fully operational, working with 7 PC's (6 with modems), 12 phone lines (6 for computers, 6 for calls); they are trained in financial aid matters; copy, fax, and long distance phone services provided by offices in the Enrollments division. Housing provided by residence halls.

Wednesday, Thursday, September 2–3

Office of Financial Assistance Services works on projection analysis of how financial assistance needs to students would change due to the hurricane. Paul Orehovec meets with Foote and Glaser to update them on financial assistance information.

Friday, September 4

University officials meet with Secretary of Education Alexander. The secretary visits with financial assistance and registration staff in financial arena.

Monday, September 7: Labor Day (UM closed)

Tuesday, September 8

Plans made for orientation and registration.

Thursday September 10

Orientation begins, following initial schedule with some slight modifications (e.g., the President's Parents reception is held at 6:15 P.M. to accommodate city curfew).

Friday, September 11

President's Freshmen Convocation held in the Lane Center as scheduled. The center was filled.

II. What We Have Learned

1. In retrospect, it's clear that we cannot underestimate the potential damage and havoc wreaked of any hurricane, especially one such as Andrew. Had the hurricane hit the Coral Gables campus directly, the damage would have been far more extensive, and we might be facing the potential loss of important data and records.

2. It's also clear how much the university—if one can speak of the university in the abstract—cares for its employees. Its efforts to call all staff, counsel employees, and express personal concern were all very gratifying to those affected by the hurricane. The outpouring of university support and help has been truly remarkable.

III. What We Need to Do to Prepare for Another Hurricane

1. Develop a hurricane emergency contingency communication strategy from the top on down. The division of enrollments will compile an internal phone and address directory (to be kept confidential) and create telephone pyramids to be able to communicate quickly with all staff. To facilitate communication, geographical centers arranged according to the residence of staff will be created and key staff in those areas will be provided with cellular phones or walkie-talkies.

2. Back up all important computer files.

3. Generate a hard copy master list of all students so as to ensure communication with those students should our computer systems fail.

4. Secure all vital information in a "hurricane proof" vault system.

5. Request that hurricane shutters be provided for the Ashe Building.

6. Divide UM employees into their respective zip codes and office, and by zip code create "Team A," "Team B," "Team C," etc. Each team will have a "captain" or "captains" who, in the case that a divisional officer is affected by the hurricane and cannot fulfill his or her responsibilities, will be deputized to act on behalf of that officer.

7. Develop a detailed contingency plan for evacuating students. Had the university been in session and an evacuation order been given, where would those students have gone? Perhaps pre-reserved contracts should be made with transportation and housing facilities elsewhere in the state of Florida (e.g., high school gymnasium in Orlando).

EXECUTIVE VICE PRESIDENT AND PROVOST

FROM: Luis Glaser
               Executive Vice President and Provost

SUBJECT: Hurricane Andrew

You have asked all of us to comment on our experiences with Hurricane Andrew and to present something of a chronology. In my own case, other than the written record that has been kept by others, I neither kept a diary nor does my mind seem to have sorted out the time frame of the events in a very precise way. I will, therefore, divide them into two components: one is a set of personal reactions; second is to me a set of important milestones in the events that happened.

Personal Reactions

The major reaction that I have to the whole hurricane episode is an extraordinary positive feeling about people. With perhaps minor exception, everyone in the system, starting with the president, rose to the occasion in an extraordinary way. The commitment to the university, sometimes at the expense of a great deal of family and personal inconvenience/risk, is something that I will always remember and treasure. It provides a totally different assessment of many people and their priorities than one could have gotten in other ways. There is a silver lining in tragedies, and certainly that is the most striking event here.

It is perhaps sad that, with normalcy, some of the wonderful spirit of working together for a single cause is rapidly evaporating into many of the parochial and bickering attitudes that have always been here. But human nature is what it has always been, and we will not be able to change it.

The Hurricane Events

1. Preparedness. We were remarkably well prepared and whether we would have been able to do well had we been closer to the eye of the storm, we do not know, but overall, we should congratulate all involved in their ability to be ready. It is very difficult to get people focused on getting prepared for rare events, and certainly we were ready.

2. What flaws did we detect? One is communication. Our communications are not as secure and fool-proof as they might be. I have already asked Lew Temares to harden our facilities, and I am sure he will come

up with appropriate guidelines. This is extremely important. An ability to communicate in the upper echelons of the university is very important.

3. The Medical School was saved from extraordinary problems by the quick thinking of Bob Rubin, who deployed a lot of people, God knows from where, to clear the construction sites that our contractors had not dealt with adequately. It is essential that we pursue this issue with our contractors. . . .

After the Hurricane

We did many things extremely well. The presence of senior management at all times, even though I think we contributed less to the outcome than we might imagine, helped significantly stabilize and calm the system. Whatever else happens in a future disaster, that presence is absolutely required.

We were overly optimistic when we first arrived on campus, in spite of the evident disaster, on how long it would take us to go back; and if we created any confusion, it was in our notion that power and other things could be restored rapidly. Everyone else in the whole city was just as confused, but we need to remember that for the future.

Of the events in the first few days, we collectively did so many things right. Housing and feeding everyone as best as we could was clearly the right thing to do, and sending the students home at some cost was absolutely essential. Even if we could have maintained them on campus, it is not clear that they would have had anything to do, and we could have had a very discouraged and unhappy group of people on campus. The investment in travel funds was clearly the best thing that we could have done. Our deal with the airlines was both misunderstood as well as mishandled by them and created more grief than good.

Rapid communication with students was a clear winner. The letter that went out under my signature on the 27th of August, just three days after the turmoil, was a clear success and restored confidence. It highlights the importance of successful communication in the system. Communicating, and communicating in a truthful, but clear way is obviously very important; it gave us a great deal of good will and restored the confidence of the students and their parents in us.

Searching for our employees was successful. While in many ways finding them did not help them, the fact that we cared came through loud and clear and also allowed many of those who were lucky enough to be relatively unscathed to participate in an endeavor that helped their colleagues. It was a very positive event.

Our housing search operation, from a distance, looks like a gesture of goodwill that may not have generated as much relief as we might have hoped for. Most people had to and did find housing on their own, but to make the gesture was indeed important.

In my estimation, one of the flaws in the system that has come out is that, in the future, we should be prepared in some way to be able to provide money for people who may not be in a position to either write a check, go to an ATM, etc., because they have a fundamental cash-flow problem. There must be a way in which we can do this in an orderly manner, not necessarily on an ad-hoc basis. We were flexible in the cases that came to the attention of upper management, but I wish we had a better system to take care of it.

There may be a lesson in the housing area that I would like to see explored. I was totally convinced that we were going to see an enormous problem in housing students off-campus. While there were problems, they were not overwhelming.

In terms of simple, raw facility issues, I would like to see us have the following:

1. Better facilities for water. Water is an essential component of how we function and the ability to provide drinkable water for a large population is essential.

2. We need to develop a plan for emergency power to manage food, the health center, and the basic communication network of adequate power. Anything else, like our full maintenance of computers, probably is so expensive as to be impossible. An adequate analysis of this needs to be carried out. My impression is that the Medical School is far better equipped in this arena than is Coral Gables, for obvious reasons, but the system was not fully tested by these last events. An assessment there, as well as at the Marine School, is clearly needed.

3. In terms of security, it is clear that our department of public safety was stretched to its limits. Our arrangement with Coral Gables needs to be revisited because the commandeering of our police department by Coral Gables brought us close to the breaking point.

Finally, I would like to strongly recommend that once a year we go through a drill, which includes everyone who would have some responsibility in a future disaster, and devote half a day to make sure that all understand where they are and that all the systems are properly in place. We cannot prepare for everything, but a certain level of awareness is certainly important.

Additional Comments

Dr. Glaser noted that the emergency brought out the inventive abilities of the university community. Dr. Glaser's position was to urge people to go ahead and do what they chose providing it was not outrageous. Employees responded by doing the right things. The campus created a great deal of autonomy for staff. With that autonomy they appeared to work more effectively.

Leadership found it was important to be on campus at all times.

The physical plant people were the heroes because they had the campus cleared in three weeks, and also housed and fed 200 people in the basketball arena.

The president sensed almost immediately that people needed something to physically hold; the newsletter that was distributed to everyone appeared important for people not only to read but to hold.

At the time of this interview, Dr. Glaser described the campus as still not whole. Most are sensitive to the tension of those who as yet are not settled. People are still displaced and that means that their travel to work may take several hours while they are trying to resettle themselves.

INTERIM DEAN OF GRADUATE SCHOOL

FROM: Jo Anne K. Hecker
               Interim Dean, Graduate School

SUBJECT: Hurricane Chronicle

The Graduate School
Chronicle of Hurricane Andrew
8/24/92 - 9/4/92

August 31st–September 4th, Monday–Friday

Graduate school staff all present and accounted for. Two of the five members had extensive home damage; one member had light car and home damage. Two others experienced little damage, except loss of power and the inconvenient water ban. Some brought containers and filled them with water from the tank truck parked near Eaton Residence Hall. All had difficulty traveling to and from the university because of debris-laden streets and non-working traffic signals. Graduate assistants and work study students did not appear all week.

Complete lists of all new and continuing graduate students' names and phone numbers were hand carried to all main campus offices—and sent by messengers to the RSMAS and medical campuses with the following memo:

The provost has asked that all our current and new graduate students be contacted by phone. I'm enclosing a list of names and phone numbers for your area. If you do not have sufficient staff to make these calls, please contact Carrie Edmondson, phone 284-2318, who is coordinating a group of volunteers. She can assign helpers to assist you.

We need to tell graduate students:

- Registration will be September 10th and 11th, and classes will begin September 14th. The semester will end December 18th as formerly scheduled. Prior to registration, students should see their advisors and obtain a signed course request form.
- Delta and several other airlines are waiving the 14-day advance purchase requirement for returning students.
- Emergency loans are available for students who have suffered losses in the local area. They can be applied for in 158 Ashe Building.
- Local students may need to have their Financial Aid package reassessed. Contact the Student Financial Aid Office, phone 284-5212 or 284-4908.
- The Graduate Student Association orientation and the new teaching assistant orientation have been postponed. Students should contact their departmental advisors or the main graduate school, 284-4154, if they have questions.
- The University Health Center and Pharmacy are open each weekday, 8:30–5:00, and will treat all students who need health care.
- Above all, assure students that the campus and its environs are safe. Power is on, and all facilities are operating. Everyone is looking forward to welcoming them to a full year of academic success.

DEAN, COLLEGE OF ENGINEERING

FROM: Martin Becker
        Dean, College of Engineering

RE: Hurricane Chronicle

After the Storm

An administrator of the dean's office living close to the university, came into the building in the early evening of Monday, the 24th, 1992, to check out potential storm damages. The building was cool, the electricity was working, and no apparent damages were noted in the dean's office area. Recorded messages on the office answering machine from concerned parents were returned, and a new message was entered reflecting the 1-800 number for university information. As additional faculty and staff came in to inspect damages, all employees who were reachable were called to determine their status. Hurricane relief information, as received, was immediately placed on the main hallway bulletin boards.

The university was closed for the week of August 24 through August 28, 1992, due to hurricane damages county-wide. Officially opening on August 31, 1992, most staff and faculty returned. Telephone calls were made to all students who were reachable assuring them and their parents that the university would be open September 10, 1992, and informing them of the new registration dates and addressing, where possible, any hurricane-related problems they were experiencing. As of September 24th, a total of 1141.5 hours of administrative leave for staff alone was granted for the College of Engineering.

Although staff and faculty have been availing themselves of flexible work time to deal with personal problems associated with the hurricane, we are still experiencing higher than usual personnel being ill with stress-related illnesses.

SCHOOL OF MEDICINE

SUBJECT: Hurricane Andrew's Effect on the School of Medicine

Per your request, following is a chronology and assessment of the School of Medicine's preparations and activities related to Hurricane Andrew. Though the school performed well—and there were many heroes—we have learned a great deal to help prepare us for the next "big one."

Hurricane Preparations

We started talking about the possibility of Andrew's arrival as early as our August 18th cabinet meeting. Each area was advised to review hurricane preparedness plans and to keep a close watch on the progress of the storm.

As late as Friday, facilities and support departments met, but admittedly did not feel that the hurricane was a serious threat. However, some vulnerable areas such as the Sylvester Comprehensive Cancer Center and the DRI construction site were evaluated. By Friday night, work began to secure those areas. On Saturday, major debris on the campus was removed or secured. By 10:00 P.M. before the storm, 90 security and physical plant personnel and their families were on campus to support facilities.

Other departments across campus followed university procedures in preparing for the storm in securing offices and equipment.

At UMHC/Sylvester, waterproof locks were put into place, sandbags were filled and put on standby, all technical equipment was "brought down" for technology and information safety, and plans were made to man the building throughout the storm.

At Jackson Memorial Hospital, the chiefs of service were called in to ensure proper emergency staffing levels and adequate supplies. OB patients, especially those with complications, were called into the hospital. Third and fourth year medical students were called in to assist.

On South Campus, with the director of veterinary resources in France at a meeting on Friday before the storm, preparation was difficult. Greg Parmeter, a manager in the division, implemented the hurricane preparedness plan for securing animal facilities on three of the four campuses on Saturday. Hundreds of animals from outlying facilities were relocated to safe caging in the center of the medical campus. Special precautions were taken to provide emergency ventilation for animals in case of power failure (which did occur), saving thousands of lives. Cages for the animals on South Campus were secured.

The Day of the Storm

There were many heroes who risked their lives to secure broken doors and restore emergency power to critical areas during the storm. On Monday morning, security and physical plant personnel began to assess the damage on the Medical Campus, most of which was on roofs. In less than four weeks after the storm, this damage was repaired.

The damage to South Campus was extensive, including $1.2 million of caging. Dr. Joe Wagner, director of veterinary resources, returned from France approximately 10 hours after the storm and resumed control of the effort to secure the cages, to keep other species alive in the absence of air conditioning, and to recapture 363 escaped monkeys raised for an NIH-funded breeding project. An erroneous report that the monkeys had AIDS led local citizens to shoot 12 monkeys. Adding to the confusion was the release of approximately 1,500–1,800 monkeys, including baboons, from the Mannheimer Foundation in Florida City, Monkey Jungle, and several breeders. In the media, the University of Miami was initially being blamed for all of it. After intense work with the media to quell the rumors, a "monkey control hot line" was set up to help people deal with the monkeys and give us information about where to capture them. As of this date, 23 of our monkeys remain unaccounted for.

Jackson Memorial Hospital was filled to capacity, but responded well during the storm and its aftermath. Because the hospital was prepared for a mass casualty disaster, the relatively moderate level of admissions following the storm did not adversely affect operations.

The Aftermath

Week One.   Of course, work hours and class time were suspended the first week for all but a few essential employees who provided information and support to employees and students in need, essential medical personnel, physical plant and security personnel, and others assessing damage and restoring their work areas to normal.

UMHC/Sylvester was open to receive patients on Tuesday and full service was up on Thursday.

The decision was made to provide medical care at UMHC and Daystar for university employees for the rest of August and September, regardless of which insurance plan employees had. For the first week, Daystar was open 24 hours a day.

When we learned that there was critical need for drinking water and toilet facilities at the Coral Gables campus, 10 medical physical plant personnel scoured the campus to find and deliver over 100-five gallon plastic jugs to Coral Gables. Medical facilities planning also found 50 portable toilets and had them delivered to the Coral Gables campus.

On the day of the storm and during the following weeks, six faculty members and approximately a core of 20 medical students and residents volunteered in approximately six clinics in under served areas in South Dade, mostly in the migrant labor camps and impoverished areas where several faculty or students had begun outreach efforts well before the storm hit. Dr. Pedro Jose Greer, associate dean for homeless health care and medical director of the Camillus Health Concern, coordinated the medical school's effort along with Dr. Art Fournier, Dr. Marc Edelstein, Dr. Walter Lambert, and Dr. Dan Moran. Dr. Gwen Wurm, assistant professor of clinical pediatrics, assumed her role as the regional health services coordinator for the Florida Department of Health and Rehabilitative Services.

The school's community health initiatives in South Dade created a lot of media interest, and a free-lance media relations specialist was hired to coordinate news coverage of the School of Medicine's and School of Nursing's clinics in South Dade. The result to date has been more than 45 local, regional, and national placements.

Weeks Two, Three, and Beyond.   Internal communication was extremely important the first two weeks, during which two school-wide meetings with departments were held. Systems were set up for needs assessment, backed by resource distribution systems. UMHC set up a buddy system, matching employees in the North who could get resources with those in the South who could not, which became a model for other departments in the school. Each employee was surveyed to determine assistance needs and the compilation of these surveys were used to develop needed on-site resources and external referral sources. More than six hundred employees volunteered as resource provider buddies. UMHC/Sylvester set up a dry-goods trading post and a refrigerator truck for perishables and ice. A newsletter—detailing a variety of policies, procedures, resource availability, and general information—was produced four times over three weeks and distributed to each employee.

Classes began on Monday of week two, just one week after Andrew hit. First and second year students lost a week, but with the help of instructors willing to teach out of phase, we were able to present the same material that would have been presented, though in a truncated form. Because of the hurricane, sophomores were given an extra week to study for medical boards. Third and fourth year students lost no time.

There were no other changes in regular education programs, but an issue came up about the supervision of students working in South Dade clinics. The Community Clinical Experience Program, AHEC, Camillus are working on a program to get students involved, but we are working on getting that integrated into curriculum with some clear educational goals and to ensure proper supervision.

When the university officially opened the week after the storm, the school's clinics were nearly empty. During the last week of August and first three weeks of September, patients canceled appointments or simply did not show up, and referrals dropped significantly. In some cases, physicians, who were taking care of hurricane damage to their homes, were not able to report to work. The net effect on PIP revenues was significant: at least $4 million. To shore up the hemorrhage of patients and dollars, a public service announcement and advertising campaign was developed and implemented. In addition, letters, advising patients that the school was open for business, were mailed to each patient (67,000) who had been treated at UM for the past six months.

As of this date, some services have returned to near normal volume. But historically after such a disaster, people tend to delay their health care for anything other than major problems. After Hurricane Hugo, it took the University of South Carolina medical school's primary departments at least six months to return to their pre-hurricane patient load.

A number of business-related procedures had to be developed and implemented, including the timely opening of the University Credit Union (medical campus), emergency cash availability, revision of patient receivables (no payments due until November), employee leave issues, as well as various accounting and bookkeeping procedures. Extensive work began with FEMA and other government agencies to determine special grants and reimbursement of expenses.

The Office of Grants and Contracts worked with principal investigators and government agencies to obtain application deadline extensions as well as information about special reimbursements of costs of interrupted research due to the hurricane.

To aid in the South Dade relief efforts, a mobile clinic, donated by the Children's Health Fund in New York, helped our pediatricians fulfill their mission. The project to obtain the van began several months ago but was hastened when the hurricane struck. When the South Dade situation stabilizes, the van will go to Liberty City, Overtown, and other inner-city locations.

The Department of Psychiatry has established a network of training for community mental health workers, teachers, and other care-givers to assist them in dealing with post-traumatic stress disorder. The department also developed a flier to assist university personnel in dealing with the problem.

To date, the net effect of Hurricane Andrew on the school's revenues is $6 million. The toll in terms of employees who were seriously affected by the storm is 403.

There have been many heroes, who saved human and animal life as well as significant amounts of school property:

Recommendations

1. The School of Medicine should have its own hurricane plan. The university's and hospital's plans do not specifically address the medical school's unique situation. Work is beginning on using what we've learned to develop a medical school hurricane plan.
   a. An effective means of communicating with clinical faculty must be developed, as their role during a disaster is quite different from other faculty.
   b. An effective means of communicating with patients is being established. Systems are being developed to begin direct communications with affected patients within a week following the storm.
2. From Jackson's standpoint, and possibly the school's:
   a. Improve communications between high level medical staff and hospital administration during the emergency. The importance of this is to ensure that the hospital itself has medical input regarding concerns about its water supply, air conditioning, possible in-

creased rates of infection, the need to cancel elective admissions, surgery, etc.

b. The need for the hospital to provide leadership and support for outreach programs and the delivery of health care to areas that might be devastated by another natural disaster, such as what occurred in South Dade.

c. Medical staff needs to establish guidelines to determine manpower needs, performance, and decision making.

SCHOOL OF MEDICINE FACILITIES AND SUPPORT SERVICES

PREPARATION FOR ANDREW: SCHOOL OF MEDICINE FACILITIES AND SUPPORT SERVICES

The facilities departments and support service groups of the school met Friday afternoon before the storm to review and implement our hurricane preparedness plans. In all honesty, we did not feel that Andrew was a serious threat at that time. In the process of evaluation, we did identify specific activities that would be required to protect the new Sylvester Cancer Clinic which had sustained significant water damage recently due to design errors. In addition, we identified the . . . construction site as a location of serious concern due to the large amount of construction material that lay about on the ground and as an integral part of the scaffolding.

By Friday night, when it was apparent that Andrew might be a serious threat, a plan was developed to police the DRI site and sandbag Sylvester. By Saturday morning, Sylvester was prepared with steel barriers on the doors and 500 sandbags were set in place along with the placing of numerous pumps and water receptacles in anticipation of major water influx. The whole medical campus was then prepared for high winds by removing debris, tying down loose equipment on roofs, and generally securing the entire structure of our buildings.

Most physical plant and security staff were then told to go home to prepare their personal homes and to return by 10:00 P.M. Meanwhile, we attempted to get the contractor to police their . . . construction site. Very little effort was made on behalf of the contractor; thus, by 9:00 P.M., physical plant brought roughly 20 men to the . . . site and began the process of securing the site. Most security personnel also arrived and began to settle in with many of their families. Thus, when the winds began we had approximately 90 men available to support the facilities.

Immediately after the storm Monday morning, security and physical plant personnel began to quantitate and document the damage. When we learned that there was a critical lack of drinkable water at the Coral Gables Campus and a critical need for toilet facilities there as well, Medical Physical Plant took 10 men and scoured the medical campus for bottled water finding and delivering over 100 5-gallon plastic jugs to the Coral Gables Physical Plant division. Medical Facilities Planning then found 50 portable toilets and had them delivered to Coral Gables.

South Campus

The situation at South Campus was much more serious, and we had far less support people to deal with the situation. The entire DVM group of veterinarians were at a meeting in France when the danger became apparent late Friday night. An administrator, Mr. Greg Parmeter, who along with his pregnant wife physically lived at South Campus, was forced to assume direction of the preparation process for the animals at all sites of the university, which included all four campuses. He accomplished amazing things with a small group of dedicated animal care workers. Hundreds of animals were relocated to safe caging in the center of the medical campus. Special precautions were made to provide emergency ventilation for the animals since we expected to lose power and AC. We did lose AC, and this action saved the lives of thousands of animals.

Greg then moved to South Campus and spent the rest of Saturday preparing this campus plus the Perrine site that we manage. He sent his wife to Miami Children's Hospital, and he moved into the Rosenstiel building. Monday, after the storm had passed, he returned to South Campus to find his home gone entirely. His wife was unreachable, and he devoted the next two days attempting to recover the monkeys that had been released, having to deal with Coast Guard personnel who had heard an inaccurate report that the monkeys had AIDS. Many monkeys were shot during this period. Our director of animal care, Joe Wagner, flew back from France and immediately took over control of the effort to secure both the monkeys and keep other species alive in the absence of air conditioning. Physical plant provided portable AC and much technical help in repairing the facilities. At this writing, all but a few monkeys are back in "custody" and the damage to South Campus is small and covered by insurance.

DEAN, LAW SCHOOL

FROM: Mary Doyle
             Dean, Law School

DATE: September 18, 1992

SUBJECT: Hurricane Response

Reconstructing and recounting our hurricane response now might make it appear that we knew what we were doing, when in fact we were making it up as we went along. Our efforts were successful, I think, because we acted as quickly as we could on each problem as it emerged, and because our people, administrators, students, and a couple of faculty, worked really well as a team, with everyone taking responsibility.

1. The First Three Days

Several administrators were able to leave their homes and get to the law school on the day after the storm; they formed the nucleus of the response team. We sought news of our colleagues by word of mouth, and by telephone. The student leadership and later our alumni office did the same.

We found it very comforting, and useful, to gather everyone who happened to be at the school (staff and faculty and student leaders) together in our one air conditioned meeting room every morning at 9. This meeting proved a good source of information about our people who had not yet reported in.

The university crisis meeting, held at the law school at 10 A.M., was crucial for us. There we received essential information (like the payroll plans) to carry back to our people. Issues were raised in those meetings that we had not thought of, so our nucleus group would assemble immediately afterward to figure out how to address those issues and how to get the information we received out to our community.

I had to make a fast decision on whether and for how long to postpone the start of school. I reached my decision after listening to a discussion of the question in the 9 A.M. gathering. The consensus was that we had to delay two weeks to give our people who had been devastated time to get control of their crises.

2. The Next Week

When most of our employees had been accounted for, we turned to the task of reaching out to our 425 entering students, who had been scheduled for orientation activities on the day the storm struck. Almost half of them had moved to Miami to start school. We were worried about the students' safety and concerned about whether a significant number would cancel their plans to enroll. Our student leadership was great. At our request, they organized a team to call every first-year student during the weekend after the storm. The message communicated was that the school was fine and we would be ready to go on September 14th. We also invited the first years to an open house on the law school campus on September 1. This event was organized to help entering students begin to feel a part of the law school community, despite the disruption. We used radio announcements to spread the invitation, and 250 students showed up. We had informal discussion groups for students and faculty scheduled throughout the day, and offered library tours, meetings with law school administrators, and pizza for lunch. The open house was very successful and made us all hopeful that normal life could be restored.

I wrote a letter that was mailed to every law student, and we had every secretary working one afternoon to telephone every second- and third-year student, conveying the same message that went to entering students.

The outreach to students worked. On September 14th, the entire student body, plus a few unexpected first years, were in attendance.

We also made an effort to reach out to our staff. Through radio announcements, we asked all staff who could do so to report for work on Monday, August 31st. We welcomed them that morning with hot coffee and pastries and a big group get-together in one of the classrooms. I greeted them, and we brought them up to date on the news. Then we encouraged them to spend time together, hearing each other's stories. They were delighted to be reunited.

3. (Preliminary) Conclusions

Reaching out for information and providing offers of help to people was the key for us. These efforts have resulted in the return of students and staff to a renewed sense of community. Now we are working on ways to make it last.

DIRECTOR OF LIBRARIES

FROM: Frank Rodgers
      Director of Libraries

SUBJECT: Impact of Andrew on the Library

As soon as an official hurricane warning was issued, steps were taken to make sure that the Richter Library Building was adequately prepared. Physical plant also covered the ranges of books nearest to the stack tower windows with plastic, as protection in the event that any stack windows were broken. Scheduled library opening hours for Sunday afternoon and evening were canceled.

The first floor group study room ("The Zoo") was made available as overnight accommodation for families of university workers on night shift duty.

In the days following the storm, our efforts were concentrated on making contact with every library staff member and with retirees, and offering help to those in need. Five staff members were homeless; four more had very severe damage. Many staff members were involved in making calls or tracking down their colleagues. My secretary, Gladys Blanco, was the nerve center for this operation, making many calls herself, and coordinating information from others. Overall, the morale of those who suffered serious losses was excellent.

IN RICHTER LIBRARY WITH ANDREW BY RONALD NAYLOR

After boarding up my house I moved my family—wife Sally, 14-year-old son Kenneth, and 10-year-old Doberman Duchess—to the Richter Library at 6:00 in the evening. We settled in my office on the second floor. The campus was peaceful. John, Jr., and his crew were putting up the aluminum siding to close off the breezeway. Seven window shutters were stuck so they couldn't be lowered, and he banged them into place.

I opened the group study room on the first floor to provide shelter for families of Ogden employees working on campus. At least 50 people, including some students, used it. I checked the windows in the stack tower and found a few that were not properly fastened. Two mechanics responded to my call to physical plant and the windows were bolted in.

At midnight, we settled down to sleep on the floor. We were wakened at 3:30 A.M. by the noise of gravel and debris hitting the metal shutters. Sounded like a machine gun. A section of window shutter came loose and began banging against the frame. It finally tore off and blew away. We moved into a corridor area with no windows. By this time the power was off, and we were using flashlights. The emergency generator provided a few lights in the building.

The worst water penetration was from the skylight domes. Water cascaded down the central staircase and puddled on the second floor before descending to the first. The floor was swimming but books were dry. The Ogden cleanup crew mopped valiantly. We went back to sleep at 5:30 A.M. At 7:00 A.M., I awoke and checked the building from the ninth floor down. An alarm was signaling that a door to the emergency stairs was open. The drop in air pressure had caused the doors on the 9th, 7th, and 6th floors to burst open despite being securely locked. One was torn off its hinges. But no water came in.

SCHOOL OF MUSIC

ANDREW CHRONICLE
SCHOOL OF MUSIC

Preparations

Requested that the sump pump be tested and fully operational.

A large pump was brought to Gusman to pump out water in case the lower level flooded.

In the lower level (below ground) of Gusman Hall, the bottom two drawers of desks and filing cabinets were placed on top of desks and tables in the event of flooding. The harpsichords were moved from the warm-up area downstairs to the elevator and raised to the stage floor level. Important software was moved to safety.

All electrical equipment was unplugged.

Faculty and staff were advised to move computers, keyboards and other musical instruments away from windows, to unplug electrical equipment, and to clear desks.

Response

As faculty and staff were reached or as they called in, information concerning the resources the university was making available to its employees was shared, as was information about the state of the university, the well-being of colleagues, and the revised academic calendar. A revised orientation/advising schedule with a cover letter from the dean was mailed to all faculty and staff. Numerous calls were received from students and/or their parents during the early period following the storm.

Since the Music Complex lost power, employees were advised not to return to work until notified by the dean's office to do so.

The Foster Practice Building did not reopen for students until the school's security guards were able to resume their normal work schedule.

With the return of faculty and staff, a closer damage assessment was made and claim reports were submitted to risk management.

All faculty and staff for whom it was not a hardship were asked to be in their offices for academic advising and other matters on Saturday and Sunday before the beginning of classes on Monday, September 14th.

A called meeting of department chairs was held on the first day of classes, and a full meeting of faculty and staff was held at the end of that week to report on the state of the school and the university and to discuss any concerns related to the revised academic calendar.

VICE PRESIDENT FOR UNIVERSITY ADVANCEMENT

FROM: Roy J. Nirschel, Jr.
        Vice President for University Advancement

DATE: October 13, 1992

Development

Development Communication is housed on the fifth floor of the Plumer Building. The cost of leasing space in both buildings is $7,406.25 per month.

The damage to the Ponce Building resulted in the loss of time, space, and equipment. In the immediate aftermath of the storm, the development department moved into the Alumni House. For the first two weeks after the storm, development and alumni staff shared space as temporary working quarters were arranged for development personnel. In the interim, 106 members of the development department, including several individuals who had recently lost their homes, assisted the volunteers with the UM CAN effort, based at the Alumni House.

As a result of this effort, 4,800 faculty and staff members were contacted, information was obtained about others, and search teams were sent out to find the last few missing employees. In addition, the UM CAN effort succeeded in identifying 419 members of our faculty and staff who either lost their homes or experienced severe damage. The development department was also instrumental in assisting faculty and staff who were left homeless. For the first two weeks after the hurricane, several development personnel were in charge of finding suitable and affordable housing for university victims of Andrew.

The estimated cost of the damaged computers is $69,821.64. Although four computers were rented from Rent-A-Computer, most of the development staff was without computers until September 30th. In terms of computer capability, the department is currently only 60 percent functional, but we expect to be completely operational by October 19th.

A post-hurricane letter was sent to 30,000 alumni on September 28th, describing the effects of Hurricane Andrew on the university's campuses, as well as soliciting alumni for the Hurricane Relief Fund. Another letter, which will be sent to freshmen parents in October, will also solicit parents for the Hurricane Relief Fund.

University Relations

The university relations department was the university's central communication point during the first three weeks following Hurricane Andrew, and, as a result, the division performed additional work and incurred expenses in two major areas: documentation of storm damage, and communication with employees and students.

Immediately after the storm, the department was asked to document, both on video and in photographs, all of the damage done to the university's campuses. Total costs incurred in the documentation process were $12,032.50.

Several communication efforts were made to contact students and staff after the hurricane. Advertisements in the *New York Times*, *USA Today*, and the *Miami Herald*, letters to students, and two telephone campaigns—one aimed at reaching all 7,600 undergraduates and the other aimed at contacting all 6,993 faculty and staff—were effectively utilized to communicate vital information to faculty, staff, and the students. In addition, six issues of a special internal newsletter—Hurricane Update—were produced and distributed throughout campus. Total costs incurred in the communication process were $52,010.78.

Media activity was constant throughout the crisis. News about the hurricane's impact on the university appeared nationwide. Recently, media strategy has shifted to focus on making faculty expertise available to the media. Faculty and students from the Schools of Nursing and Medicine have been featured on network news as well as local TV for their volunteer efforts in the areas hardest hit by Hurricane Andrew. Faculty from architecture and engineering have been frequently interviewed locally and have appeared nationally in *The Wall Street Journal*, the *New York Times*, and on the "Today Show." In addition to local coverage, faculty from RSMAS has been quoted in the *New York Times* and the *Washington Post*.

For three weeks after the hurricane, university relations personnel were scattered throughout the university, due to the lack of electricity at the Corniche Building.

Alumni Relations

Although the Alumni House suffered no damage, and had electricity one week after the hurricane, the alumni relations department was unable to function normally because of the temporary relocation of the development department to the Alumni House. In the interim, alumni personnel assisted with the UM CAN effort.

VICE PRESIDENT AND GENERAL COUNSEL

FROM: Paul T. Dee
               Vice President and General Counsel

SUBJECT: Hurricane Recovery Survey and Diary
HURRICANE RECOVERY-OFFICE OF GENERAL COUNSEL

August 26th

Most legal questions related to recovery and contract issues. Communication restored with cellular phone. Three attorneys on staff worked this day without office.

August 27th

University effort to locate and assist employees begins. Working with attorneys in office finally contact all employees. All 12 are OK. Three have lost homes. All are without power, water, phones. University effort to locate property for homeless begins. University determines to rent apartments for employees. We review leases and draft subleases. Still no power in offices.

August 28th

Questions regarding storage of art objects at Lowe come in. Research and drafting of storage documents undertaken by staff. Medical School operation going on almost regular basis.

August 29th–August 30th

Housing issues arise for faculty and staff. Attorneys continue working on leases and subleases. Issue regarding use of university police officers by city of Coral Gables discussed.

August 31st

Contact made with city regarding police. Begin working on agreement with state university police officers. Staff meeting. Eleven of 12 employees report. One who lost home unable to come to office. Medical school office back to full operation. Coral Gables office closed due to lack of power. Attend hurricane meeting. Work on solving individual employee problems.

THE OFFICE OF UNIVERSITY RELATIONS

Susan Bonnett wrote the following in the CASE District III entry "Hurricane Andrew Communication Program."

Hurrican Andrew Communication Program

The University of Miami has had a comprehensive hurricane plan in place for many years. The plan includes preparing facilities on all campuses; providing emergency supplies of water, food, gas, and first aid supplies; informing students in residential facilities of precautions and the university's policies during and after a hurricane; establishing an emergency telephone system; and communicating internally and with key constituencies. Each year the plan is circulated and updated, and a hurricane planning meeting is held just prior to hurricane season.

On August 22nd when a hurricane warning was issued for South Florida, the president convened the hurricane planning group. We were confident that our planning was thorough and that we were adequately prepared. However, no amount of planning could have prepared us for what has been called the worst natural disaster in U.S. history.

Not yet knowing the severity of the storm, we issued a media advisory on August 24th stating that orientation activities were canceled and that the university would be closed Monday, August 24th. The assumption behind the hurricane plan was that we may be without power and water for two or three days. But when the storm was over some sources predicted several weeks without power and water. No water meant no toilets. Sanitation became an immediate concern with over four thousand people in the residence colleges. Decisions on when to reopen were made and remade as damage reports came in. Two days after the hurricane, the decision was made to postpone the start of classes to September 14th and to close most of the housing facilities for repairs.

Next to the safety of students and employees, communication became the highest priority and concern. While some of the following strategies had been planned, the need was much greater and continued for a longer period of time than that anticipated. Initial communication efforts were made more difficult by the lack of power and impassability of roads which prevented staff from coming to work.

The primary communication objectives were:
- To provide a means for families of students who stayed on campus to obtain information immediately after the storm.
- To determine the safety and housing status of all employees and to provide assistance where needed.
- To inform students, parents, faculty, and staff of the schedule changes.
- To keep students from returning to the residential facilities during the clean up.
- To dispel rumors and misinformation about the condition of the campus and to encourage out-of-town students to return.

Strategies—Students

- 800 line—An 800 line was installed and staffed during and after the hurricane. The number was provided to all students in the residential colleges to give to their families in case regular phone lines were overloaded or not functioning.

- Local news media were asked to carry information on the schedule changes. All of the contacts were done by phone since there was no electricity for fax machines and courier service was nonexistent. The president was made available to broadcast media for live sound bites several times a day.

- National and regional media were targeted based upon those areas with our largest student bases. Initial placements were made by phone, faxes were used for later efforts.

- Advertisements were placed in the *Miami Herald* to reach staff and local students. After reviewing the cost of advertising in our key markets we decided to run one ad in *USA TODAY* intended to reach the broadest spectrum of our national audience.

- Letters containing information on the status of the university were sent to all undergraduate students.

- A telephone campaign was conducted to contact undergraduates or their families to let them know about the changes, answer any questions they might have about the status of the university, and to inquire about their plans to return. Approximately 4,840 of the 7,600 students were contacted directly.

Strategies—Faculty and Staff

- A telephone campaign was immediately organized to contact the 6,993 faculty and staff to inquire about their safety and to provide assistance to those with critical needs. Information about the reopening of the university was also provided. Staff and volunteers reached 4,600 employees in three days. Information was obtained about the others and search teams were sent to find the last few missing employees. Through the phone campaign 419 families were identified as homeless, and many were assisted in finding temporary housing.

- A telephone script was distributed to all operators and staffed offices. Administrators were asked to use the information in the script in answering calls and to record the script on their voice mail.

- Local news media were used to carry information on the status of the university and to urge homeless employees to contact the university.

- In addition to the schedule changes, the local advertisements included information on when employees should report to work and where to call for assistance.

- Since local mail could not be counted on, letters containing status information and where to call for help were distributed with all employee paychecks.

- Post-hurricane meetings were held several times a week beginning the day after the storm. Status reports were given by key areas such as student housing, the health center, public safety department, facilities management, computer services, and volunteer services.

- Information shared at the above meetings was edited into a special newsletter, *Hurricane Update*, and was published several times a week. The newsletter was distributed by student volunteers to employees arriving to work on the reopening day, delivered to key offices, distributed via fax machines and displayed on the e-mail system.

- Separate editions were produced for the medical campus during the same period.

- The regular issue of *Veritas*, the internal tabloid, was replaced with a special edition containing coverage of the hurricane and its aftermath. A feature on the hurricane's impact on the university was added to the university magazine which is sent to all alumni.

- A letter from the president was sent to all alumni outside of the affected zip code areas. The letter contained a status report on the university and an appeal for a UM Hurricane Relief Fund.

- Various types of assistance were offered to employees through special seminars on dealing with insurance claims, publishing lists of reliable contractors, and distributing information on coping with stress after disaster.

Results

- The results of this type of effort are difficult to measure since it is impossible to determine what would have happened if we did not do any or all of the above. Most importantly, students understood and followed the hurricane instructions. There were no accidents or any serious injuries to students or staff during and after the storm.

- There were a great number of anecdotal reports. Volunteers making phone calls to employees received many comments of appreciation for the calls and the offer of support. Parents who used the 800 line told the staff how much they appreciated having someone to call when they were worried. And students who were contacted by phone said they were happy to have someone from the university call and answer their questions.

In terms of student retention, the efforts were highly effective. With the delayed opening and all of the adverse national publicity of the storm's devastation, the undergraduate enrollment was just 25 students below the projected number of 8,609. Given the market conditions, this would be considered a good number even without the hurricane.

Of the nearly 2,000 students on campus during the hurricane, after the first few days only 350 remained in the residential colleges. Students were encouraged to return home so that the facilities could be cleaned and repaired. Almost all of the students who remained on campus became involved in volunteer work on campus and in the community.

When the university reopened nearly all employees reported for work. Those who did not had severe damage to their homes or complications with family members as a result of the storm.

The letter to alumni informing them of the status of the university also asked for donations to a UM Hurricane Relief Fund. To date nearly $300,000 has been raised from that letter.

COMMENTARY

The preparedness checklist presented by Vice President Lieberman is one schools may want to copy, especially arranging for an 800 number in anticipation of the storm. That phone line was answered by the Public Safety Office. Additional phones were added and tested before the storm. The school learned after the storm that cellular phones operated when other phones did not; many offices are now equipped with cellular phones. The school's amateur radio station was used to relay messages when the other communication lines failed.

Because the university population had little or no access to information, the daily, open, president-led hurricane advisory committee meeting was a chance to keep current.

Enrollment management wisely decided that a hard copy of the student directory information should be available in the event of wanting to reach students when computers are down.

The realization that it would be quite difficult to rehabilitate the campus when the students were present led to the decision to invite students to return home and to deduct that cost from the spring semester tuition. That action hastened the return to full operation.

The commandeering of police by the city and the further denial of the campus' right to use other officers reinforces our memory that occasional stifling bureaucratic arbitrariness is not impeded by hurricanes.

Having the president on national radio networks helped the school contact students to announce the delay in school opening. Because students come from all over, ads were also taken out in USA Today and other papers with nationwide circulation.

The school's "We Will Rebuild" campaign was enhanced with the active help of the board and political leaders. The timely calls to alumni by the volunteers gave further support to the campaign. The campaign and its title had to create a spirit of hope and recovery for everyone associated with the university.

One department was made responsible for collecting damage reports. Those reports were then given to risk management for the insurance company, which allowed for quicker reimbursement.

The university made cash available because banks were closed or inaccessible and the ATM's were not working

The university initiated UM CAN, UM Cares about its Neighbors, to provide relief to the people in the devastated areas. Not only did students volunteer immediately, but the campus hosted volunteers that came from around the country. The volunteer effort continued on weekends through the semester.

Employees appreciated the university-sponsored seminars on insurance, selecting contractors, and home-renovation loans.

The housing director urged parents of new students to stay on campus and then assigned all who stayed in housing to groups that would share the same buildings. They were assigned flashlights, asked to stay together, eat together, and get information from the assigned resident assistants.

No mention can be made of any hurricane or other natural disaster preparation without planning for alternate supplies of water. Some water was trucked in from other states. Bottled water was available in very limited quantities.

The university generated hurricane preparation and response guidelines for fraternity houses and for commuters. A housing-availability card catalogue gave commuter students a purview of off-campus housing. Staff were given information about renting to students.

A massive telephone outreach to students together with the media announcements were credited with the high student return rate. One of the graduate schools advised students that the buildings were safe.

The placement office anticipated that local stores would need additional help and personally visited those businesses to make them aware of student availability for jobs.

The suggestion that the campus test out its emergency preparedness and review and update its plan once a year is an appropriate suggestion for all institutions.

PART

3

* * * * * * * * *

CHAPTER
eleven
❋ ❋ ❋ ❋ ❋ ❋ ❋ ❋

Summary

The following points may be used to help college personnel in various divisions understand how the whole university functions during an emergency. The guiding principles for the actions in each school studied were to help those in need and to prevent further harm to anyone. What schools did, whether or not they were properly prepared to face such crises, was to allow the staff to respond creatively. The all night meeting in the residence hall following the death of a student, for example, was a spontaneous idea, not one written in a plan or checklist. Nevertheless, there are steps campuses can take to help their departments respond compassionately and efficiently.

It is important to have representatives of many offices participating in guiding the institutional response to crises. The different officers raise consciousness for the needs of the particular constituency they represent. For example, in the case of the campus rape where the student was the perpetrator, spokespeople for women's groups on campus may have influenced the executive committee's actions. The open daily meetings some schools had during crises provided for more inclusion in planning.

CRISIS RESPONSE COMMITTEES

Several schools whose crises were studies had committees that continually planned for how their institutions' would prepare for and respond to emergencies. Other schools had a committee that could be convened if needed. All provided help for the victims, and all recognized that secondary victims were also in need of support. For those schools whose crises required immediate responses, committees met daily to keep people informed and to identify needs to be met. In the cases of the serial murders and the hurricane, schools encouraged individual administrators to find ways to relieve the pain the community as best they could.

PREPARING FOR CRISES

Despite the fact that several of the schools studied had crisis response committees, the first crisis revealed gaps in planning. At UC, for instance, campus officials learned after responding to the fire that decision-making power wasn't clearly defined. As a result, the crisis response committee revised its procedures to designate a decision maker during crisis situations. Unfortunately, the campus had to respond to a tragedy shortly after the fire, but the new procedures allowed the committee to respond more efficiently. Such flexibility and willingness to learn from mistakes is key to campus planning efforts.

Visibility of Senior Administration

Staff members in many of the universities described the importance of the visibility of senior staff and the presidents during their crises. Students and staff spoke with admiration about the presidents' personal kindnesses toward victims and their families. Several mentioned how empathetic staff members were with people in despair. Without exception, the personnel interviewed referred to such examples to explain their pride in the schools.

Victim Services

All schools offered counseling services to victims, and to their roommates and friends. Both École and UC offered services to the affected external community following their crises.

Several schools directed information and help to students and later realized that staff and faculty were equally distressed. Two had formal employee assistance counseling service. The conference on post hurricane reactions was an example of a way to reach out to many.

When UF's housing director allowed students to make physical changes in their rooms to enhance their feelings of safety, families and students reported feeling more secure. Such flexibility makes a real difference.

Community victim services supplemented campus services. Sometimes they extended attention given to dealing with a past tragedy for longer periods of time than the campus did.

The Information Officer

The information officer needs to be fully informed about everything as quickly as possible and on a continuing basis no matter who is giving out the messages. An effective rumor control program can begin immediately when the institution speaks in a unified voice. When a school faces an emergency, administrators learn fast how quickly rumors spread and how promptly the press calls. The information officer should reflect the intent of the institution to be candid, to be circumspect, and to be open, but at the same time should make sure that the university does not assume responsibility for problems outside its purview.

Media Relations

Several information officers helped reporters meet deadlines. One school, which was not permitted to release information because facts of the investigation could only be divulged by another agency, was perceived by the press and the campus community as stonewalling. The president was put in a difficult situation as a result.

The news media are perceived in many roles: adversaries demanding schools give information; ghouls searching for victims to televise and situations to sensationalize; noble guardians of the community demanding details so a public can better protect itself. Universities court them, avoid them, befriend them, and need them.

In "The Athlete as the Perpetrator" the sports information officer anticipated that the reporter would be interviewing teammates of the perpetrator. The athletic director, therefore, selected articulate spokespeople who would be able to well represent the team and the school. The AD stated that his decision to suspend the student from play was because the athlete's name had appeared in the paper as the perpetrator. Some other schools' responses appeared driven by the worry about media reaction.

Staff in several schools noted that student reaction to the media's interviewing has changed over the years. Fewer students are now willing to be interviewed. Attitudes ranged from lack of interest to anger at the intrusion of cameras, lights, and reporters.

All information officers agreed that the university needs to develop good working relationships with the press before a crisis occurs. Responding to tragedy requires the help of the media. The media are a quick, effective way to inform parents, students, alumni, the local community, and legislators about serious crises.

UF's information officer said that the institution wanted to let it be known that it was in control, that is, that it is actively protecting the community and has plans for coping with the crisis.

When violent tragedies occur on campuses, the world treats those events differently from the way it treats such happenings when they occur off-campus, whether or not they involve students. Campus crises are looked at, rightly or wrongly, as the institution's problem. Using the media wisely can help to alleviate this situation.

Communicating with the Campus

Identifying who needs information may be the first decision. Is the information for everyone on-campus, for the total community, on- and off-campus, or for students alone? In several situations cited, employees were in the same danger as students and needed the information.

TSU communicated with the faculty and staff instantly through e-mail after the second rape. That required a reminder to people to read the monitors. In the future, TSU will use a pyramid telephoning system to ask users to read the e-mail.

UC's building-coordinator communication system, together with the local radio and television, proved a very efficient method for evacuating 38,000 people during the bomb threat.

UM used two-way radios; they will rely more heavily on cellular phones in the future. Their daily newsletter pyramids and daily open meetings with the president kept people up to date.

Police

All the police chiefs and chiefs of public safety were academy-trained police officers. Their powers differed depending on the state. Police were differently integrated into the academic community at each school. In some they were more identified with the campus; at UC, for instance, they served on campus committees not relevant to their specific duties.

The police chief at M College had completed his undergraduate degree while in office. He was working on an advanced degree when interviewed. He said that experience enabled him to better understand students.

On three campuses the officers were not armed. Chiefs described the occupation of campus police as comparable to that of other noncampus police. Some reported how identifying with the ethos of the institution influenced the style of their work and that of their staff's.

Chiefs reported choosing to work on campuses. Officers who leave university positions frequently go to other campuses. As campus staff, they want students to know the university is sensitive and empathetic. The more they are integrated into campus committees and campus planning, the more they can help the university in crisis.

Some offices in the university were surprised that campus police investigated serious crime and were not aware they were academy trained.

A rape victim complained that the police interrogating her during several interviews made her feel further victimized. When police requested additional meetings, rumors started that the rape victim was not credible. It appears that when police first meet rape victims, officers know that the victim is in crisis and an officer may treat the victim compassionately without many challenging questions. In subsequent meetings, the officer, after interviewing the alleged perpetrator and relevant witnesses, must verify facts and resolve contradictions in statements. It's about that time that victims complain that police questioning them cause them further victimization. Victims are apt to report that police are acting as if victims are not credible.

Some schools have assigned officers to different residence halls where, as in the case of the University of Miami, the dormitory population get to know them. Such police presence both discourages crime and increases reporting.

Telephones

The telephone rings incessantly when crises happen, and the callers are frequently demanding information. Judging from the kinds of questions callers asked, universities found it wise to have informed people answering the phones at such times. Some had recordings to report the most frequently requested information.

Some schools logged all calls to better understand what kinds of questions arose during the crisis. The phone calls reportedly were mostly from parents, media, and vendors. Two universities installed additional lines.

The University of Miami anticipated that many people from around the country would call after the hurricane; they installed an 800 telephone number for the duration of the crisis. Phone calls from parents continued for a very long time after things appeared to return to normal.

UF's offering the alumni office's bank of phones for students to call free of charge and tell their families they were safe saved staff time and lessened parents' anxiety.

Searching for Information

FIU provided scripts to their volunteers who called employees to learn their status. All people answering phones were continually given the most current information. The daily meetings at many campuses during crises allowed for up-to-date intelligence.

Campus Attorneys

University lawyers did not report being directly involved in the campus response. They were more involved in the business following the tragedies. Risk managers were in the same role.

Students

Student participation in campus response to crisis varied in the different schools. Students served on planning committees. Several schools described the active safety programs that student groups conducted. Student newspapers received the press releases distributed to the media.

Including students on the crisis response committee was exceptionally helpful at UF.

Other Campus Resources

Campus ministry supplemented many campus services. At UF a minister was on the crisis committee. In addition to ministry services, ritual plays an important role in bringing the community together and healing. Ceremonies, flags at half-mast, shared moments of silence, or music bring communities together with a resolve to heal.

Of Interest

Two schools had a visible number of homeless people on the campus. During the crises, these homeless left their usual spaces and returned when the campuses had returned to a quieter state. Another interesting question that comes up is when is the crisis over? To some extent it is over when the school declares it past, frequently with some symbolic act like raising the flag.

CONCLUSIONS

How serious a crisis may be and what kind of response is needed depends on some or all of the following: the nature of the event; what kind of help people need; how many and how quickly people need to be helped, informed, or both; who and how many need interpretation of the events; how accessible those people are; how much interaction with the media is necessary; what the media chooses to emphasize; who and how many people need emergency care; how much the institution needs to assert control and demonstrate that it is capable of responding and how quickly the institution needs to respond.

Each crisis is unique, and although many institutions have established crisis management processes, administrators adjust and respond differently to each situation. The same situation may be a crisis at one time but not at another. In crisis, the best of us will be candid, caring, supportive, fair, and compassionate. Different offices will almost seem to be competing as they strive to ease the pain of those affected and to make the rest of the campus population feel as safe as possible. The university bureaucracy, if it is permitted, will forget its usual internal divisions and politics, not because it chooses to, but because the common goal to mitigate the effects of the crisis supplants the usual focus on individual and hierarchical power. Several of the interviewed administrators described that short period when everyone in the institution joined forces to face the crisis together, each working avidly to help.

Everyone hopes that our higher education institutions do not become like cities that tally their murders daily. Each crime in our midst, regardless of its severity, is a violation of our entire community.

CHAPTER
twelve
✦ ✦ ✦ ✦ ✦ ✦ ✦

Suggestions from Others

PREPARING FOR CRISIS

The following suggestions, reprinted with the permission of the author and CASE (Council for Advancement and Support of Education), are listed in the CASE Issues Paper for Communications Professionals:

Before a crime occurs:
1. Prepare information about your institution's security and safety policies. Also, have available information on drug and alcohol abuse programs, rape prevention programs, and other materials to educate key publics and document that your institution takes crime seriously and has prevention programs in place.
2. Plan how the public information office will operate . . . you may need to line up additional staffing during an emergency. . . . plan such small details as notifying your campus telephone operators where they should switch various calls.
3. Identify student, faculty, and other campus leaders who can serve as volunteers to help communications efforts during a crisis.
4. Discuss with community leaders, local law enforcement officials, and members of your campus crisis team how you can effectively work together during a crime incident. Identify, for instance, community groups you should alert if a crime occurs. Determine campus policies and procedures for allowing the media to photograph or film on-campus sites such as residence halls.
5. Identify your campus's most knowledgeable spokespersons and provide media training for these individuals.
6. Select and equip sites for news conferences and media use during an emergency.[1]

Linda Gray, assistant vice-president and director of Information Services, University of Florida, suggests the following preparation before the crisis.

1. Have a close working relationship with key university staff people. Crisis is not time to get to know people.
2. Have close working relationships with key public relations professionals in the community and community leaders.
3. Keep an up-to-date media list on computer. (Office and home numbers, if possible, of key media.)
4. Have a written crisis plan that details: Who decides what information is released. Who speaks for the institution, or releases material to media. Who inside and outside the institution must be notified in a crisis. What role media relations staff will play. Composition of crisis teams that can be called together depending on the nature of crisis. Phone numbers and addresses of key people, including top administrators, crisis teams, media relations staff. Logistical details and locations where press conferences/media availabilities can be held (sizes of rooms, whom to call to reserve). Phone lines—you may need more in your office. Where are phones media can use to call in? Equipment/Space—Keep an inventory of what equipment and space you have, where cameras can plug in, where laptops can be plugged into phones, where computers can be used. Details on hotels/motels—which are closest, best, cheapest? Parking—where can media park? Set aside parking areas. Work with police. Designate satellite truck parking spots. Determine what staff support is available—clerical, technical back-up people, as well as those who deal directly with media.[2]

Eric Shoemaker, director of Public Safety of the University of Miami suggests the following preparation.

- Regular inventories and rotation of emergency supplies to include traffic control equipment
- Detailed plans for action to be taken at the "watch" and "warning" phases
- Identify essential personnel and support they will need
- Post assignments of officers across campus (as the danger nears)
- Plan for contract security personnel to supplement the force until security integrity is restored
- Communication alternatives
- Emergency power alternatives
- A communications plan which includes physical plant and executive officers of the institution

> - A family support system for all department members which includes emergency aid, psychological and spiritual assistance.[3]

General Suggestions

All schools agreed that someone needed to coordinate the campus response, to call the essential planners together. At FIU and UC the emergency coordinator was given decision-making authority.

Every campus included in these studies considered the emotional support of the community a primary responsibility. Where students had died, some campuses held memorial services. At UD the staff met with students who had lived with the deceased. They also visited the family of the deceased. At HTU Student Affairs personnel gave students the phone numbers of resident staff and urged them to call. This was supplemental to an all night open meeting and counseling. UC distributed fliers advising the community what reactions were appropriate to the distress they had witnessed and which responses indicated a need for further help. All of them provided counseling for victims, their families, and friends.

Schools conducted open meetings, group meetings, and communal memorial services in addition to counseling. TSU continued weekly meetings until no one came. The UF community placed the flowers from the memorial services near a tree; people stopped to look and remember.

UC provided counseling for police officers while officers were leaving a confrontation with a killer. Police officers in Florida were encouraged to move into the headquarters with their families.

In most schools leaders commented that following the events described in this book people would not be the same for the rest of the year. Leadership supported everyone's being more flexible about when assignments were due and some schools further agreed to allow a year's extension for faculty who could not meet requirements for tenure. FIU convened workshops on the aftereffects of the hurricane to help people understand how much they were all suffering from the effects of the storm.

Both UM and FIU reached out to offer care, consolation, and supplies to the many who had sustained losses.

UC needed to update the telephone numbers for those who were on-call for emergencies. They distributed all the numbers on a business card to all staff on-call for an emergency. Some suggested including the known and proven volunteers like the ministry and leaders from service organizations and further suggested including those volunteers in planning meetings. UC had given people on the emergency call list IDs that identified them as personnel needed for emergencies.

At UF, national and local media representatives converged on the campus requiring parking spaces, equal access to information, and help with housing. When the information officer wanted to announce some change, she placed notices in each of the hotels where press were staying in addition to calling each reporter she knew.

With no radio, television, or telephones, information circulars distributed to all the buildings on-campus were the first ways to communicate during natural disasters. Schools wanted everyone to know where to get help and information, and they wanted to let them know when the institution would resume functioning.

For schools whose students come from all over the nation, it was helpful to get on national television and to advertise in a national paper about the state of the university.

The University of Miami discovered that the cellular phone worked when regular telephone service had ceased.

Several campuses mentioned pyramid plans to get word across campus quickly .

The FIU on-call agreements with contractors enabled the campus to have skilled help when such personnel were not otherwise available.

Help can be offered through recorded messages that afford access to such varied data as what to expect from police, judicial, and criminal justice procedures, and how to find a particular building. TSU has an information tape system with instructions for the accused and victims to understand their rights and the availability of resources.

RESPONDING TO THE CRISIS—OTHER SUGGESTIONS

Telephones

Update information for people answering the phones. Those who are working at the phones will need relief. Consider adding additional emergency telephone lines. Is the emergency such that you should add a line for calls from the media? Inform them if you do. It probably is best if several people rotate in answering the phones.

Death Notification

If the crisis involves a death or serious injury, verify the identity of the person before any notification is made. Identify the people on-campus who need notification such as roommates and fraternities, as well as bureaucratic offices.

Rumor Control

Plan ways to control rumors. Regular information dissemination may not be sufficient. Consider information telephone lines. You may want to put recordings on answering machines and change the messages as new information becomes available. Consider open meetings where the latest information will be available. Try putting the latest information on computer bulletin boards, marked with date and time. Be sure to remove the data when no longer current (assign someone to do this when it is first posted).

Informing the Community

Decide who needs what information and how quickly they need it. You will want to tell the resident students first thing in the morning that someone was hurt by a mugger at 3:00 A.M., but the rest of the campus could learn it from the school newspaper. Announce the death of a resident student to immediate neighbors as soon as possible. In general, decide whether all or part of the campus population needs to be told that it is or is not in danger.

Disseminate information identifying what people may do to feel more in control of their own destinies. You probably have distributed such information before, but at this moment students and employees are more likely to pay attention.

Inform the community of the university's actions. Include in your information what help and service campus personnel gave to victims, friends, family, and roommates. The community wants to know how the victim is faring.

We Don't Always Need Professional Help

In addition to counseling help, consider urging community members to help each other.

After the Crisis

Inform faculty about students who may have been especially affected. Provide opportunities for the community to learn what happened, how the university responded, and what new steps the school is taking to prevent the occurrence of such events. Invite their participation in assessing the reaction and improving preparedness for the future.

Offer support services where students are located such as the residence halls and the Student Union. Make it convenient for the community to get help.

Make no guarantees of safety.

Recognize the many who will have worked under difficult circumstances during the crisis. Many clerks and secretaries will have been first-line responders to anxious and angry people.

Consider letters to the community, students, and/or parents to assure them that the institution is on course and to again inform them about the availability of services. When appropriate, commend those whose responses were of exceptional help.

Evaluate how your campus responded. An assessment soon after the event will be helpful, but another review six months later may also be useful.

The Information Officer and the Crisis

The CASE Issues Report recommends that when a crime occurs:

> Outline your audience's short and long-term communications needs. Your audiences will need varying degrees of information: some will need a personal approach; others will require frequent updates; still others will want information long after the crime has occurred. How personal and frequently your communications will be depends on the type and nature of the crime, the size of your campus, and the resources available to you."

The communication continues identifying the audiences that may need to be addressed: students, parents, the victim's family, alumni, and the community, if the crime involves people other than students on-campus.

The report recommends the use of one media-trained spokesperson. The issue continues, "If the crime is receiving significant media attention, you should hold a formal news conference . . . to correct any rumors.

Information officers are urged to send copies of press releases to trustees and friends.

Linda Gray of the University of Florida makes the following suggestions about media relations during the crisis:

- Always return media calls, . . . even if they are hostile.
- Really communicate with press when you are talking with them; that means both talking and listening. Don't rush them.
- Avoid antagonizing media representatives, if possible. A sharp tone can affect your future relationship with an individual and with any other media reps who may hear the conversation.
- Consider establishing a dedicated call-in phone line that will offer information to media or others who phone in. Information on news conferences, rumor control information, and newly acquired information can be placed on a tape that can be updated. This system is particularly useful when your regular phone lines are tied up with calls.
- If things you say will result in media calling other agencies or individuals, you need to call them first to warn of impending calls.

- When talking to media, be sure to give credit to other agencies, groups, or individuals working on the crisis, including your own staff.
- Try to be pro-active with new information. Even though things may be frantic, if you acquire new information regarding the crisis, reach out to the media. Everybody's looking for a "twist" on the story that no one else has. If you can provide some media with a special angle, it can pay off later.

Linda Gray makes the following suggestions about news conferences and availabilities:

- When you notify media of news conferences/availabilities, be sure to define what kind of event you are actually having. Usually, if you announce a news conference, media expect you to provide them with information, or to announce something. A press availability can simply mean you are making individual(s) available to answer questions from the media.
- Don't call unnecessary news conferences/availabilities.
- If holding a news conference, try to tell media in advance some details of what you will be announcing.
- Gauge the size of your crowd carefully when reserving a room; better to have too much, than too little space. Make sure microphones, chairs, lighting, and water are in place at least 30 minutes before an event.
- Decide format in advance. Who will introduce speakers, who decides when question/answer period ends, and other details.
- Check to see what else is happening on campus and in the community. Don't lose effectiveness through time conflicts with other events.
- Consider whether you need to let other organizations and agencies know you are having a news conference. (You may wish to invite others to attend.)
- Try to plan length of news conference/availability, but be flexible.
- Consider the time of the news conference availability. If you want to make the noon, 6:00 P.M., or 11:00 P.M. TV and radio news, you need to allow time for crews to travel and edit tape. Remember, the time scheduled for a news conference/availability can send a signal to the media; sometimes right, sometimes wrong.

- If you have a satellite hook-up or other equipment, be sure to let media know in advance.
- You may want to pre-plan still photo opportunities.
- If you are going to set restrictions on an event try to put it in writing and communicate it to media representatives at least 24 hours in advance.[4]

REFERENCES

1. "Crime Incidents on Campus," CASE Issues Paper for Communications Professionals, *Public Affairs Services*, December 1990, No. 3, Council for Advancement and Support of Education.
2. Gray, Linda S., "Dealing with University Crisis," unpublished paper.
3. Shoemaker, Eric, "When the Wind Blew Through 'Cane Country," *Campus Law Enforcement Journal*, January–February, 1993.
4. Gray, "Dealing with University Crisis."

CHAPTER
thirteen

❋ ❋ ❋ ❋ ❋ ❋

A Crisis Preparation Checklist

GENERAL PREPARATION

Choose a person or group to be responsible for crisis management and response. Because the plan should include preparation for such diverse crises as crime, natural disasters, plant failures, threats to community safety including riots and bomb threats, planning will require participation by those responsible for public safety, physical plant facilities, media relations, student services, and administration. Most campuses will not be totally self-sufficient in meeting the needs for each emergency but can have resources available to them by contractors, whose services they have agreed to provide on-call.

Keeping the Plan Current

Emergency preparedness requires that a plan be reviewed at least every six months to update the following:

- Telephone listings for all people who may need to be notified—parents, emergency resources
- The chain of command—who will assign responsibility and convene members
- Current telephone listing, including fax and cellular numbers, for all essential personnel for any crisis
- Plan for supplemental police services
- Review of emergency communication
- Pyramid telephone plan
- Plans for reaching people who are out of touch—those at athletic fields, etc.

- Back-up people for essential personnel
- Evacuation plans
- Campus maps

Who and What May Be Needed

Emergency resource people should be available for the following:

- Person in emotional crisis, suicide attempt
- Victim assistance
- Specially trained assistance for victims of sexual assault
- Victim assistance for secondary victims including roommates, friends, family, staff
- Emergency resources for drug and alcohol emergencies
- Building maintenance
- Locksmith on-call
- Resource people who can de-escalate tense situations

In the event of a natural disaster, you may need any or all of the following:

- Emergency supplies—accessible site for storage with keys available near the potential users
- Drinking water
- Cellular phones or two-way radios
- Portable toilets
- Generators independent of existing fuel supply
- Trained emergency personnel

In the event of physical plant failure, you may need:

- Emergency repair services
- Alternate facility for resident population
- Plans to protect property—computer data, records, safes
- Evacuation plans

In the event of protests or riots, racial and ethnic conflict, the following should be available:

- Skilled prevention staff
- Sensitivity training and awareness of the perceptions of minority populations
- Fair and sensitive institutional policies and procedures

To respond to a threat to the public welfare—e.g., crime with perpetrator at large, the following will be needed:

- Increased police services
- Opportunity for campus to learn what the institution is doing with regular updates
- Emergency directions to community —how to be safe

After a crisis

- Emergency information available to parents—media communication, volunteers to answer phones
- Temporary relocation of student(s)
- Ceremonies and rituals to help the community heal
- Help for students to adjust to academic demands. Helping all affected populations to heal.
- Notify faculty
- Procedures in emergency for disabled persons
- Alternate facilities

General Advice

- Have written procedures for suicide, suicide attempt, for victim crime, fire, natural disaster, riot, protest, evacuation of each building on campus
- Let the campus know how you are responding
- Clear parking spaces for the press
- Keep media from intruding on classes, meetings, ceremonies, and privacy of individuals. Assign them space in meetings so they do not become center of meeting
- Evaluate your response

A Crisis Has Occurred

The first step is to call the relevant people from the crisis response committee, the people on the list. After contacting the appropriate officials, the following questions need to be considered:

Is a person present who has responsibility to organize all communications for the internal and external publics to hear consistent messages from the institution?

Who needs to be notified and how will each be contacted? For example:

- Parents
- Students
- Friends and Roommates
- Physician
- Victim assistance
- President
- Campus community
- Residence community

What emergency service does the victim need?

What emergency services do secondary victims need?

Will parking spaces need to be set aside for television crews?

Should an answering message be created to inform callers?

Will volunteers be needed to answer the phones?

What, if any information, should be announced on radio or television?

Are any locks, doors or windows in need of emergency repair?

Will any group need to be fed? Who needs to hear about food needs?

Is special housecleaning needed—or should it be prevented in event of police investigation?

If evacuation is needed, are sleeping bags or other bedding available? Should evacuees bring bedding?

Will people need:
- water
- radio
- two-way radios or cellular phones

Should referral be made to:

- alcohol or drug program
- clergy
- counseling
- rape crisis resource

Will faculty need to be informed about any student?

Does any member of the community need additional support?

Should university representatives visit or call anyone?

If a death has occurred, have all offices been notified not to send registration and other information; how will any final bills be handled?

Will there be opportunities for the community to attend the funeral?

If a student allegedly commits a violent crime consider the need for temporary removal of the student from residence or from the university.
Does the victim need any special protection or help?
Will police need to redirect traffic?
Will the school need increased security?
Will special crowd control techniques be needed?
Does the information officer know everything that is happening?

INDEX

❋ ❋ ❋ ❋ ❋ ❋ ❋ ❋

Compiled by Janet Perlman